Y0-ADX-153

Words from Abroad

K

K R I T I K

German Literary Theory and Cultural Studies
Liliane Weissberg, Editor

*A complete listing of the books in this series
can be found online at http://wsupress.wayne.edu*

© 2005 BY WAYNE STATE UNIVERSITY PRESS,
DETROIT, MICHIGAN 48201. ALL RIGHTS RESERVED.
NO PART OF THIS BOOK MAY BE REPRODUCED WITHOUT FORMAL PERMISSION.
MANUFACTURED IN THE UNITED STATES OF AMERICA.
09 08 07 06 05   5 4 3 2 1

LIBRARY OF CONGRESS CATALOGING-IN-PUBLICATION DATA

GARLOFF, KATJA.

WORDS FROM ABROAD : TRAUMA AND DISPLACEMENT IN POSTWAR GERMAN JEWISH WRITERS /

KATJA GARLOFF.

P. CM. — (KRITIK : GERMAN LITERARY THEORY AND CULTURAL STUDIES)

INCLUDES BIBLIOGRAPHICAL REFERENCES AND INDEX.

ISBN 0-8143-3245-5 (CLOTH : ALK. PAPER)

1. GERMAN LITERATURE—JEWISH AUTHORS—HISTORY AND CRITICISM. 2. GERMAN LITERATURE—20TH CENTURY—HISTORY AND CRITICISM. 3. AUTHORS, EXILED—FOREIGN COUNTRIES. 4. GERMAN LITERATURE—FOREIGN COUNTRIES—HISTORY AND CRITICISM. 5. PSYCHIC TRAUMA IN LITERATURE. 6. JEWISH DIASPORA IN LITERATURE. I. TITLE. II. KRITIK (DETROIT, MICH.)

PT169.G37 2005

830.9'8924'009045—DC22

2004022775

∞THE PAPER USED IN THIS PUBLICATION MEETS THE MINIMUM REQUIREMENTS OF THE AMERICAN NATIONAL STANDARD FOR INFORMATION SCIENCES—PERMANENCE OF PAPER FOR PRINTED LIBRARY MATERIALS, ANSI Z39.48-1984.

Words from Abroad

Trauma and Displacement in Postwar German Jewish Writers

KATJA GARLOFF

WAYNE STATE UNIVERSITY PRESS
DETROIT

To My Parents

Contents

Acknowledgments *ix* Abbreviations *xi*

Introduction:
Trauma and Displacement *1*

1.
The Inability to Return:
German Jewish Intellectuals after the Holocaust *21*

2.
Peter Weiss's Skeptical Cosmopolitanism *55*

3.
Nelly Sachs and the Myth
of the "German-Jewish Symbiosis" *95*

4.
Paul Celan's Revisiting of Eastern Europe *131*

Conclusion:
Toward the Possibility of a Diasporic Community *173*

Notes *187* Works Cited *221* Index *237*

Acknowledgments

I WOULD LIKE TO thank the first readers of this project, who inspired and supported me throughout years of research and writing: Sander Gilman, Katie Trumpener, Eric Santner, and Michael Geyer provided invaluable guidance and encouragement. Heartfelt thanks to Julia Hell, Rochelle Tobias, Uta Werner, and Ülker Gökberk, who read drafts of one or more chapters of this book and made wise suggestions for revisions. Stefani Engelstein read many different parts of the manuscript in many different stages and improved it on all levels, in both substance and style. William Diebold and Jan Mieszkowski gave me valuable stylistic tips and helped with the translations. I am indebted to many other colleagues and friends for useful suggestions, critical responses, or invitations to present my work, including Ken Calhoon, Robert Cohen, Dagmar Deuring, Elizabeth Duquette, Jeffrey Grossman, Jonathan Hess, Alexander Honold, Volker Kaiser, Roger Porter, William Ray, Gerhard Richter, Jürgen Schutte, Jochen Vogt, Steven Wasserstrom, and Marc Weiner. My students at Reed College responded to the ideas of this book in several literature courses with enthusiasm and perspicuity, and I wish to thank them for that.

During this project I received generous fellowship and research support from the Levine Fund, the Stillman Drake Fund, and the Reed College Faculty Paid Leave Awards Program. They enabled me to carry out additional archival research and gave me the time to write the final version of this book, for which I am very grateful. Thanks are also due to the staffs at the Stiftung Archiv der Akademie der Künste in Berlin,

ACKNOWLEDGMENTS

the Stadt- und Landesbibliothek in Dortmund, and the Deutsches Literaturarchiv in Marbach, who helped me locate and obtain archival materials.

I would like to express my gratitude to Liliane Weissberg, who took a kind interest in the project when it was reaching completion and recommended it for publication in the *Kritik* series. Leslie Morrison and Karen Remmler, the outside readers for Wayne State University Press, provided perceptive comments that were crucial in bringing the manuscript into its final form. At the Press, Kathryn Wildfong, Kristin Lawrence, and Kathleen Fields made editing and publication a smooth, efficient, and enjoyable process, and they deserve thanks for that.

Most of all, I need to thank my husband, Asher Klatchko, for his love, inspiration, and unflagging support throughout the years, and our sons, Benjamin and Jonathan, for being in the world.

Parts of chapter 2 of this book have previously been published as "Peter Weiss's Entry into the German Public Sphere: On Diaspora, Language, and the Uses of Distance," *Colloquia Germanica* 30, no. 1 (1997): 47–70, and as "Cosmopolitian Leftovers and Experimental Prose: Peter Weiss's *Das Gespräch der drei Gehenden*," in *Rethinking Peter Weiss*, ed. Jost Hermand and Marc Silberman, 1–19 (New York: Peter Lang, 2000). A section of chapter 1 has appeared as "Essay, Exile, Efficacy: Adorno's Literary Criticism," *Monatshefte* 94, no. 1 (Winter 2002): 80–95. The Francke Verlag, Peter Lange Publishing, and the University of Wisconsin Press have kindly granted permission to use this material here.

Note on quotations and translations: In the introduction and chapter 1, which set up the theoretical framework of my study, I quote in English only. In the remaining chapters, I quote in both German and English for literary texts and in English only for archival materials, notebooks, letters, and so forth. I have used published English translations whenever possible; all other translations are mine.

Abbreviations

C *The Conversation of the Three Walkers and The Shadow of the Coachman's Body* by Peter Weiss, trans. S. M. Cupitt (London: Calder and Boyars, 1972)

E *Eli* by Nelly Sachs, in *Zeichen im Sand: Die szenischen Dichtungen der Nelly Sachs* (Frankfurt am Main: Suhrkamp, 1962)

Ex *Exile* by Peter Weiss, trans. E. B. Garside, Alastair Hamilton, and Christopher Levenson (New York: Delacorte Press, 1968)

F *Flucht und Verwandlung* by Nelly Sachs, in *Fahrt ins Staublose* (Frankfurt am Main: Suhrkamp, 1961)

GS *Glottal Stop: 101 Poems by Paul Celan,* trans. Nikolai Popov and Heather McHugh (Hanover, N.H.: Wesleyan University Press/University Press of New England, 2000)

I *The Investigation* by Peter Weiss, trans. Jon Swan and Ulu Grosbard, rev. Robert Cohen, in *Marat/Sade, The Investigation, The Shadow of the Body of the Coachman,* ed. Robert Cohen (New York: Continuum, 1998)

N *Und niemand weiß weiter* by Nelly Sachs, in *Fahrt ins Staublose* (Frankfurt am Main: Suhrkamp, 1961)

Nb *Notizbücher, 1960–1971* by Peter Weiss (Frankfurt am Main: Suhrkamp, 1982)

ABBREVIATIONS

Nr	*Die Niemandsrose* by Paul Celan, Tübinger Ausgabe, ed. Jürgen Wertheimer (Frankfurt am Main: Suhrkamp, 1996)
OTC	*O the Chimneys: Selected Poems* by Nelly Sachs, trans. Michael Hamburger et al. (New York: Farrar, Straus and Giroux, 1967)
PPS	*Poems of Paul Celan,* trans. Michael Hamburger. (New York: Persea Books, 2002)
S	*Sternverdunklung* by Nelly Sachs, in *Fahrt ins Staublose* (Frankfurt am Main: Suhrkamp, 1961)
SG	*Speech-Grille and Selected Poems* by Paul Celan, trans. Joachim Neugroschel (New York: Dutton, 1971)
SP	*Selected Poems and Prose of Paul Celan,* trans. John Felstiner (New York: Norton, 2001)
SNL	*Suche nach Lebenden* by Nelly Sachs (Frankfurt am Main: Suhrkamp, 1971)
T	*Noch feiert Tod das Leben* by Nelly Sachs, in *Fahrt ins Staublose* (Frankfurt am Main: Suhrkamp, 1961)
TS	*The Seeker and Other Poems* by Nelly Sachs, trans. Ruth and Matthew Mead and Michael Hamburger (New York: Farrar, Straus and Giroux, 1970)
W	*Werke in sechs Bänden* by Peter Weiss (Frankfurt am Main: Suhrkamp, 1991)

Introduction:
Trauma and Displacement

This study examines the responses of German Jewish writers to the geographical and cultural displacement that is one of the lasting consequences of the Holocaust, or Shoah.[1] The project sprang from my observation of a curious discrepancy: several authors who after 1945 lived outside of Germany but continued to write in German paradoxically experienced their favorable reception in West Germany after 1960 as a traumatic return of genocide and mass expulsion. This is true for at least three writers who attained high visibility and distinct profiles: Peter Weiss, who became the showcase exile writer of West Germany's leading literary group, the Gruppe 47; Nelly Sachs, who became a celebrated symbol of reconciliation between Germans and Jews; and Paul Celan, who began to be recognized as one of the most important German-speaking poets of the twentieth century. The sense of crisis is most evident in the cases of Celan and Sachs, both of whom experienced a massive return of persecution fears, which were linked to their experiences during the Third Reich. But Weiss's recognition as a German-language writer around the same time, commonly treated as his literary breakthrough, was also accompanied by strong feelings of ambivalence and a renewed sense that his own biography was vitally shaped by his family's departure from Germany in 1935. Similarly, several German

INTRODUCTION

Jewish intellectuals whose postwar thinking revolved around the "break in civilization"[2] that is Auschwitz, including Theodor Adorno, Jean Améry, and Günther Anders, revisited their own experience of exile and displacement during the 1960s, often with devastating results. Grown up but not yet established at the onset of their exile, these writers and thinkers came into their own only after 1945, when the physical barriers to returning to Germany or Austria ceased to exist and a more diffuse sense of dispersal emerged.

The thesis of my study is that these authors transformed their catastrophic displacement into a meaningful and productive predicament characterized as "diaspora." In choosing this term, I enter a rich theoretical field in which attention to problems caused by globalization and mass migration goes hand in hand with a reconceptualization of diaspora as a political and cultural opportunity. The rethinking of "diaspora" began with the attempt in postwar scholarship on Jewish history to distinguish between imposed and self-chosen exile, the latter being designated by diaspora. This distinction reflects the insight that since the establishment of the state of Israel, Jewish life outside Israel has become largely a matter of choice, as it has been in previous periods of Jewish independence or compact settlement in their own land. In contrast, the term *galut* (Hebrew for "exile") refers to the forced dispersion of the Jewish people. The distinction has been codified in the *Encyclopedia Judaica*, where it is used to characterize the different epochs of Jewish history.[3] The conception of this difference is a result of the secularization and politicization of Jewish thought. Whereas the biblical term *galut* refers to exile as a divinely ordained condition, usually a punishment for the people's deviation from the path of the Torah, the notion of self-chosen exile assumes the ability of humans to determine the conditions of their own lives through political action rather than religious observance. Although the precise beginnings of this view are difficult to determine, it was foregrounded by the agitation for the emancipation of the Jews in the eighteenth century and the Zionist movement that emerged at the end of the nineteenth century. Both the proponents of emancipation, who trusted in liberalism's capacity to advance religious tolerance and civic equality, and the Zionists, who promoted the establishment of a Jewish state as a remedy against abiding antisemitism, were engaged in the creation of political conditions that would bring an end to the humiliations and persecutions suffered by Jews in the *galut*.[4] "Self-chosen exile" in this sense does not mean

TRAUMA AND DISPLACEMENT

that diaspora is a good thing but that one can do something against it. As Barbara Kirshenblatt-Gimblett notes, such a distinction between forced exile and willed diaspora remains wedded to a (Zionist) view of dispersion as pathological.[5]

The decisive shift toward a more positive understanding of diaspora occurred more recently in postcolonial criticism and Jewish cultural studies. The new conception was concomitant with a semantic expansion of the term to include a wider range of displacements in a world marked by mass migrations for economic and political reasons. As one critic summarizes: "The term that once described Jewish, Greek, and Armenian dispersion now shares meaning with a larger semantic domain that includes words like immigrant, expatriate, refugee, guest-worker, exile community, overseas community, ethnic community."[6] The most important conceptual shift accomplished by postcolonial critics is their redefinition of diaspora not merely as a place of dwelling but as enunciative position and mode of articulation. Stuart Hall, for instance, uses the term diaspora to circumscribe a form of cultural identity that, although mentally bound to a lost place of origin, recognizes the insurmountable distance between this imaginary spatial center and the lived experience of postcolonial migrants.[7] According to him, it is the gap between "here" and "there" and the refusal to cover this gap through nostalgia and idealization of the lost home that makes diasporic discourse capable of producing new places from which to speak. The acceptance of an irreparable rupture between the subject and its place of origin, Hall further suggests, prevents the hypostatization of this place as pure origin while guarding against any form of ethnocentric absolutism that would preclude an engagement with the dynamic and hybrid reality of cultural identities. In view of mass displacements that elude a clear distinction between imposed and self-chosen exile, critics such as Hall replace the criterion of willingness with that of cultural productivity.[8]

Central to the dialogue between postcolonial critics and Jewish studies scholars is their search for an alternative to the idea of national self-determination, a critical counterforce to the homogenizing tendencies of the modern nation-state. According to the postcolonial critic Homi Bhabha, diasporic voices disclose a paradox inherent in contemporary nationalisms: their attempt to homogenize society and solidify the imagined national community during "one of the most sustained periods of mass migration within the West, and colonial expansion in the East."[9] In his analyses of a range of texts reflecting on various migra-

3

tory experiences, Bhabha emphasizes the performative character of these texts, which undermine national narratives by giving expression to incommensurable cultural and historical differences. Daniel Boyarin and Jonathan Boyarin, advocates of diaspora on the Jewish studies side, similarly suggest that the experience of diaspora may serve as "a positive *resource* in the necessary rethinking of models of polity in the current erosion and questioning of the modern nation-state system and ideal."[10] They propose the Jewish diaspora as a model of how a minority group can preserve a distinct group identity while being able to share space with others who are recognized and respected as others.[11] Accepting the geographical dispersion of the Jews as a condition imposed by God, rabbinical Judaism has grounded Jewish group identity in a common genealogical origin rather than in a common spatial origin, subsequently producing cultural identities that do not need to draw strict spatial boundaries in order to mark their difference from others:

> Diasporic cultural identity teaches us that cultures are not preserved by being protected from "mixing" but probably can only continue to exist as a product of such mixing. Cultures, as well as identities, are constantly being remade. While this is true of all cultures, diasporic Jewish culture lays it bare because of the impossibility of a natural association between this people and a particular land—thus the impossibility of seeing Jewish culture as a self-enclosed, bounded phenomenon.[12]

Thus the Boyarins draw on Jewish religious tradition to launch a secular critique of the autochthonous constructions of culture implied in most nationalisms. The religious imagination that relates to the land of Israel as the Promised Land, as something that is given to humans by God and never entirely possessed by them, serves here as a model of how a sense of "coming from elsewhere" allows people to accept the fact that their own culture is always bound up with other cultures.

The points of convergence between postcolonial critics and Jewish studies scholars should not obscure the fact that their dialogue has also been contentious. As the Boyarins observe, the postcolonial expansion of the term "diaspora" often entailed a reduction of the modern Jewish experience to the Zionist project. This is most evident in Hall's polemical dismissal of the Jewish concept of diaspora as a nostalgic and politically problematic fixation on a lost home.[13] But also the attempt by James Clifford, who is aware of and sympathetic to a broader range of Jewish diaspora experience, to decenter the discussion from the Jewish model might obscure insights on how much the model has to offer. This is where the Boyarins seek to intervene and establish the relevance of the Jewish diaspora for current theoretical debates. Against Hall's fetishizing of newness they hold that the commemorative link to the homeland, which has been a characteristic of the Jewish diaspora, does not need to culminate in the idea of return. Rather, the commemoration of a past homeland can provide reference points for the continuous reimagination of the present, especially when the repeated experience of "rediasporization" refracts the image of the homeland through memories of other transitory homes: "Zion [is] longed for and imagined through Cordoba, Cairo, or Vilna, and these frequently palimpsested one on the other such that Cairo becomes a remembered Cordoba and the new Jerusalem a remembered Vilna."[14] Such dissemination of memory fosters cultural creativity and the development of new forms of political agency. The Boyarins demonstrate these "powers of diaspora" with examples ranging from "effeminate" resistance strategies of late antiquity rabbis, such as trickery and evasion, to the struggle of contemporary Hasidim to exert school autonomy while receiving public funding. The politics of the Jewish diaspora experience challenges the notion that polity must be based in territory and rights in the individual. What emerges instead are "claims of an identity dependent on genealogical and diasporic loyalty rather than individual and territorial liberty"[15] and a culturally productive tension of separation and entanglement.

My own study of German Jewish writers after the Holocaust will push the debates about the paradigmatic character of Jewish diasporas further, precisely because these writers pose such a challenge to any positive understanding of diaspora. The Boyarins programmatically bracket the negative aspects of diaspora, including the historical suffering and political vulnerability experienced all too often by minority groups. They reconstruct positive—or subversive, or creative— moments in the diaspora experience in order to valorize it. But how can one reconcile these claims of a productive force of displacement with the knowledge that it was caused by genocidal terror? In the post-Holocaust period, German and Jewish cultures have been related through what Dan Diner has called a "negative symbiosis," that is, a

INTRODUCTION

shared reference to the Shoah from radically different perspectives.[16] As my chapter on Nelly Sachs will show, the term "negative symbiosis" is not entirely adequate because it tends to blur the distinction between victims and perpetrators and to obscure the multiple affiliations of displaced German Jewish writers after the war. But for the moment it will suffice to characterize a situation in which an abyss separates the former victims and perpetrators, making an in-between position almost impossible. The crises of Weiss, Sachs, and Celan testify to the difficulty, perhaps the impossibility, of sustaining relations between the small group of Jewish survivors who continue to write in German and the German language, literary heritage, and public sphere. Whereas the Boyarins draw upon situations in which Jews enjoyed a measure of political autonomy and a positive engagement with the majority culture, I focus on a moment in which the "powers of diaspora" have been radically vacated.

The writers analyzed in this study experienced an extreme form of rediasporization. A distinct diaspora consciousness expressed through ritual reenactment of the bond to the land of Israel in prayer and liturgy, which was a constitutive element of Jewish group identity in premodern Europe, largely disappeared in the German-speaking countries during the nineteenth-century process of emancipation and acculturation.[17] The reversal of Jewish emancipation during the Third Reich and the Holocaust created a new and redoubled diaspora, composed of Jews who had fled from Germany or German-speaking Central Europe and after the war did not want to return, yet failed to feel at home anywhere else and remained linked to their country of origin through their language and memories. The diasporic consciousness now involved a rejection of the home that has turned into a site of genocide. This redoubling of diaspora gave rise to a search for new points of reference or a rediscovery of forgotten ones. In Peter Weiss's semi-autobiographical novel *Fluchtpunkt*, the narrator recounts a brief, disturbing visit to his native country soon after the war and then goes on to establish existentialist Paris as the symbolic center of his cosmopolitan map. His view of German as a universal language, furthermore, resolves the tension between this cosmopolitan identification and his clinging to a native language. Nelly Sachs similarly detaches culture from place through her recuperation of the land of Israel as a site of hope and through her idealization of the "Other Germany," a cultural community of victims and opponents of Nazism that transcends any specific location. This strategy in effect allows her to maintain and develop attachments to multiple places. Celan's and Anders's rediscovery of a historic diaspora—of German-speaking Jews in Eastern Europe—further complicates the opposition between home and exile.[18]

In order to subsume these different writerly positions under the concept of diaspora, we will have to reconsider what exactly "productivity" means and to what extent it dismantles more emphatic notions of exile as meaningful or empowering. Peter Weiss adopts a cosmopolitan ideal, which posits that leaving one's place of origin is a positive move because it allows for a subjectivity free from the limitations that result from too much grounding in a particular place and culture. This positive model becomes infused with incommensurable experiences of catastrophic exile in Weiss's texts, a tension that issues in new literary experiments with the diasporic perspective. In a different but related gesture, Nelly Sachs revives a Jewish religious model that postulates the divine intentionality of Jewish dispersal, an intentionality she reinterprets as the task of giving testimony to the Shoah. Paul Celan establishes an elegiac relationship to the destroyed Jewish diaspora in Eastern Europe—the "Wander-Osten" as he writes in one of his poems—and finds ways to represent traumatizing destruction without assuming its predetermination. His non-apocalyptic view enables him to locate in the always-already dispersed East symbolic resources for a resistance against the fascism he saw resurging in Western Europe during the 1960s. Finally, Adorno, Anders, and Améry in different ways elaborate the epistemological advantage of the exile who temporarily returns to his former home or another site of trauma. Because the term diaspora refers to a dislocation (and a consciousness) that is both forced and productive, it is appropriate to conceptualize these affirmations of an irredeemable state of dispersal together, however vexed and tenuous they are. In contrast to exile, with its connotations of a nostalgic attachment to a lost home, diaspora, as I use it in this study, signifies a violent separation that opens up a way to new affiliations and critical interventions.[19]

To understand the force of such interventions we need to look at the historical context. The crises experienced by displaced German Jewish writers, paradoxically in response to a more favorable public reception, occurred at a turning point in the postwar confrontation with the legacy of Nazism and the closely related reconstitution of German

INTRODUCTION

national identity. Anson Rabinbach speaks of a crisis of *Vergangenheitsbewältigung* (mastering of the past) in 1958 and 1959.[20] The emotions released by the staging of the Anne Frank diaries and other cultural events of the late 1950s indicated that a new confrontation with the Nazi past was taking shape, while a series of desecrations of Jewish cemeteries and synagogues in December 1959 demonstrated the failure of the attempts at denazification in the immediate postwar years. The almost simultaneous publication of Heinrich Böll's *Billiard um halb zehn* (*Billiards at Half-Past Nine*), Günter Grass's *Die Blechtrommel* (*The Tin Drum*), and Uwe Johnson's *Mutmaßungen über Jakob* (*Speculations about Jakob*) in 1959 further signaled a new openness toward a confrontation with the Nazi past. In the early 1960s, then, there was a wave of re-remembering the Holocaust inaugurated by the public's attention to the Eichmann and Auschwitz trials.[21] Jeffrey Herf has attributed the changes in public memory to the departure of Konrad Adenauer from the political scene.[22] Chancellor since 1949, Adenauer had pursued democratization through the integration of former followers of Nazism. At the same time, he had instituted a politics of restitution for the Jewish victims of the Holocaust, focusing his efforts on positive relations with the state of Israel rather than confronting the responsibility of Germans in the Holocaust. However, the findings of the Central Office for the Investigation of National Socialist Crimes (established in 1958), the Eichmann trial, and the debates on the statute of limitations on the crime of murder alerted the public to the price that had been paid for Adenauer's approach: the silencing of memory. As Herf shows, the restitution politics in West Germany was fueled by hopes to facilitate the integration of the Federal Republic into a Western political framework.

In their study *The Inability to Mourn*, the psychoanalysts Alexander and Margarethe Mitscherlich give reasons for this delay of remembrance. They argue that a genuine confrontation with the atrocities of the Nazi past in postwar Germany had been hampered by the prevalence of a sociopsychological disposition that they characterize as repressed melancholia following a massive narcissistic injury. The loss of Hitler and the National Socialist order, with which large segments of the German population had identified narcissistically, would normally have provoked a melancholic reaction. However, melancholia was fended off by the deployment of a set of defense mechanisms, such as the shift of identifications from Hitler to the democratic allies and a reinvestment of libidinal energies into the economic machine of the *Wirtschaftswunder*. Because the fundamentally narcissistic patterns of identification had not been disrupted, the Nazi genocide against the Jews—that is, the "others" on whose violent exclusion the imaginary German identity propagated by Nazism had been based—had not even begun to be recognized, let alone be mourned. As Eric Santner analyzes the structural impasses of the mourning process: "The paradoxical task faced by the postwar population was thus to mourn for losses incurred in the name of a society that was in its turn founded on a fundamental denial of mourning in its (self-) constituting capacities. Germans had to mourn *as Germans* for those whom they had excluded and exterminated in their mad efforts to produce their 'Germanness.'"[23]

The evasion of mourning was facilitated by symbolic acts that functioned as surrogates for a deeper confrontation with the responsibility for, and complicity in, Nazism for large segments of the German population. Many of these acts were, in fact, focused on the Holocaust and its main victims, the Jews. Rather than being simply ignored, the genocide against the Jews was made visible in the political sphere of postwar West Germany in complex and highly symbolic ways. For instance, the financial reparations treaty (*Wiedergutmachung*), which was implemented by the West German government in 1956, was limited to Jews, excluding other victims of Nazism, such as Gypsies and homosexuals; it thus "sanctioned the substitution of the Jewish Question for the Nazi question."[24] At the same time, an ostensible philosemitism shaped public and private behavior. The philosemitic syndrome developed in the immediate postwar years in the Western zones of occupation, where the Allied authorities measured the success of Germany's denazification and democratization by the treatment of the Jews.[25] After 1949, philosemitism was used in domestic and foreign policy to demonstrate the overcoming of Nazism and thus to foster the integration of the newly founded Federal Republic into a Western political framework. Writing in 1965, Eleanore Sterling recognizes that philosemitism "signifies the exploitation of a symbol, which by proxy is supposed to certify as already completed a process and product as yet only in the state of emergence: namely, a true democracy and a positive attitude toward the Jewish minority. Philosemitism—like anti-communism—is part of the 'confessional' character of the as yet unrealized German democracy."[26] This symbolic anticipation of democracy, we may add, hampered a genuine progress toward democracy since it helped to sustain the repression of the past; appraisals of "Jewish accomplishments" diverted from the horrors of genocide, and the philosemitic inversion of traditional antisemitic stereotypes adapted lingering prejudices to the present rather than removed them.

Beginning with the crisis of *Vergangenheitsbewältigung* in the early 1960s, certain shifts in the public discussion of Nazism took place. There was a turn toward an analysis of the sociopsychological structures that had sustained Nazism and persisted into the Federal Republic and a concomitant emphasis on pedagogy as a means of working through the unmastered past. The pedagogical impetus cut across political lines, reaching from Theodor W. Adorno's article "The Meaning of Working Through the Past" (1959) to Konrad Adenauer's call for an improvement of historical education in the same year. This appeal was followed by proposals for new school curricula that would allow for a more intensive study of Nazism and antisemitism. Rabinbach suggests that these efforts, while ending the fifteen years of public evasion about Nazism, produced new symbolic displacements. In particular, the proponents of the emerging New Left, while relentlessly disclosing the legacy of Nazism in the Federal Republic, abstracted and internationalized the problem of fascism and focused on political actions exclusively aimed at the present: "the struggle against contemporary 'fascisms,' e.g., in the Federal Republic, Mozambique or Israel, became a surrogate for the missing antifascism of the postwar generation."[27]

By situating the literary production of writers in the context of the West German public sphere during the 1960s, I intend to specify some of the problems that marked the new critical confrontation with Nazism. This confrontation entailed a growing reception of German-speaking authors in exile, mostly refugees from Nazism who chose not to return to their former homes after the war. The crises Weiss, Sachs, and Celan suffered in response to their reception in Germany may help us better understand how historical violence was replayed in the cultural public sphere. As I will show, the constructions of exile and Jewish authors by the West German public issued new exclusionary principles, such as the privileging of political over "racial" exile by the Gruppe 47 and the fusion of Christian religious language and political idiom in the cultural spectacles of the *Woche der Brüderlichkeit* [week of brotherhood]. My focus, however, is on the authors and their texts. In contrast to empirical reception studies, I do not attempt an exhaustive reconstruction of the authors' de facto critical impact to describe the cultural ambiance in West Germany; rather, I analyze salient features of their public reception to illuminate the critical intention, or potential, of their texts. What writers like Weiss, Sachs, and Celan have in common, despite their very diverse aesthetic projects and political views, is their attempt to transform their own displacement into a critical stance and their inability, or unwillingness, to arrive at a position of strength and detachment.

Read against the backdrop of the contemporary ideological discourses of healing and recuperation, this "failure" turns out to be productive in and by itself, as it provides a new ground for critical intervention. I already mentioned that Peter Weiss's cosmopolitan view, which establishes exile as a privileged site of critique, is complicated in his prose texts by the evocation of catastrophic forms of exile that continue to undermine the cosmopolitan promise of freedom and critical distance. Rather than speaking from a stable position of measured distance, these texts fluctuate between numbing distance and uncanny proximity. Weiss's experimentation with different incarnations of the narrator-as-stranger produces critical perspectives on West Germany in texts that do not narrate but perform for an imagined German audience the violent rupture between the subject and its place of origin. Nelly Sachs's work, in contrast, seems much less critical. She constructs symbolic spaces in which biblical place names such as Ur come to encapsulate her own conflict between German and Jewish origins, a survival strategy that, by dehistoricizing the conflict, facilitated her appropriation as a figure of reconciliation by sectors of the West German public. However, Sachs's nervous breakdown shortly after her first visit to postwar Germany to receive a literary prize is symptomatic of the instability of her position, and the attempts at cultural mediation in her poetry are undermined by textual crises. Finally, Paul Celan's remapping of the East European Jewish diaspora in *Die Niemandsrose* [*The No-One's Rose*] presents an example of a more self-reflexive deployment of figures of trauma and loss. In response to a charge of plagiarism that was leveled against him in 1960 and that amounted to a second expulsion from home, Celan composed elegies on exile, dispersal, and the East, elegies that evoke redemptive resolutions only to corrode them. Celan's insistence on the incompleteness of mourning, as well as the increasing recalcitrance of his poems and their encrypted historical referentiality, work against the philosemitic appropriation of his texts.

INTRODUCTION

In the first part of this introduction I have described the shift in postcolonial criticism and Jewish cultural studies from a concept of diaspora as self-chosen exile to one of diaspora as coercive yet culturally productive. What scholars such as Homi Bhabha, James Clifford, and Daniel and Jonathan Boyarin find valuable in diaspora is not a purported freedom of choice but the possibility of fashioning new cultural identities in the absence of a clearly defined homeland. I also suggested that the renewed contact between Jewish diaspora writers and the West German public in the 1960s substantiates this idea of a positive force of displacement—and it goes without saying that "positive" can refer here only to the critical power of texts, not to the psychical well-being of people. In what follows now, I suggest some parallels between this idea and the invocation of the emigrant as a privileged figure of witness in recent trauma theory. Trauma theory is relevant for my study because it offers an explanation for the temporal lag between the first public notice of the death camps after the war and the re-remembrance of the Holocaust in the early 1960s. This delayed remembrance, which was not confined to Germany but also noticeable in other countries, indicates that Holocaust remembrance as a whole is marked by the *Nachträglichkeit,* or deferred action, that Freud has identified as the central structure of traumatic experience. Even more important, recent trauma theorists have invoked figures of displacement to explain how the transmission of traumatic experience is possible. If postcolonial criticism has historicized and politicized poststructuralist concepts including difference and displacement, trauma theory uses such concepts to figure the possibility of testimony. In what follows, I will distinguish between (1) the psychoanalytic notion of the emigrant's return as a form of "working-through" and (2) the more radical understanding of testimony as incomplete speech and emigration as irrevocable departure in the work of the Italian philosopher Giorgio Agamben.

The interest in testimony as a literary genre has altered the debate about the "unsayability" or the "unrepresentability" of the Holocaust. Originally concerned with the question of how human language could ever furnish words for this unique act of mass destruction, the debate has shifted toward the insight that the Holocaust has disrupted not so much the referential function of language but its ability to address. As Shoshana Felman and Dori Laub put it, the Holocaust is an "event without a witness" not only because the Nazis killed or silenced most physical witnesses of the Holocaust but also because the bureaucratically administered genocide destroyed the ethical dimension of language, its capacity to forge bonds between human beings.[28] Holocaust testimony both expresses this crisis of language and restores some of the lost capacity by opening up a communal and communicative space in which the truth can emerge. The witness to trauma does not possess the truth but rather is part of an ongoing quest for the truth, a quest that involves an audience willing and able to endure the silences that accompany all Holocaust testimony. In her interpretation of Claude Lanzmann's film *Shoah*, Felman focuses on the emigrant-survivor whose return to the site of trauma initiates a process of working-through. *Shoah* begins with an account of how Lanzmann went to Israel and found Simon Srebnik, one of only two survivors of the Chelmno death camp, and convinced him to return to Chelmno in order to describe what happened there. Felman argues that this return restores a sense of agency to Srebnik. Originally too young and too numbed to bear witness, Srebnik is able to describe the events he had seen in Chelmno only much later, when he revisits the former death camp with the inner distance granted by his postwar life in Israel. Residence in Israel, "the place of the regeneration and the locus of the gathering of Holocaust survivors,"[29] has provided him with a new "frame of reference" that relativizes the frame of death and destruction governing the camps and enables him to become "an articulate and for the first time fully *conscious* witness of what he had been witnessing during the war."[30] Felman places particular emphasis on the expansion of Srebnik's cognitive horizon and his development of a double perspective after his move to Israel. In thus invoking the emigrant's epistemological advantage, she mobilizes a hermeneutic of exile to argue for the possibility of testimony.[31]

In *Remnants of Auschwitz*, a meditation on the writings of Primo Levi, Giorgio Agamben similarly describes testimony as a form of speech that is marked by lacunae and a constitutive incompleteness. In testimony, the speech of the survivor is conjoined with the silence of the *Muselmann*, the camp jargon for those who had grown so weak in body and spirit that they seemed doomed to selection. (The *Muselmann* is an important figure in all of Primo Levi's writings.) Testimony depends on an asymmetrical dialogue between the survivor, who can speak but has not fully experienced the camps, and the *Muselmann*, who has the experience but can no longer speak. The crux of Agamben's argument is that

INTRODUCTION

the witness does not primarily testify to the historical facts, such as the existence of the camps, but rather to someone who can no longer speak or to something that can no longer be spoken. Like Felman and Laub, who read testimony as a product of human interaction—the attentiveness extended by the empathetic listener to the traumatized survivor—Agamben never detaches testimony from the concrete agencies of speech. In the act of testimony, two different kinds of impossibilities, the impossibility of experience and the impossibility of speech, collide in a way that splits the monolithic idea of "unspeakability" into instances of a process of transmission. The language of testimony does not simply falter and stammer in the face of the unspeakable but rather expresses the silence of another human being, thus founding a relationship between the speaker and the mute.[32]

Though figures of displacement are less prominent in Agamben's work, one appears at the crucial juncture when he develops his idea of the "remnant." Agamben cites a remark by a famous German Jewish emigrant, the political philosopher Hannah Arendt, who in 1961 stated that "what remains" is "the mother tongue."[33] Taking his lead from this remark, Agamben forms a new conception of how the speaking testify to the speechless by reenacting the loss of language: "to bear witness is to place oneself in one's own language in the position of those who have lost it, to establish oneself in a living language as if it were dead, or in a dead language as if it were living—in any case, outside both the archive and the *corpus* of what has already been said."[34] Agamben's choice of the former refugee Arendt is no coincidence. The refugee who is alive because she escaped the camps is a paradigmatic survivor, able to bear witness precisely because she has not, as Agamben cites Primo Levi, "'touched bottom' in the camp."[35] Exile is a paradigmatic predicament that forces one's own language to be reborn. Exile literature—or as I will call it later on in this study, diaspora literature—is a form of writing that arises neither from the corpus of what has been said nor from the writer's subjectivity. For the exile writer's words are dislodged from what is being said at home, and her self has first to be reconstituted after the loss of all existential certainties. Of course, this idea of the constitutive newness of exilic language does not necessarily hold true in reality—indeed, such a language is just as likely to be conventional as any other—but it is significant that Agamben invokes the experience of emigration to figure the possibility of testimony. Suggesting that she who speaks in a mother tongue experienced as dead performs the same crossing of the boundary between life and death that characterizes testimony, Agamben projects a paradoxical experience of time onto the spatial movement of emigration.

The use of figures of displacement in these theorists of testimony is neither arbitrary nor merely illustrative. Rather, it captures their shared idea that in testimony the possibility of transmission emerges from the impossibility of speech. It is precisely because an experience cannot be fully verbalized that it demands to be rearticulated in search of new addressees.[36] However, while Felman and Laub locate the experience of the Holocaust in the psychical structure of the witness, which can be gradually articulated within a community of first- and second-degree witnesses, Agamben posits a more radical disjunction between language and experience. According to Felman and Laub, the return to a site of trauma is an important step in the survivor's recuperation of linguistic agency and the establishment of new idioms to talk about the Holocaust. Agamben's focus on a different impediment to speech, the incomprehensibility and irretrievability of the *Muselmann*'s words, is reflected in his different use of the figure of the emigrant. Whereas for Felman and Laub emigration and return make up the spiral movement that is working-through, Agamben cites emigration as an instance of departure without arrival and without return. Likewise, testimony, if it is at all possible, is a departure to new expressive possibilities rather than a recovery of lost speech or memories. In this study I argue that Agamben's idea, more so than the model proposed by Felman and Laub, sheds light on the "impossible returns" of postwar German Jewish writers.

The vicissitudes of return transpire in recent memoirs by Ruth Klüger and Peter Gay. Both Klüger (from Vienna) and Gay (from Berlin) are intellectuals versed in the language of psychoanalysis as well as former Jewish refugees, and both chose to frame their memoirs by scenes of return. In the epilogue to *weiter leben* (1992) [*Still Alive*], an account of a childhood spent in fascist Vienna and in concentration camps, Klüger details how she began writing the book during a two-year visit to Germany, or more precisely, after a cerebral hemorrhage (the result of being run down by a bicyclist) necessitated a long stay in a German hospital. This accident and her recovery reiterate her original trauma because they are products of chance and create a constant tension between terrifying fear and elusive moments of hope.[37] It is significant that the accident takes place in Germany, where Klüger spent

INTRODUCTION

some time after the end of the war. However intimately linked Germany is to her sufferings, it is not itself a site of trauma, or at least this is what we have to infer from Klüger's observation that a return to a site of trauma in the strict sense is impossible. For the survivor of Auschwitz, the camp is a *Zeitschaft*,[38] a place that existed only at a distinct moment in time and whose meaning cannot be recovered by visiting its remnants; only someone who has never lived in a camp will visit it in search of remembrance. Nor is it possible for Klüger to return to Austria, a place that signifies the all-pervasive hostility she experienced there as a child, regardless of the meanings Austria may since have acquired. The Germany of the present, however, provides a setting in which it is possible to have a new kind of dialogue with the former enemies. In the epilogue Klüger describes how she wrote her memoir in cooperation with German friends, to whom she dedicates the book, and throughout the text she reflects on what it means for a Holocaust survivor to address a German audience. This situation is often vexing, as becomes clear in the text when she warns her readers against cathartic readings or reminds them of all that remains unspeakable in conversations with Germans. But the fact that these hesitations can be articulated and the boundaries between her and her German interlocutors redrawn marks the minimal difference the writing of a memoir can make.

Peter Gay's memoir *My German Question* (1998) offers another example of a return to Germany that sets the stage for a process of working-through. The book, the first half of which relates the experience of a Jewish teenager in Nazi Germany trying to protect his threatened sense of self from an environment that labels him subhuman, starts out with a reminiscence of Gay's first trip to Germany in 1961. This return is construed, if not as the beginning of writing, as the beginning of a new encounter with his native country that ultimately enables him to articulate the refugee's trauma. Symptomatic of the ordeal of return is an incident that occurred right after he and his wife had crossed the border to Germany and that subjected him "to the most disconcerting anti-Semitic display I had endured since I left Germany."[39] While exchanging currency, Gay noticed that the woman behind the counter "looked at me coldly, her eyes registering pure hatred as I handed her my passport. A glance at her had left no doubt in my mind: murderous anti-Semitism was alive and flourishing in my native land."[40] Sometime later, however—it is not clear when exactly,

16

but certainly not at the time of the incident—Gay corrects this impression, thinking that the woman was probably simply indifferent and her hatred a product of his own projection: "The fact was that this clerk did not hate me; she barely registered my existence. I hated her."[41] In this scene Gay carries out the affective and cognitive labor Freud considered crucial for successful working-through; he recuperates the affect that was missing in the original experience while submitting the experience to critical reflection. It is for this reason, perhaps, that his return to Germany was one of his steps toward "reconciliation"[42]—or at least toward the resolution of his own internal conflict between the refugee who is passionately opposed to his former home and the exile who harbors some nostalgia for his native city, Berlin.

These accounts of trauma and working-through suggest that the act of returning does not mark the reclamation of a lost home but at best the discovery of a language in which historical events can begin to be articulated. More precisely, Gay's and Klüger's return to Germany furnishes not so much new words but new communal relations that aid the verbalization of traumatic experience. Just as Klüger enlists the help of her local friends to compose her memoir, Gay deems his conversations with German friends, whom he first met at Stanford and later visited in Germany, the decisive turning point in his relationship to his own past. The memoirs thus illustrate the shift from reference to address conceptualized in recent trauma theory. At the same time, these memoirs undermine the idea of return as condition of working-through. It is in Germany that Klüger remembers her childhood in Vienna and Auschwitz, and it is on the border between France and Germany that the crucial incident between Gay and the clerk takes place—and it is in yet another place that he grasps the meaning of this incident. As in Agamben, the emigrant embodies a disjunction between place and memory that founds the possibility of testimony, understood as a speech act that continuously reopens the abyss between the speaking and the speechless. Elsewhere I have argued that the late W. G. Sebald similarly postulates the existence of an unbridgeable gap between the victims and their witnesses, though in Sebald the gap separates victims from nonvictims—often Jews from non-Jews—rather than survivors from *Muselmänner*.[43] The inability to return indicates here the unavailability of a testimonial community in the emphatic sense. The emigrant who refuses to get settled again embodies the willingness to live with that situation—or at least the necessity of living

INTRODUCTION

with it. This idea of the productivity of permanent displacement throws into sharper relief the critical force of German Jewish writing after the Holocaust.

The writers analyzed in this study, I propose, help us better understand the ways that displacement can be both traumatic and productive. Chapters 2 to 4 of this book are case studies of Weiss, Sachs, and Celan that are structured around crises in the public reception of these authors. These crises coincided with a transformative moment in the history of Holocaust remembrance, its first generational reimagining in the wake of a number of highly publicized criminal trials. Around the same time, Weiss's sudden recognition as a German-language writer, Sachs's celebration as a figure of reconciliation between Germans and Jews, and the plagiarism charge against Celan reaffirmed, modified, or radically questioned the ways that these authors made sense of their own displacement after the Holocaust. These case studies are framed by reflections on displacement in three German Jewish intellectuals who embody different forms of—incomplete, impossible—return: Theodor W. Adorno went from his exile in the United States to the German city of Frankfurt; Günther Anders moved to Vienna, a city tied to German language and culture yet remote from his Eastern European birthplace and the German cities in which he used to live before the war; and Jean Améry, a survivor of Auschwitz who was born and raised in Austria, moved to French-speaking Belgium, where he continued to write and publish in German. The inclusion of Adorno in this study required a slight expansion of its spatial frame, since Adorno permanently resettled in West Germany. Yet as I hope to show, Adorno provides us with a powerful example of a diaspora position within Germany while furnishing important paradigms of the textual articulation of diaspora. Adorno provocatively realigns exile and textuality in his redefinition of the essay as a quintessentially diasporic form of writing. While he shares this definition with Jean Améry, their respective choices of residence have an analogue in their critical strategies: whereas Adorno mobilizes the inner heterogeneity of the German language by punctuating his essays with equivocations and foreign words, Améry adopts the spatial and discursive position of a traveler to challenge from without the repression of the past in Germany. And whereas Améry claims the survivor's disrupted sense of time as a source of moral knowledge, Adorno translates temporal discontinuity into strategies of "retroactive diasporization." This projection of spatial and temporal rifts into the past reverses the gradual disappearance of a diasporic consciousness among German Jews over the course of the nineteenth century. Günther Anders pursues a similar goal in describing the dynamic of Jewish assimilation and dissimilation in turn-of-the-century Eastern Europe. By fracturing the monolithic image of the past and disrupting the impression of an automatic drive toward catastrophe, both Adorno and Anders attempt to restore the possibility of mourning and resistance. Whether performed in the present or projected into the past, the concepts of diaspora implied, if rarely made explicit, by these German Jewish intellectuals provide a point of departure for the recharting of the German Jewish diaspora after the Holocaust.

1
The Inability to Return:
German Jewish Intellectuals after the Holocaust

Theodor W. Adorno: Essay, Exile, Efficacy

Theodor W. Adorno has figured quite prominently in recent discussions on exile and diaspora. Building on texts from Adorno's exile in Los Angeles, Edward Said has established him as a paradigm of the émigré intellectual whose critical acumen derives from a sense of separateness from his place of residence, a condition that enables the emigrant to historicize phenomena of everyday life and put them into critical perspective.[1] Los Angeles is also the focus of a chapter by Nico Israel that attempts to differentiate the widely accepted view of Adorno's nostalgia for European high culture by analyzing his complex relationship to the city he loathed but also recognized as a prototypical site of administered culture.[2] Less has been made, however, of the meaning of displacement in Adorno after his return to Germany in 1949. This return was not easy. Apart from Adorno's own doubts as to whether postwar Germany offered a climate of genuine reflection and discussion, his professional career moved slowly and was tainted by attempts to dismiss his appointments as measures of restitution and compensation. In 1953 he was given a "Compensation Chair" (*Wiedergutmachungslehrstuhl*) and upon his appointment as a full professor in

1956, several of his colleagues attributed his success to his status as a Jewish re-migrant rather than his professional accomplishments.[3]

If the image of Adorno as a successful re-migrant nonetheless prevails, this might be so because he himself at times emphasized the measure of cultural continuity that was possible despite the rupture that the Holocaust brought about for Western concepts of civilization and subjectivity. In his 1965 essay "On the Question: 'What is German?'" he famously bases his decision to return to Germany on the affinity between the German language and his own philosophical project. He seems to embrace an essentialist notion of an authentic language the expressive potential of which cannot be fully utilized by a non-native speaker: "At least the native German will feel that he cannot fully acquire the essential aspect of presentation or of expression in the foreign language."[4] Yet upon closer inspection, even in this essay he comes to valorize the effects of a displacement that forever changes a person. If Adorno values the intimate knowledge of a native language, it is in the figure of the returning emigrant, who has lost the natural bond with this language, that he locates a form of authentic language beyond the "jargon of authenticity"[5]: "The returning émigré, who has lost the naïve relationship to what is his own, must unite the most intimate relationship to his native language with unflagging vigilance against any fraud it promotes."[6] In this section, I will examine Adorno's postwar valorization of diaspora by tracing his definition of the essay as a quintessentially diasporic genre and tool of critical intervention. In a close reading of his essay "Heine the Wound," I will show how he deploys strategies associated with exile and diaspora in an effort to disrupt the systemic continuity of fascism in postwar West Germany. I will also suggest that Adorno's essays shed new light on recent debates about the modes and functions of post-traumatic writing, and in particular the roles of historical reference and force of address in such writing.

In their famous *Dialectic of Enlightenment,* written in Californian exile in 1944, Adorno and Horkheimer ground their valorization of diaspora in the historical experience of the Jews and the theological foundations of Judaism. As Anson Rabinbach has shown, they draw on the Judaic taboo on mimesis, or *Bilderverbot,* to propose a model of enlightenment that would not, in the name of historical progress, regress to the merely mimetic and blindly destructive. Rabinbach also provides evidence that Adorno and Horkheimer explicitly associate this model with the historical condition of diaspora in letters and notes exchanged during the conception of the book.[7] This valorization of the Jewish diaspora and the prohibition on graven images is predicated on the notion that both mark intermediate stages in the process of enlightenment, the critique of which is the main subject of *Dialectic of Enlightenment*. Mimesis, according to Adorno and Horkheimer, allows for a nondominating relationship with nature but also presents a step toward instrumental rationality in its attempt to control and even annihilate an other that is both feared and desired.[8] The Judaic taboo on mimesis, then, both deepens the separation from nature and diminishes the destructive force of mimesis, thereby investing enlightenment with a moment of hope: "The disenchanted world of Judaism conciliates magic by negating it in the idea of God. Jewish religion allows no word that would alleviate the despair of all that is mortal. It associates hope only with the prohibition against calling on what is false as God, against invoking the finite as the infinite, lies as truth."[9] If Adorno associates the Judaic proscription on idolatry with nomadism, however, this idea is never fleshed out in historical detail but pertains to the "imaginary prehistory of the Jews"[10] he developed during the early 1940s. This construct posits that nomadism freed the Jews from local gods and symbiotic ties to a native soil, thus advancing abstraction and universalism, and at the same time represents a state that precedes the enslavement of modern man through routine labor and a fixed homeland. In the antisemitism chapter of *Dialectic of Enlightenment*, this dialectic is tangible in the invocations of different historical roles of Jews, who as merchants helped to spread civilization in the Roman Empire and as adherents of the idea of a promised land attracted the hatred of those who were forced to repress their sensuous and mimetic desires.

However, already in *Dialectic of Enlightenment* the speculative link between Judaism, diaspora, and enlightenment tends to recede in favor of a broad understanding of civilization itself as an exile from myth and nature. With Odysseus figuring as the prototype of the wandering Jew—he is described as an "oriental merchant"[11] and a typical middleman—and the odyssey as a model of enlightenment predicated on the departure from home, the critical force of exile is displaced from Hebrew to Greek culture. This displacement of nomadism from Jewish into new contexts continues in essays Adorno wrote during the 1950s. In an essay on Joseph von Eichendorff, for instance, he attests the poems of the German Romantic poet an observation of the *Bilderver-*

CHAPTER 1

bot and a special sensibility for poetic valences of foreign words.[12] And whereas he compares foreign words explicitly with Jews in *Minima Moralia*—"Foreign words [Fremdwörter] are the Jews of language"[13]—he elaborates their critical potential in much more general terms in "Words from Abroad." In "The Essay as Form," published in 1958 as a self-reflexive overture to *Notes to Literature* 1, Adorno cites further markers of Jewishness without explicitly naming them. In his description of the prejudices against the essay form in Germany, he mentions not only the yellow star but also the traditional epithet of ostracized Jews, mostly of Eastern European provenance—*Luftmensch*—to describe the essay's lack of canonicity and the nature of literary interpretation: "The person who interprets instead of accepting what is given and classifying it is marked with the yellow star [der gelbe Fleck] of one who squanders his intelligence in impotent speculation, reading things in where there is nothing to interpret. A man with his feet on the ground or a man with his head in the clouds [Luftmensch]—those are the alternatives."[14] These lines redeem the antisemitic image of the hyperintelligent Jew whose critical acumen derives from a lack of creativity through the idea that a similarly excessive, unsystematic, and displaced intelligence helps the essayist to push a literary text beyond its author's intentions.

This link between the uprooted Jew and the essay indicates that Adorno transposes his philosophical valorization of diaspora onto the very form of the essay. In fact, he defines the essay as a quintessentially diasporic genre, emphasizing its lack of origins and originality in both form and subject matter. As a form of commentary whose "efforts reflect the leisure of a childlike person who has no qualms about taking his inspiration from what others have done before him,"[15] the essay necessarily relates to something preexisting and preformed. Adorno contrasts the essay's nonoriginal character with what he perceives to be a problematic invocation of primordiality (of Heidegger, though this name is never mentioned) that in a world of reification cannot be but false. Against such a celebration of origins Adorno sets the transformative power of the essay, its tendency to develop further what exists rather than tracing it back to origins. On a philosophical level, this means that the essay exposes the pseudonatural, mythological character of cultural phenomena. On a linguistic level, it means that it employs strategies such as equivocation. Whereas equivocation in rhetoric weakens and manipulates the listener, in the essay it reveals a hidden truth, namely the affinities between different things or phenomena denoted by the same word. Yet unlike Heideggerian etymology, essayistic equivocation does not imply that these are primordial connections of the past but rather points to possible, aesthetic, fragile "cross-connections between elements, something for which discursive logic has no place."[16]

This latter point is important because it assigns to the essay a special temporality and openness toward the future. The essay's ability to open up new possibilities derives at least in part from its lack of conceptual grounding and refusal to provide exact definitions of concepts. Whoever insists on such definitions overlooks, Adorno argues, that "all concepts are already implicitly concretized through the language in which they stand. The essay starts with these meanings, and, being essentially language itself, takes them farther; it wants to help language in its relation to concepts, to take them in reflection as they have been named unreflectingly in language."[17] This does not mean that every essay is critical; on the contrary, bad essays affirm the existing order by presupposing and reproducing the abstractions and clichés that inform mainstream society. The essay's critical potential and orientation toward an open-ended future are once again captured in the image of a person away from home. Adorno compares the treatment of concepts in good essays to "the behavior of someone in a foreign country who is forced to speak its language instead of piecing it together out of its elements according to the rules learned in school."[18] In both cases, the possibility of erring is outweighed by the possibility of a genuinely open spiritual experience. Adorno's use of figures of displacement is not incidental but rather reflects his conception of the essay as a genre whose critical force derives from intratextual motion.

In this way, figures of displacement contribute to the peculiar public effect Adorno's essays had or at least aimed for. To be sure, Adorno's focus on essay composition coincided with his withdrawal from more immediate forms of public education. After his return to Germany he had participated in the Group Experiment, an opinion research study that supplemented quantitative with qualitative analysis to gauge the presence of fascist dispositions among the German population and that was consistent with the American policy of education for democracy. After the completion of the project in 1955, he increasingly recoiled from empirical sociological research, a decision he explained in a 1957 manuscript with the increasing divide between criticism and empiricism. Yet a portrayal of Adorno as a theorist removed from praxis would obscure the fact that he was also a public intellectual who sought to intervene in contemporary German society through teaching and writing.[19] Many of the literary critical essays collected in his *Notes to Literature* were originally conceived as radio lectures, though even then they resembled essays more than public speeches. In his theory of the essay, Adorno provides some justification for the absence of address or appeal in his lectures, writing that the essay has a historical affinity to rhetoric but sublimates the rhetorical gratification of the audience into "the idea of a happiness in freedom vis-à-vis the object."[20] Adorno's self-distancing from the idea of a direct impact is crucial. Intervention for him exists not in interaction with an audience but in discursive work on reified concepts and their linguistic expressions in slogans and stereotypes, a procedure that may release the unfulfilled truth potential of these concepts.[21]

Adorno's 1959 essay "Words from Abroad" further elucidates the connection between displacement and critical intervention in his own writing.[22] The essay describes the critical function of foreign words (*Fremdwörter*) in the German language and generally complicates the question of what is native and what is foreign in a language. Adorno vindicates there his own use of foreign words as a strategy to evoke dissonance from within the German language, in which Germanic and Latin elements were never successfully fused. He argues that foreign words introduce a tension into language that reveals what is true for all language; namely, that it neither possesses an organic form nor grants an immediate access to reality. The argument for a healthy dose of linguistic heterogeneity is compounded by the idea of the greater precision achieved through the thoughtful use of foreign words, with precision meaning not referential exactitude but connotative plenitude and mimetic adaptation to complex subjects. Read against the backdrop of the claims Adorno makes a few years later in "On the Question: 'What is German?'" the essay "Words from Abroad" can be said to expose a tension between heterogeneity and continuity in language. As Thomas Levin put it, the moment Adorno discovers the continuity of self grounded in a native language is "the moment that he recognizes that this language is not his at all."[23]

This tension is in part resolved through a retroactive fragmentation of space, a strategy that is most tangible in the concrete, physiognomic elements of the essay, such as the introductory autobiographical remarks. Adorno relates there three episodes of his life in which his use of complex language aroused resentment in his surroundings. First, after the recent broadcast of his Proust lecture, he had received letters of protest against his allegedly excessive use of foreign words. To illuminate his point that these listeners resisted the foreignness of his thoughts rather than that of his language, he then relates another situation, when, during the time of his emigration, he presented provocative ideas in a lecture given to an audience of émigrés. As an experiment, he carefully eliminated all foreign words from the lecture, but afterward nonetheless was accused of using too many of them. Finally, he remembers a third situation from his childhood, in which he spoke High German on the street only to be rebuked by a dialect-speaking neighbor. The combination of these episodes is especially interesting because it in no way prepares the way for the rest of the argument but rather serves to establish a temporal continuity. No mention of foreign words is made in the case of the child (at least not initially) and, by selecting the second episode from the time of his emigration, Adorno shifts the focus away from what is otherwise an important argument of the essay, that foreign words may serve as an antidote to German nationalism. In other words, the use of complex language appears as a form of cultural dissent that bridges spatial and temporal distances, including that of the Holocaust. The ability to relate to such a tradition of cultural dissent might explain why Adorno found the possibility to express himself in German still intact or, in his own term, not "damaged." Yet the childhood scene also shows that this assertion of cultural continuity is contingent upon a retroactive fragmentation and dispersion of space, namely the creation of a rift between the (Jewish) child and his neighbors. The temporal gap potentially opened up through emigration is, paradoxically, closed though the creation of spatial gaps.

Adding parenthetically that the child is Jewish means, of course, to evade a problem—namely the fact that Adorno himself never uses the word Jewish. However, the High German-speaking boy who is being rebuked by his dialect-speaking neighbor brings to mind the historical process of assimilation, during which Jews adopted High German rather than local vernaculars and became major proponents of the universalist, humanist strains of German culture. The impression that Adorno taps here into a cultural archive of images of Jews and Gentiles is confirmed by the following image of the boy timidly watching his neighbor being carried home in a state of total intoxication.

CHAPTER 1

Furthermore, the portrait of a petit bourgeois filled with resentment against the privileged and ready to project it onto the weakest members of society (here children, but in historical reality often the Jews) offers a microstudy of antisemitism. Jews, on the other hand, figure somewhat stereotypically as both victims of and critical counterforce to cultural parochialism. The way in which ethnoreligious stereotypes are implied rather than made explicit in the text reveals the position from which Adorno speaks, a position both inside and outside of the culture in which he lives and writes. Just as his dispersal of the German language is contingent upon the assertion of continuity within this very language, his inscription of ethnoreligious difference depends on an intimate knowledge of, and participation in, a native discourse on non-natives.

Reading Heine, Reading History

Adorno's essay "Heine the Wound" presents an important example of how his critical position depends upon strategies of retroactive diasporization, that is, the projection of moments of difference into the past. "Heine the Wound" was first broadcast on the 100th anniversary of Heine's death in 1956. At first sight, Adorno's reading of Heine's exile as a largely negative predicament seems to contrast with his valorization of the Jewish diaspora in *Dialectic of Enlightenment* and related texts. The word he uses in the Heine essay is *Heimatlosigkeit* (homelessness), referring to the marginalization of the Jewish author of the *Book of Songs* in Germany rather than the isolation of the German poet in France. Following in the vein of Karl Kraus and others, Adorno indicts the smoothness of Heine's poetic language as an expression of the increasing commodification of culture before he analyzes it in more complex ways. More precisely, he redeems the supposed aesthetic faults of Heine's poems by reading them first as a symptom of failed Jewish emancipation, then as a product of projection—Heine's Jewishness, he argues, served as a pretext for those who sought to deny the effects of increasing commodification on everybody's life—and finally as an anticipation of a post-Holocaust state of alienation.

As Peter Uwe Hohendahl has pointed out, these claims do not go together very well.[24] In particular, there is a tension between a projection theory of antisemitism, according to which the choice of the victim would be arbitrary, and the notion that there is something real in the Jewish condition that attracts hatred, here the lack of identity and authentic language resulting from failed assimilation. One may add that a similar tension exists in *Dialectic of Enlightenment,* which describes antisemitism as a blind projection of aggressive wishes generated by the renunciation of instincts and simultaneously reads the Judaic injunction against idolatry as one of the major forces pushing toward a greater renunciation of instincts. Hohendahl argues that in the Heine essay, Adorno "becomes caught up in conflicting discourses that he is unable to control,"[25] in part because he himself is still haunted by Heine's problem, the inability to be at home in a native language: Adorno was aware of the fact that his own language was marked by a complexity and heterogeneity traditionally associated with Jewish intellectuals.[26] Such a symptomatic reading of the inconsistencies of the Heine essay has much validity. However, there is a greater rationale to these inconsistencies, which result from the ways Adorno translates his philosophical valorization of diaspora into a textual deployment of figures of dispersion. In his essay on Heine, Adorno uses two strategies he associates in other places with exile and diaspora, essayistic equivocation and the use of *Fremdwörter.* These strategies allow him to read history in a way that disrupts the mechanisms of projection and the systemic continuity of fascism he analyzed so eloquently in his 1959 essay "The Meaning of Working Through the Past."

On a thematic level, in the Heine essay Adorno elaborates the critical impact of Jewish assimilation, which he interprets as a form of mimetic behavior. He initially attributes Heine's purely instrumental use of language to his fairly recent entry into German culture, thus aligning Jewish assimilation with the advance of capitalism, both of which are held to deprive things of their essence and reduce them to exchange value. After mentioning that Heine's mother was not fluent in German, he suggests that Heine's own linguistic versatility reflects the cultural outsider's lack of sensitivity to the semantic and emotional depth of words: "His lack of resistance to words that are in fashion is the excessive mimetic zeal of the person who is excluded."[27] In terms of Adorno's own theory, Heine's use of language would be mimesis in a negative sense, a mere imitation that ultimately affirms the existing order, rather than a critical adaptation that will eventually change it. Adorno's initial verdict is modified, however, through the invocation of the figure of the virtuoso: "So great was the virtuosity of this man, who imitated language as if he were playing it on a keyboard, that he raised even the inadequacy of his language to the medium of one to whom it was granted to say what he suffered."[28] Musical performance is Adorno's principal example of mimetic understanding, that is, the constructive appropriation of an artwork that releases its critical-utopian potential.[29] The virtuoso, who isolates moments of an artwork and fetishizes their technical challenge, easily undoes this critical potential. However, as we know from Adorno's *Aesthetic Theory*, the virtuoso also reveals a truth about all art, namely the antinomy that follows from the impossible striving for aesthetic autonomy.[30] Analogously, Adorno seems to be suggesting, the desperately assimilating Jew exposes the impossible striving for community in a world torn apart by economic and social conflicts. In fact, if we read the virtuoso here as a pure performer who empties an artwork of essence by exalting its technical difficulty, we may compare his activity to what Homi Bhabha calls "colonial mimicry," that is, a mode of imitating a national culture that ultimately undermines it by revealing the performative nature of all national identity.[31]

This reconceptualization of Heine's *Heimatlosigkeit* as a positive force is underwritten by two textual strategies associated with exile and diaspora. One of these is essayistic equivocation, especially around the word "wound." Adorno begins the essay: "Anyone who wants to make a serious contribution to remembering Heine on the centennial of his death and not merely deliver a formal speech will have to speak about a wound; about what in Heine and his relationship to the German tradition causes us pain and what has been repressed, especially in Germany since the Second World War."[32] This sentence, which likens Heine to a wound that causes discomfort in those born after him, sets the tone for the description of his reception, which is throughout the essay associated with annoyance, embarrassment, and shame. But there is also the opposite tendency to describe Heine himself as wounded. The sentence "since that time Heine's aura has been painful and guilt-laden, as though it were bleeding,"[33] for instance, first depicts Heine's aura as a cause of pain, that is, a wound, before suggesting that the aura itself is bleeding, that is, wounded. The dissemination of adjectives and verbs associated with the wound creates an ambiguity as to whether Heine *is* a wound or *has* a wound. This ambiguity is readily audible in the German title, "Die Wunde Heine" [Heine the wound], which is almost indistinguishable from "Die Wunde Heines" [Heine's wound]. In the concluding passage of the essay, this ambiguity entails a leap from the past into the present. This passage interprets Heine's damaged life and language as an anticipation of the homelessness and alienation experienced by contemporary humanity:

> Now that the destiny which Heine sensed has been fulfilled literally, however, the homelessness has also become everyone's homelessness; all human beings have been as badly injured in their beings and their language as Heine the outcast was. His words stand in for their words: there is no longer any homeland other than a world in which no one would be cast out any more, the world of a genuinely emancipated humanity. The wound that is Heine will heal only in a society that has achieved reconciliation.[34]

This passage performs what Adorno calls in "The Essay as Form" a quintessential essayistic movement, namely a temporal leap through equivocation, here evolving around "Heine the wound" and "Heine's wound." As we have just seen, the equivocal use of words may uncover hidden affinities between different things or phenomena without implying that these are primordial connections of the past. One may argue, however, that the utopian work of the essay, its opening up of new possibilities, undermines its critical intention. For the leap from the past to the present is accompanied by a tendency toward identification and inclusion. Heine, who is the wound of German culture and history, now appears as "injured"—that is, he has the wound everybody suffers today—and the focus is on the condition of woundedness rather than the process of its infliction. These shifting meanings of the wound are symptomatic of a process of conflation, a bracketing of difference and conflict that culminates in Adorno's use of the indefinite pronoun "all." Equivocation turns into equation as the problem of a social minority in Germany turns out to be the universal predicament of contemporary society. And yet, if we take Adorno's claim seriously that equivocation points to possible rather than factual affinities, we may discern here something other than an abstract and all-inclusive utopianism based on the assimilation of the past to the present. As a quintessentially diasporic genre that construes rather than unearths and invents rather than discovers, the essay would be expected to resist the logic of prefiguration and its identificatory grasp on the past.

It is possible to read these inclusionary gestures as subterranean strategies of intervention. More precisely, we may discern here an

CHAPTER 1

attempt on Adorno's part to make his readers capable of self-reflection. Self-reflection is what the antisemite lacks, according to the theory of antisemitism as "false mimesis" developed in *Dialectic of Enlightenment*. Whereas true mimesis allows for a nondominating relationship with nature or otherness, modern antisemitism arises when, in a world of total reification, the mimetic impulse has become a taboo and is lived out—or rather, perverted—in the strictly delimited realms of fascist rituals. Unlike true mimesis, which relates the inner to the outer world, false mimesis confuses inner and outer world; the subject experiences part of himself as hostile and projects, blindly and without self-reflection, this hostile part outward. The concluding passage of "Heine the Wound," then, exposes one such projection mechanism. This is the tendency of many West Germans to translate repressed guilt feelings into a fear of punishment that is projected onto the victims, leading to the charge that the Jews were seeking revenge for the Holocaust and thus responsible for the continued disruption of German identity.[35] Read against the backdrop of this problem, Adorno's insistence that Heine's problem is everyone's is not so much a quick generalization as it is an attempt to prevent this kind of projection, the projection of a sense of stigmatization and fragmentation onto the image of the ostracized Jew. We may even say that the essay constitutes a form of mimetic practice, an address through identification. Aware of the latent antisemitism in postwar West Germany, Adorno first evokes antisemitic projection mechanisms before dismantling them.

There is another important instance in which Adorno combines a leap from the past to the present with a textual strategy associated with exile; he accomplishes this shift through the use of a foreign word. This passage discusses Heine's relevance in today's German society, which relies on mechanisms of repression and exclusion similar to those that hampered Heine's reception in Germany in the first place. The passage is closely related to Adorno's concerns in "The Meaning of Working Through the Past" in its attempts to uncover the continuity, and the no less problematic displacement and inversion, of antisemitic stereotypes in postwar West Germany:

> [Heine's] impertinence sprang from the impulse of the person who wants for the life of him to be accepted and is thereby doubly irritating to those who are already established, who drown out their own guilt at excluding him by

holding the vulnerability of his adaptation up to him. This continues to be the trauma [Trauma] of Heine's name today, and it can be healed only if it is recognized rather than left to go on leading an obscure, preconscious existence.[36]

Why does Adorno use here *Trauma* (rather than *Wunde*), a word that shifts the emphasis from the physical to the psychical and that is strongly associated with psychoanalysis? *Trauma* is the Greek word for wound, as well as a psychological term that would not have been as familiar to Adorno's German contemporaries as it is to American academics today. It would in fact stand out as a foreign word, one of the *Fremdwörter* whose function Adorno analyzes in his essay "Words from Abroad." There, Adorno argues that foreign words carry a special affective tension that derives from libidinal cathexes; their attraction is grounded in the erotic desire for the exotic, a form of linguistic exogamy. But this affective tension, if repressed, can easily turn into hatred, which makes foreign words both seductive and threatening. Given the collective resistance to psychoanalysis in postwar Germany diagnosed in "The Meaning of Working Through the Past," the shift from *Wunde* to *Trauma* is apt to induce just such a negative affect, the uncomfortable feeling that Heine's suffering cannot be fully assimilated by postwar Germans. This deployment of affect in the text complements, but also curiously undermines, its more explicit appeal to the faculty of cognition.

Adorno's use of the word *Wunde* for Heine's haunting proximity, for his anticipation of the state of alienation in contemporary society, is interesting in other ways as well. One might perceive here a tension that characterizes Adorno's work as a whole, between a view of the Holocaust as a radical rupture in history and, as Ulrich Baer puts it, "the contention that the effects of this rupture, if not its actual occurrence, were foreshadowed in pre-Holocaust works."[37] However, rather than reading this tension in terms of a failed attempt to integrate the Holocaust into a larger historical narrative, I suggest that it reflects the impact of trauma on the essay itself, with trauma understood as an experience that profoundly unsettles our ability to place events in time or history. The word *Wunde*, I will argue, testifies to the ways in which the theoretical reflection on trauma is bound up with its textual reenactment.

CHAPTER 1

The word *Wunde* appears at least twice in places in which Adorno reflects on the psychoanalytic model of enlightenment, which he himself had espoused in response to the impasses of the traditional concept of *Bildung* that troubled his pedagogical project. Whereas the concept of *Bildung* depends on a notion of individual autonomy that has become untenable in late capitalism, psychoanalysis acknowledges the subject's limited access to his own subjectivity and allows him to recognize and work through the resistances arising from his deformation in society.[38] However, some strands of psychoanalysis forego this critical effect. In *Minima Moralia*, Adorno uses the word *Wunde* in his critique of the transformation of psychoanalysis into therapy in the United States. By reducing psychical suffering to a set of symptoms that can be discovered and treated individually, American deep psychology obfuscates and ultimately affirms the social pressures that deform the individual. This observation is framed in terms of Adorno's and Horkheimer's critique of the culture industry: psychoanalytic concepts have become facile labels and stereotypes that deny the individual access to her experience instead of enabling her to engage in self-reflection. As Adorno concludes the passage:

> Moreover, psychoanalysis itself is castrated by its conventionalization: sexual motives, partly disavowed and partly approved, are made totally harmless but also totally insignificant. With the fear they instill vanishes the joy they might procure. . . . The last grandly-conceived theorem of bourgeois self-criticism has become a means of making bourgeois self-alienation, in its final phase, absolute, and of rendering ineffectual the lingering awareness of the ancient wound [Ahnung der uralten Wunde], in which lies hope of a better future.[39]

It is not entirely clear what the referent of the word *Wunde* here is. Most likely, it is sexuality, or a related expression of the unconscious, which could be the cause of both pain and hope in that it would both inspire fear and instigate social change were its force not blunted in the American version of psychoanalysis. This blunting itself is called a "castration" of psychoanalysis, that is, another kind of wound, a debilitating wound that lacks the utopian impulse of the "uralten Wunde." And yet *Wunde* connotes pain and suffering in a way that is not fully born out by the reflections on sexuality that precede it. Furthermore, the attribute *uralt*, which connotes a prehistorical time from which no written records exist, situates the wound both inside and outside of history. There is a certain tension between the attempt to historicize sexuality—that is, to explain its expressions in terms of changing historical conditions—and the contention that it is in some fundamental way ahistorical, or rather, as the word *Ahnung* suggests, that it is not yet historical because it eludes cognitive registers. The word *Wunde* functions here as a suggestive figure that allows Adorno to intimate relations between sexual and historical experience without detailing these relations any further.

Adorno's "The Meaning of Working Through the Past" advances a related critique of a discursive use of psychoanalysis, or rather of its pop-psychological variants, that hampers its recuperation as a model of critical self-reflection. As an example he cites in this essay the psychological diagnosis of a German "guilt complex,"[40] which may serve to fend off feelings of guilt that are more than justified and generally obviates questions of agency and responsibility. Adorno strives to undo such pathologization through rhetorical inserts such as "the tendency toward the unconscious *and not so unconscious* defensiveness against guilt,"[41] thereby suggesting that what has become know as the German "inability to mourn" is an unwillingness to mourn. After listing a number of strategies employed by Germans to disavow responsibility for the crimes of Nazism, including the equation of Auschwitz and Dresden, Adorno again uses the word *Wunde:* "The idiocy of all this is truly a sign of something that psychologically has not been mastered, a wound, although the idea of wounds would be rather more appropriate for the victims."[42]

This side remark on the possible inappropriateness of the word *Wunde* has two implications. First, it indicates a conceptual uncertainty about the nature of what one may call perpetrator trauma. Even though Adorno criticizes the tendency to disavow responsibility by labeling reactions as "unconscious," he also concedes that there is indeed something traumatic about these reactions. His claim that the "effacement of memory is more the achievement of an *all too alert* consciousness than its weakness when confronted with the superior strength of unconscious processes"[43] recalls the notion of both Freud and Benjamin that hyperconsciousness itself is a response to trauma, a protective mechanism that serves to fend off stimuli before they fully

CHAPTER 1

register.[44] Adorno's analysis, which concludes that the collective identification with the National Socialist regime boosted the individual's self-confidence and that the demise of the regime inflicted a narcissistic injury, points into a similar direction. This thesis was later taken up by Alexander and Margarete Mitscherlich and, more recently, expanded by Eric Santner into a theory of mourning according to which the loss of an object of narcissistic identification would have required forms of mourning that first constitute a subject's ability to recognize an other as other.[45] Secondly, Adorno's simultaneous use and revocation of the word *Wunde* brings into focus his own participation in the discourse he criticizes, that is, the blurring of the distinction between victims and nonvictims, signaling, perhaps, a certain unease with his in-between position.[46] Adorno's self-questioning use of the word *Wunde* thus makes a double point: it renders defense mechanisms legible as traumatic symptoms while guarding against the use of the discourse of trauma for apologetic ends.

Adorno's own uncertainty about the nature of, and the adequate response to, perpetrator trauma explains, perhaps, why this essay has been cited by at least two critics in support of opposing views of Freud's concept of working-through. Dominick LaCapra understands working-through as a process that helps people overcome traumatic fixations and obtain, if not a total mastery over their lives, at least some form of closure, a measure of control, and a reinvestment in social life. LaCapra tends to privilege the cognitive aspects of working-through, for instance, the historical knowledge that allows for "the specification or naming of deserving victims," and he cites Adorno as one of the major witnesses to the loss of historical consciousness defined as the ability to make such distinctions.[47] In contrast, Werner Hamacher postulates that genuine working-through begins with a disruption of the very ability to name, a disruption that opens up a potentially infinite process of transference. He bases his idea on a reading of one of Freud's key articles on the subject, titled "Remembering, Repeating, and Working Through." Toward the end of the essay, Freud shifts into an anecdotal tone and relates various complaints he received from other analysts about the slow progression of a cure even when the patient's resistances were recognized and given a name. The interaction with a traumatized patient, Freud realizes, confronts the analyst with the limits of his interpretive powers and forces him to adopt an attitude of patience and openness. He even has to turn to another analyst for help so that "the dialogical dyad, the definition of work as normalization and idealization and the interpretation of the analysis as the work of identificatory naming, is left behind and abandoned in favor of a principally open, no longer simply naming, a *transidealizing* and virtually interminable polylogical process."[48] According to Hamacher, Adorno advances a similar idea of working through as an inherently interminable process and in so doing elaborates hidden semantic possibilities of the word *aufarbeiten*, with its implications of openness and futurity.[49] One can in fact marshal further evidence to corroborate Hamacher's view that working through in Adorno begins with a crisis of representation. In the first paragraph of the essay, Adorno speaks of the difficulty of uttering the name of the events he writes about, speaking about "a domain from which even now there emanates such horror that one hesitates to call it by name."[50]

What the disagreement between Hamacher and LaCapra illustrates is the difference between locution and illocution, or historical reference and force of address, in the writing of trauma. Adorno would certainly support LaCapra's view that the faculty of historical judgment and the ability to distinguish between different forms of trauma are indispensable for an adequate response to it. Yet in his own writing he resists the closure of the hermeneutic circle that LaCapra at least implicitly demands: Adorno leaves the traumatic ambiguity of the word *Wunde* unresolved while countering its tendency to elide historical difference. At the same time Hamacher, who refers to Adorno as a witness to the simultaneous breakdown and proliferation of communication in the aftermath of trauma, does not fully consider the difficulty of comparing the speech in a psychoanalytic session with the writing of essays. As I have suggested, Adorno shifts the focus from the rhetorical dimension of the essay—the way in which it attempts to persuade or more generally engage a reader or listener—to the essayistic mobilization of ossified words, concepts, or ideas. The small shocks he administers, for instance, through sudden changes of linguistic register, are remnants of a pedagogical gesture that has otherwise become untenable. Figures of displacement are instrumental in creating Adorno's distinct public voice, which modulates between distance and proximity, separation and entanglement. We may probe this idea once more in a passage that gives quite explicit instructions about what needs to be done to work through the past, the conclusion of "The Meaning of Working Through the Past." There Adorno argues that reminding Germans of their own suffering during World War II might prevent a recurrence of

CHAPTER 1

fascism, but he continues that such an appeal to the instinct of self-preservation, as one may call it, is insufficient if the causes of the past are not removed at the same time:

> Despite all the psychological repression, Stalingrad and the night bombings are not so forgotten that everyone cannot be made to understand the connection between the revival of a politics that led to them and the prospect of a Third Punic War. Even if this succeeds, the danger will still exist. The past will have been worked through only when the causes of what happened then have been eliminated. Only because the causes continue to exist does the captivating spell of the past remain to this day unbroken.[51]

Referring to the Third Punic War, which resulted in the final destruction of Carthage, Adorno appeals here to the reader's historical consciousness to prevent a repetition of the past in the future. His implication is that if Germans fail to learn the lessons of two highly destructive wars, they might provoke a third war that will end them within history altogether. Yet the figurative use of the Third Punic War in this passage produces effects not fully contained in such a straightforward reading. This usage not only enacts a whole new set of displacements—mapping, for instance, the conflict between Germany and the Allied Forces onto one between Carthage and Rome—but also unsettles the relations between past, present, and future. By choosing the expression "Third Punic War" instead of the "Third World War" one would expect here, Adorno aligns the possible future with a past that precedes World War I and II, thus creating the impression that the future has already happened. At the same time, the combination of the "Third Punic War" with an indefinite article turns the war from a one-time historical event into a metaphor. The war whose specter Adorno raises signifies both a catastrophic event and the impossibility of placing this event in time; as such it is symptomatic of the retroactive effect of trauma, its unhinging of events from their place in history. This paradoxical temporality continues in Adorno's subsequent claim that the past will be truly worked through once its causes will have been eliminated. To be sure, on a conceptual level this is not at all paradoxical: the idea that only profound changes in the socioeconomic conditions will guarantee a future free of fascism complements Adorno's earlier arguments about the systemic continuity of fascism. But the wording here is peculiar, for to say that not the persistent conditions but the "causes of what happened then" will have to be changed creates the paradoxical impression that the past itself can be changed. In Adorno's essays, the tension between an appeal to the reader's historical consciousness and a force of address that derives from the inability of placing events in history is never entirely resolved. But it is precisely this tension that makes his essays a rich resource for contemporary debates on trauma, displacement, and representation.

With the Heine essay and its hollowing out of the logic of progression, Adorno participates in a wider intellectual trend of rethinking German Jewish culture before the Holocaust in light of the destruction wrought upon it. Whereas many scholars regarded the Holocaust as the ultimate proof that Jewish emancipation and assimilation had been doomed from the beginning, others attempted to distinguish between different strands of German Jewish culture. The political philosopher Hannah Arendt, for instance, discovered a "hidden tradition" of Jewish pariahs who resisted the assimilatory pressures to which their parvenu counterparts yielded and who turned their own ostracism into social critique.[52] This political awareness is most purely embodied in the "conscious pariah," a term Arendt adopts from Bernhard Lazare (1865–1903), a legal adviser to the Dreyfus family and author of a book on the causes of antisemitism. According to Arendt, Heine embodies a different kind of pariah; his sensibility for mechanisms of exclusion does not turn into political action but into disdain for social conventions and delight in popular culture that enables him to prefigure, in his poetry, genuine freedom. Like Adorno, Arendt associates the recalcitrance she values in the pariah with displacement when she remarks that "the refugee was to become, in the guise of the 'stateless,' the living symbol of the pariah."[53] Their readings of Heine differ mainly in that Arendt held to be authentic what Adorno believed to be a product of commodification, popular culture. Arendt further locates Heine's resistance in his own mind, whereas Adorno argues that it has been gradually brought out by history, in Gustav Mahler's intonations of his poems as well as in Adorno's own reading of him.

    Adorno's reading of Heine is, of course, indebted to Walter Benjamin's idea that the work of art successively unfolds its meaning in criticism. In a broader sense, Adorno continues the model of historiography established by Benjamin, elaborating the possibilities of the past in order to energize the political struggles of the present. Both thinkers reject the ideology of progress in favor of a view of the past as permanent catastrophe, a chain of human suffering. At the same time, they conceive of this past not as a fixed entity but as an assemblage of events whose meaning can be mobilized and changed in the act of reading. Like a text, history is punctuated by fissures to be filled in by commentators. To be sure, Adorno's idea of history is less hopeful than Benjamin's. Whereas Benjamin attempts to "blast open the continuum of history" by isolating moments of possible happiness,[54] Adorno finds little in Heine but protest against his own exclusion. And whereas Benjamin recuperates the unfulfilled promises of the past in order to fuel revolutionary practice, Adorno recovers its traumatic moments in order to hold these up, as a warning, to a post-Holocaust German audience.

A more recent adaptation of the paradigm established by Benjamin and Adorno is Michael André Bernstein's critique of narrative backshadowing in Holocaust literature.[55] Backshadowing, or retroactive foreshadowing, comprises various strategies of connecting two temporally distant events in a way that suggests that the later event is the predictable outcome of the first or in other ways inevitably linked to it. Though frequently encountered in Holocaust literature, backshadowing is problematic because it implies a deterministic view of history and presents destruction as the inevitable outcome of the history of European Jewry. According to Bernstein, only a non-deterministic view of history, which affords a minimal freedom to imagine the possible future of that which is lost, makes mourning—and resistance—possible. He therefore advocates sideshadowing, or narrative strategies that restore a sense of possibility to the past by associating an event not with its apparent outcome but with other possibilities that it overshadows without eradicating. In representations of pre-Holocaust Jewish life in Europe, sideshadowing brings into focus the enormity of loss precisely because it undermines any apocalyptic view that presents European Jewry as always-already doomed to destruction. One form of such sideshadowing is what I have called retroactive diasporization, that is, the projection of heterogeneity into German Jewish culture before the Holocaust. This may be accomplished by highlighting Jewish cultural, ethnic, or religious difference or by focusing on a historical moment or a geographical region in which the integration of the Jews into German society is not yet complete. In turning to the nineteenth century, Adorno retrieves the recalcitrance of Heine's poetry, which he first reads as a reflection of the laws of capitalist society but then reinterprets as an outcry against social prejudice. In what follows, I will argue that Günther Anders attempts a similar revaluation of Jewish life during his postwar visit to Silesia in Eastern Europe, a region in which German hegemony has been historically unstable. Like Adorno, Anders revisits the process of Jewish emancipation and assimilation at a moment when it has become overshadowed by the Holocaust and, like Adorno, he attempts to counteract a sense of doom through strategies of retroactive diasporization.

Günther Anders's Uncanny Return

Born in Breslau in 1902 to an assimilated German Jewish family, Günther Anders studied philosophy with Martin Heidegger, among others, before taking his doctor's degree with Edmund Husserl in 1924.[56] After his plans for a *Habilitation* in music philosophy failed, he began to work as a journalist at the *Berliner Börsen-Courier* and in 1929 married Hannah Arendt. In 1933 he left first for Paris and then for the United States, where he worked a number of odd jobs. He returned to Europe in 1950, yet instead of settling in either of the two German states, he decided to move to Vienna, the native city of his second wife. As a philosopher Anders developed a critique of technology that, similar to that of the late Heidegger, indicts the reduction of all living beings to raw material for technological exploitation. He accorded equal importance to Auschwitz and Hiroshima as turning points of human history and proof of the destructive potential of modern technology: whereas the atomic bomb threatens the physical survival of the human race, the death camp epitomizes the destruction of human dignity. In diaries from the 1950s and 1960s, published in 1967 under the title *Die Schrift an der Wand* [The Writing on the Wall], Anders grapples with the question of what return can mean for people whose departure from home was intimately bound up with this unprecedented historical violence. He attends to the difficulties of his postwar life in Vienna, voicing frustration over the city's inhabitants' preoccupation with their own suffering, their unwillingness to acknowledge the plight of the Jews under National Socialism, and their own complicity in it. Yet more fundamentally, he is concerned with the psychological structure of the former emigrant. At one point he uses the metaphor of the kink [*Knickung*] to describe the disintegration of the emigrant's life into unrelated segments:

> Characteristic for us is not that our life has been interrupted by an intermezzo that we cannot remember, but that the disintegration of our life into several lives has become irrevocable. That means that the second life stands off from the first at an angle, and so does the third from the second. It means that a "bend" occurred each time, a *kink* that makes it impossible—I would almost have written physically impossible—to look back.[57]

The metaphor of a kink that inhibits the process of memory recalls the perception of many German Jewish refugees—among them, as we shall see, Jean Améry—that the violent separation from their homeland as a result of Nazi persecution retrospectively invalidates their former life and self. Anders's description of his return to Europe as an uncanny visit to a land of the living dead suggests that this perception derives from an inability to establish a dynamic, mournful relationship to the lost home and self. This "inability to mourn" means, of course, not the narcissistic longing for a lost grandeur described by the Mitscherlichs but the traumatic fixation on an experience so extreme that it cannot be integrated into a life story. The work of mourning, minimally defined as the rites and psychical mechanisms that enable a mourner to survive loss by laying the lost object properly to rest, achieves a delicate balance between continuity and discontinuity. In psychoanalytic terms, successful mourning first displaces the libido from the lost object onto transitional objects or substitutes—often memory images—before it can be attached to new objects. While attending to the lost object, mourning rituals in fact distance the object from the mourning subject, thus ensuring a separation between the dead and the living. A commemorative speech, for instance, may preserve a memory of something while marking it as past.

One reason for the pervasive sense of uncanniness that accompanies Anders's return to Europe is the absence of symbolic forms that would ensure such a separation between past and present. Freud's observation that the uncanny is marked by a disruption of the temporal order—an illicit intrusion of the past into the present—is here extended to the realm of history. Anders is irritated by elegant upper-middle-class apartments that have outlasted the war and whose interior still seems to promise the security of a bourgeois life—displaced remnants of a world whose foundations were shattered by World War II and the Holocaust. He is appalled by the absence of traces of catastrophe: "The shamelessness of random objects, which survived the apocalypse as if they had not been concerned by it; they keep their mouths shut and say nothing about the dead."[58] The returning exile experiences the absence of change as a recurrence—continuity as horror rather than comfort—since for him the Second World War and the Holocaust have destroyed the prewar European world so thoroughly that the continued presence of any of its objects and symbols seems absurd. The encounter with real objects from prewar Europe consequently makes these objects appear as revenants, markers of a shadowy world that uncannily undoes the reality of history.

Anders's relationship to prewar Europe is diametrically opposed to nostalgia, which Susan Stewart has powerfully analyzed in her book *On Longing*.[59] Whereas the nostalgic keeps the object of his or her desire—the idealized past—at a distance in order to preserve an unblemished image of it, Anders alternately experiences a distanced indifference regarding the past and an overproximity to it. This overproximity culminates, in "Der Überfall" (1962) [The Assault], in a surrealist vision of schizophrenic doubles splitting off from his body and attacking him with demands for attention.[60] This short prose text depicts a captain on a ship being followed by his own former selves who suddenly band up to attack him, causing the ship to interrupt its journey and drift around aimlessly. The ship is generally a symbol of departure and movement to new horizons—in fact, the destination of this particular ship is the future—and the disruption of this journey is a pointed image of stasis and repetition. The quintessential experience of catastrophic exile, that is, according to Anders, the absence of any kind of mnemonic or imaginative mediation between past and present, thus entails a reification and spatialization of the past, rendering it alternately inaccessible and all-consuming.

If Anders's return to Europe is marked by distanced numbness and emotional devastation, two symptoms of trauma, his later visit to Eastern Europe suggests that this traumatic fixation is only enhanced by a sense of historical predetermination. This visit, which led him first to Auschwitz and then to the city of Breslau, in which he spent the first

CHAPTER 1

twelve years of his life, is described in the last part of the published diary, titled "Besuch im Hades" (1966) [Visit to Hades]. Surprisingly, only a relatively small portion of the text deals with Auschwitz. In fact, Anders never describes his actual visit in the camp but only his departure from it, thus establishing the departure from Auschwitz as the vantage point of recollection. Even the title "Visit to Hades" does not, as one would expect, refer to the Auschwitz death camp but to the space and time of Anders's childhood, which appears as a realm of uncannily resurrected corpses, or more precisely, of ghosts who have never really died.[61] The proximity—both textual and geographic—of Auschwitz and Breslau indicates that Anders's perception of his birthplace cannot be separated from the Holocaust. On the most explicit level, the knowledge of everything that happened after he left forces him to reevaluate the German political hegemony in this region, which had intermittently been, and was once again, Polish. While his assimilated German Jewish parents had uncritically supported this hegemony, Anders analyzes the motives for their (in retrospect, naive) German patriotism. His travelogue soon turns into a meditation on the contradictions and impasses of assimilation, dwelling upon the figure of Edith Stein—a brilliant philosophy student, first of Anders's father and then of Edmund Husserl, who later converted to Catholicism and ultimately perished in the Shoah—before moving to his father's various attempts to secure himself a place in German society. Anders's critique of Jewish assimilation is underwritten by backshadowing strategies that link his birthplace to the Holocaust. In reading Edith Stein's journey from Germany to Poland in 1919 as a prefiguration of the flight of Jewish families in 1939, for instance, Anders implies that later historical events could or should have been anticipated in the past.

Throughout the Breslau diary, Anders records moments of a sudden and uncanny proximity of childhood events, a symptom of a traumatic loss for which no symbolic frame of mourning exists. This absence reflects not only the shattering of traditional frames of reference by the Holocaust but also the writer's troubled sense that the German-speaking Jewish population was unwittingly complicit in its own destruction. Indeed, he seems to be disturbed by the possibility that he himself perpetuates the naïveté of his parents, especially when he reproduces past scenery in his memory despite the radical changes that have occurred: "In front of us I see—*not* the castle museum. Behind us—*not* the synagogue."[62] While the emphatic negation in the quote stresses the nonexistence of the buildings, Anders's use of the pronoun "we" a moment later and his lapse into present tense as he narrates Germany's rise to imperial power indicates his own absorption into the remembered past: "When you consider that we are about to embark upon our world-domination over the sea . . ."[63] The relief he feels in view of signs of the passing of time betrays a desire to repeal this identification by restoring a proper diachronic order to things: "It is bad enough that things perish. At times, though, their survival is even worse, because it causes something else to perish: namely the time and reality of one's own life lived in the meantime. I stand here, and it is 1910 again. And all that has occurred since then has been erased. That which has remained is the death of that which was. . . . Away from here! Away from here! And back to the ruins, the good ruins which prove that today is not the day before yesterday, but is today."[64]

One of Anders's strategies to get beyond the impasses of mourning is a retrospective diasporization of Breslau, the inscription of Jewish ethnic particularity into an otherwise homogeneously German past. This strategy is especially tangible in the description of his mother. Like many other passages in the book, this passage takes the form of an (imagined) dialog between Anders and his wife, who is accompanying him on his trip. After reminiscing about his mother's typical turn-of-the-century Central European appearance of a "fantastic scarecrow" (English in the original), Anders corrects himself and finds that she looks "just like pretty Jewish women presumably looked in Galilee two thousand years ago, and later in Spain."[65] He imagines his wife unveiling the face that is hidden behind the fashions of the time. "For if you . . . lifted the rim of her hat, you would see a melancholic, Greco-like face, one of those delicate Jewess faces of which we just saw innumerable examples, I mean in Auschwitz, on those hundreds of numbered passports of Jewesses."[66] The link here between the imagined unveiling of his mother's Jewishness and the faces of those who perished in Auschwitz is another instance of backshadowing. To be sure, there are traces of sideshadowing in Anders's diary. He reminds us, for instance, that despite the similarity between the mother's youthful face and the faces of those perished in Auschwitz, she could not have known about the future genocide and, furthermore, that she herself ended up in New York rather than Auschwitz. Yet as a whole the diary shows how difficult it is to sustain a sense of historical open-endedness. Anders easily lapses into backshadowing strategies that, though mostly devoid of the

CHAPTER 1

judgmental tone Bernstein ascribes to this technique, effect a sense of doom that makes it almost impossible to recuperate anything positive from the culture he revisits. Both assimilation and the occasionally maintained—and retrospectively emphasized—Jewish particularity seem inevitably to lead into the Holocaust. Anders's tendency to locate a redemptive difference on the female Jewish body compounds the impression of a mythic past removed from history. In a telling passage, he invokes his mother's "Oriental" beauty as the sign of a difference that could have counterpoised the uncritical assimilation of Jews to Prussian society had it not been suppressed first by the mother's anxious family and then by her conformist husband.

> Certainly Father was alarmed again and again whenever he saw his oriental looking young wife in the circle of the wives of his colleagues, half-Prussian, half-Slavic, and often vacant-looking. As a Jewish lecturer who dreamed of one day becoming a professor—which was already unusual enough—he naturally had to avoid any additional conspicuousness. Presumably, he thanked God that Mother did not behave as exotically as she looked, that she did not—as she of whom Salomon sung did—conduct herself like the fiery Rose of Sharon, but rather sat quietly within the circle, the embodiment of all imaginable taboos and manners, so that nobody could have found fault with her.[67]

Anders's association of Jewish difference with the female Jewish body, which is compounded by a citation of the biblical Song of Songs, both recalls and obfuscates the gender dynamics in the historical process of assimilation. At the beginning of Jewish emancipation and assimilation, when the goal was primarily to acquire the language and customs of the non-Jewish environment, Jewish women came to embody the desire for acculturation.[68] While we should not confuse the life of Rahel Varnhagen or Henriette Herz with that of the average Jewish woman, these Romantic "salon Jewesses" emblematize the openness of Jewish women to secular Western culture at a time when their place in Jewish religion and culture was less clearly defined than that of their male counterparts. However, with the relocation of religion in the domestic sphere during the nineteenth century, it fell upon Jewish women to keep traditional rituals and create Jewish homes while their husbands increasingly absented themselves from synagogues and pursued assimilation in the economic and political spheres. To locate Jewish difference on the female body thus means to essentialize a social role bestowed on Jewish women at a particular historical moment. Instead of making the past available again by highlighting its heterogeneity and contingency, Anders's retroactive diasporization of Eastern Europe further distances the past from the present. The association between Breslau and Auschwitz around which he structures the text explains, perhaps, why there is ultimately no alternative for him other than to leave Breslau and forget it anew.

The reification of the pre-Holocaust past in Anders's diary parallels a relatively strict distinction between private and public voices in his work. To the extent that they are unhistorical and limited to the local, indeed familial, sphere, Anders's observations follow the traditional generic markers of the diary, which describes personal experience without necessary claims toward larger historical significance. The voice he construes here differs decisively from his other important contribution to the debates on the Holocaust and German *Vergangenheitsbewältigung*. In 1964, he published an open letter, titled "Wir Eichmannssöhne" (We, Eichmann's Sons) and addressed to Klaus Eichmann, the son of the notorious Adolf Eichmann who had been executed after a famous trial in Jerusalem three years earlier.[69] In this letter Anders contemplates the guilt and responsibility of the so-called desk perpetrators, concluding with an appeal to Klaus Eichmann to join the anti-atom movement in order to help prevent further crimes of the kind committed by his father. Although Anders mentions his own identity as a Jew who escaped the Holocaust only by coincidence, his use of the first person plural highlights the logic of comparability and universality that informs his argument. We are all "Eichmann's sons" because we are equally capable of becoming cogwheels in the machinery of destruction if we do not actively resist the blind rule of technology in the modern world. In what follows, I will show that Jean Améry, another German-speaking Jewish intellectual who in the 1960s revisits his own experience of exile and persecution, proposes a different relationship between the particular and the universal and the public and the private. Rather than containing the vulnerability of the victim within a genre marked as private, Améry claims this vulnerability as a source of moral knowledge and the very basis of his public voice.

CHAPTER 1

Jean Améry's Resentments

Coming from a mixed Austrian Jewish background, Jean Améry had pursued literary and philosophical studies for some years before the German annexation of Austria forced him to flee to Belgium. He later joined a resistance group and helped distribute anti-Nazi leaflets, an activity that led to his arrest in 1943 and deportation to Auschwitz in 1944. After his liberation he returned to Belgium, where he wrote German-language essays and articles that he published with Swiss papers before consciously turning toward a German audience.[70] Even after that he retained a stronger sense of separation from the German language and culture than Adorno or Anders. Although Améry occasionally points out positive aspects of his linguistic situation, including the stylistic and analytical benefits of writing in a language different form that of one's environment, his sense of alienation from the German language prevailed. For the former resistance fighter and inmate of Auschwitz, this language had forever become a locus of struggle rather than a source of resistance: "The meaning of every German word changed for us, and finally, whether we resisted or not, our mother tongue became just as inimical as the one they spoke around us. . . . The words were laden with a given reality, which was the threat of death."[71] The different degrees of return among these German Jewish intellectuals are already indicated in the ways they did or did not change their names after the war. Whereas Adorno retained his mother's Italian name and continued to condense his father's recognizably Jewish name into an initial, and Anders adopted the pen name he had occasionally used before his emigration (meaning "other" in German), Améry made the most far-reaching changes by translating and rearranging the letters of his original name, "Hans Maier," into a French name. Améry was less concerned than Adorno and Anders with the historical project of Jewish emancipation, which he deemed retroactively invalidated by Auschwitz. At times he even laconically accepted a view of German Jewish identity as nothing but a mask now discarded into a lumber room. Yet he left no doubt that the identification of Jews with German culture was profound and perhaps irreplaceable for those who embraced it. "Everyone must be who he was in the first years of his life, even if later these were buried under. No one can become what he cannot find in his memories."[72] Having grown up without Jewish cultural and religious traditions, he finds that he can identify as a Jew only because of the persecution he suffered, not because of any positive connections with Judaism.

In what follows, I will examine Améry's first publication directed primarily at a German audience, titled *At the Mind's Limits*. Published in 1966, the book comprises essays on the situation of the intellectual in the concentration camp, the lasting impact of torture and exile, the survivor's inability to forget, and finally, the aporias of Jewish identity after the Holocaust. I will argue that in this book, Améry turns a sense of irredeemably catastrophic exile into a public provocation that radicalizes Adorno's model of essayistic intervention. This is not to suggest that Améry shared Adorno's philosophical orientation; his unceasing belief in the validity of enlightenment principles was rather incompatible with Adorno's view of the death camps as a product of the instrumental reason that is part and parcel of the Western idea of enlightenment. Améry once called Adorno's idiom a "jargon of dialectics," a purely speculative language that is not only unnecessarily verbose but also bound to abstract and thus to forget suffering.[73] However, in different ways, both authors worked to transform the genre of the essay into a privileged site for reflections on exile. I have shown that Adorno valorizes the nonoriginal, diasporic, even parasitic character of the essay form and in his own writing mobilizes the internal heterogeneity of the German language to infuse it with some similar qualities. Améry's insistence on the incommensurability of his experience and his textual deployment of affect dismantle whatever still remains in Adorno of the pedagogical gesture, until his writing no longer really fits the category of the essay: "I had planned a contemplative, essayistic study. What resulted was a personal confession refracted through meditation."[74]

The essays collected in *At the Mind's Limits* both invoke and dismantle the notion of exile as a positive force, for instance, as an occasion for personal growth or critical analysis. In "How Much Home Does a Person Need?" Améry emphasizes that, for a post-Holocaust German or Austrian Jew, the loss of home remains devastating because the experience of having been abandoned so easily by one's homeland and fellow citizens instills a lasting insecurity.[75] Améry neither makes an attempt to reclaim his country of origin nor does he evoke any hope for another potential, future home. Instead, out of the bleak state of banishment emerges a voice that does not attempt to mitigate loss by restoring hope to it but that challenges the Germans, reminding them of their guilt and calling upon them to remember. This intervening voice is most manifest in the essay "Resentments," which levels a bitter charge against the tendencies of normalization during the 1950s and 1960s that succeeded in establishing West Germany in a Western political framework at the expense of a deeper confrontation with its past. Traveling through the economically successful, attractive, modern West Germany, Améry notes the discrepancy between his own rage and bitterness and the Germans' complacency about the successful recovery of their country. To their seemingly natural sense of time passing and effacing the past, he opposes the shattered sense of time of the concentration camp survivor who clings to his traumatic past. He calls this disposition "resentment," an inability to forget that represents for him the only moral—as opposed to natural—reaction to the Shoah.

The word "resentment" picks up on a catchword that has after 1945 served in West Germany to exclude the voices of emigrants. With its Nietzschean undertones, the word insinuated that the refugees from Nazism were in an overly subjective state of mind, unable to abstract from their past experiences, and therefore they could not seriously and rationally contribute to the debates on Germany's responsibility for Nazism and on its future.[76] The devaluation of the victims' voices continued and grew even stronger in the 1960s, when psychological discourses of the kind of "Delayed Psychic Effects After Political Persecution"[77] were pathologizing and marginalizing these voices instead of taking them seriously as testimonies to the Nazi crimes. By referring polemically to such discourses, Améry uncovers a mostly overlooked problem inherent in the West German *Wiedergutmachung* that started in 1956. *Wiedergutmachung* encompassed a number of measures from financial aid for Israel to compensation payments for Jewish individuals who were persecuted or could prove that they were still suffering from the lasting effects of indirect persecution. As such, it not only had the potential to relieve Germans of their guilt feelings by suggesting that recompense for the crimes was possible, but it also forced the victims to categorize themselves in terms of psychopathological symptoms, that is, to recognize themselves as impaired.[78] It is in this context that we have to read Améry's insistence on the survivor's subjective experience as the only possible point of departure for understanding Nazism. By accepting the representation of the survivor's subjectivity as damaged, tortured, and overly sensitive, Améry recuperates it as a valid moral reaction, thus challenging its ongoing psychologization and marginalization. The survivor's resentments constitute for him a moral category rather than one of psychopathology.

Améry attempts to realize this idea and put pain to use for the production of moral knowledge by directing his own negative affects toward his German readership. He emphasizes throughout the text his own position as an outsider to the group he addresses: "The people of whom I am speaking and whom I am addressing here show muted understanding for my retrospective grudge."[79] The text's topography, which assigns to the speaking subject the position of a traveler who does not belong to this place but crosses through it temporarily—the first sentence reads: "Sometimes it happens that in the summer I travel through a thriving land"[80]—externalizes and enacts the tension between Améry and his imagined German readers. Améry draws and constantly reinforces a line between victims and perpetrators, for instance, by ironically addressing his readers, thus producing a distancing effect and suspending any cathartic relief they might otherwise derive from an identification with the victims: "I would be thankful to the reader if he were willing to follow me, even if in the hour before us he more than once feels the wish to put down the book."[81] As the traveler's position inscribes a peculiar distance into the text, the text becomes the site of enunciations that rhythmically modulate from proximity to distance, from the hope of being heard to utter resignation and loneliness, from emotional appeal to bitter sarcasm. Witness the last sentence of the essay: "We victims must finish with our retroactive rancor, in the sense that the KZ argot once gave the word 'finish'; it meant as much as 'to kill.' Soon we must and will be finished. Until that time has come, we request of those whose peace is disturbed by our grudge that they be patient."[82] The sarcasm of this sentence illustrates the utter absence of the benevolence of pedagogy from Améry's attitude toward his readership. His texts do not strive to educate but rather to disturb and disrupt, thus accentuating the conflict between Germans and Jews.

The textual reproduction of this conflict alters the generic categories of autobiographical writing. According to Jürgen Habermas, the autobiographical and the psychological novel originated as literary forms based on a privatized, intimate relationship between writer and reader.[83] Implicitly or explicitly, the writer would address readers as equal human beings with whom to share interests and insights into the human psyche. Autobiographical and psychological novels, in other words, invite identificatory readings that level potential differences of

CHAPTER 1

background and experience in favor of something universally human. Améry frustrates this kind of reading, thus turning his autobiographical essays into a testimony that emphasizes the conflict between his own historical perspective and that of his imagined readers.

The critical thrust of Améry's writing lies in the way it responds to, and attempts to break through, a sociopsychological disposition he perceives as specific to his German audience. Améry describes this disposition varyingly as complacency, "equanimity,"[84] and "peace,"[85] reflecting the extent to which the Germans he meets remain unaffected by the monstrosity of their past. As Moishe Postone has shown, this state of mind is by no means confined to the reactionary or politically indifferent forces in German society, but it is also palpable in the leftist inclination to theoretical models of National Socialism. These theories, Postone argues, have in fact abstracted Nazism at the expense of concretely felt horror and have been instrumental in mitigating guilt feelings.[86] Striving to break through such defense mechanisms, Améry departs from the enlightened, reasonable conversation that was constitutive for the critical function of the emerging bourgeois public sphere. Instead of initiating a dialog grounded in a common reasoning, he emphasizes the abyss between victims and perpetrators, an abyss that has to be bridged not through a rational understanding of National Socialism but through the recuperation of painful affect. The deeper meaning of acts of punishment that force the perpetrator to mimetically reproduce the victim's affects—his or her absolute helplessness in the face of violence—is the creation of a common ground between victims and perpetrators: "The experience of persecution was, at the very bottom, that of an extreme *loneliness*. At stake for me is the release from the abandonment that has persisted from that time until today. When the SS-man Wajs stood before the firing squad, he experienced the moral truth of his crimes. At that moment, he was with *me*—and I was no longer alone with the shovel handle."[87]

For contemporary Germans, the establishment of a common ground between victims and perpetrators would involve the repulsion against their own history while acknowledging it as their own and renouncing any attempt to distance themselves from it: "two groups of people, the overpowered and those who overpowered them, would be joined in the desire that time be turned back and, with it, that history become moral."[88] Any utopianism still implied in this sentence, however, is counterpoised by Améry's skepticism regarding the likelihood that such a moral upsurge against the flow of time will happen in the Germany of the 1960s. What remains is a minimal hope that his own writing may achieve a similar effect, however transient and limited. Améry thus touches upon a critical potential of diasporic discourse later elaborated by Homi Bhabha in his discussion of the ability of diasporic (postcolonial) discourse to address incommensurable cultural and historical differences. Bhabha has suggested that instead of mitigating such differences, diasporic discourse uses them as a disruptive force against the homogenizing discourse of the nation. Améry attempts to achieve a similar effect by injecting another time—that of the survivor who clings traumatically to his past—into the organic and progressive time of a West Germany rebuilding from an imagined zero hour. His resentments transform the survivor's words into signs that form a barrier to the discourse of normalization.

2
Peter Weiss's Skeptical Cosmopolitanism

> Have meanwhile become a "German-language author."
> Sit in Stockholm . . . at the drafting table where a few
> years ago I produced my films and collages. Write in the
> language which I learned as a child and lost when I was
> 17.
> —*Peter Weiss*

Written in 1961, these sentences capture a crucial moment in Peter Weiss's literary career, the moment when he became a German-language author.[1] Weiss had, in fact, written in German before, but it was only after the publication of *Der Schatten des Körpers des Kutschers* [*The Shadow of the Coachman's Body*] in 1960[2] that he gained that public recognition as a "German-language author," a label to which he refers here, as his use of quotation marks suggests, with some uneasiness. At first glance, the success of *Der Schatten des Körpers des Kutschers* ended Weiss's tenuous existence as a displaced, or more accurately placeless, artist. The son of a Christian mother and a Jewish father who had converted to Protestantism after his marriage, Weiss left Nazi Germany with his family in 1934, stayed for brief periods in England, Czechoslovakia, and Switzerland, and finally arrived in Sweden in 1939. For more than ten years, he vacillated between writing and painting, and between German and Swedish, and finally gave up writing for a period in favor of filmmaking. In the early 1960s, however, he experienced an outburst of literary productivity and a rapid integration into the German cultural scene, promoted by postwar West Germany's leading literary institution, the Gruppe 47. Yet even when Weiss's existence as an artist without an audience ceased, his exile did not. While he paid frequent visits to Germany and even considered moving back there, he ultimately decided to stay in Stockholm and observe Germany from the distant perspective captured by his image of the watcher through the window.

This chapter explores the paradox inherent in Weiss's entry into the German public sphere, the fact that he claimed a diasporic position at the very moment when he became a recognized exponent of German culture. Weiss's writings from the early to mid-1960s have thus far been researched mostly under the aspect of his politicization as a Marxist, a focus that was sustained by Weiss's own representation of his transformation from an idiosyncratic, self-centered surrealist into a politically engaged writer. From this perspective, Weiss's experimental prose texts of the time appear to be mere relapses into apolitical subjectivism and aestheticism.[3] At the same time, critics who address questions of displacement in Weiss's work often rely on the opposition between the self-expansive cosmopolitan and the victimized exile. In her analysis of representations of the Third World in postwar German literature, Arlene Teraoka recognizes that Weiss's interest in colonialism and its aftermath derived from his belated confrontation with the horrors of Auschwitz and interprets his political commitment after 1965 as a reversal of his political passivity during the Second World War.[4] Her conclusion that his political engagement with the victims of colonialism served primarily to mitigate his own sense of guilt recalls contemporary critiques of cosmopolitanism as an endless expansion of the self through projection. In contrast, Alfons Söllner emphasizes in *Peter Weiss und die Deutschen* Weiss's own victimization during the Third Reich and reads his early, pre-1953 work as an aesthetically and politically intricate expression of his "exile after exile."[5] Weiss's abiding exclusion after 1945 from the cultural sphere of the country that had forced him into exile—Germany—singularly positioned him to lend a voice to the victims of Holocaust.

The following chapter aims to go beyond the dichotomy between self-assertive cosmopolitanism and catastrophic exile by showing that both operate in Weiss's texts in a productive tension that marks his work as diasporic. During his belated integration into the German public sphere, Weiss engages in reflections on exile that are attuned to the diasporic consciousness as defined above, an attempt to render livable and productive an irreparable rupture between the subject and its place of origin. I trace a tension in his work between the development of a cosmopolitan view, which establishes exile as a site of subjective empowerment and critical consciousness, and the instability of this model in view of other forms of exile, forms of exile that result from persecution and that are most prominently embodied by Jewish figures. Jean Améry may serve here as a model of how a sense of permanent, catastrophic exile translates into a deployment of affect in texts that disrupt facile identificatory or redemptive readings. Améry's attempt to communicate the experience of extreme suffering to a public he deemed largely unreceptive for his voice sheds light on Weiss's autobiographical writings, which similarly modulate between distance and proximity, separation and entanglement. However, Weiss's project differs from Améry's in that he does not primarily expose the survivor's woundedness as a source of moral knowledge but engages in literary experiments with the diasporic perspective, experiments that lay open the hypothetical character of his critical stance. In the experimental prose text *Das Gespräch der drei Gehenden* [*The Conversation of the Three Walkers*], he projects the emergence of a new form of community from traumatic experiences of flight and persecution. In "Bericht über Einrichtungen und Gebräuche in den Siedlungen der Grauhäute" [Report on Institutions and Customs in the Settlements of the Grayskins] and *Die Ermittlung* [*The Investigation*] he performs for an imagined German audience the violent rupture between the subject and its place of origin.[6]

Entering the West German Public Sphere

That Peter Weiss was deeply ambivalent about his newly acquired status within the German public sphere, to the point that he experienced his presence in Germany as a déjà vu of the violence refugees from Nazism suffered twenty or thirty years earlier, is documented in his *Notizbücher, 1960–1971*. This collection of short notes, observations, and sketches for future projects—which is formally marked by exclamations, apostrophes, question marks, and change of pronouns—performs the traditional generic function of the diary as the site of those private emotions that do not easily find a place in public. As Weiss's visits to Germany grew more frequent, he used the notebooks to record his negative reactions toward Germany, reactions that ranged from a general sense of antagonism to outright fears of persecution. Notably, the notebooks hardly mention Weiss's stunning successes at the beginning of the 1960s but contain a number of highly critical observations that treat his artistic breakthrough in Germany with a profound skepticism: "If I really dared to ask myself how things stood with me, if I really dared to speak the truth, you would not be able to bear it—no radio station would broadcast it, no publisher would print it" (*Nb*, 102). The notebooks also testify to the collapse of linear time that occurs when the exile returns to the country that persecuted him. Like Améry, Weiss infuses the present with traumatic memories of the past, producing an uncanny superimposition of past and present. In one note, this superimposition transforms an innocent scene at a bus station into a threatening image that evokes the unloading of train passengers upon arrival at the concentration camps: "He returned to them in May of 1962. It had been two decades since they could have sent him up the chimney. Move along, move along, people, hurry up please, the bus conductor shouted to the crowd of impatient riders in front of the train station. Already three decades—" (*Nb*, 227).[7] As Weiss formulates programmatically: "I'll show you those who live today, and how they live today, and I'll erase time so that they will say to you now what they once said, but what they otherwise no longer say" (*Nb*, 233).

Emblematic for the difficulties Weiss encountered vis-à-vis the German public is his relationship to the Gruppe 47, the most important literary association in postwar West Germany, which actively pursued his establishment in the West German literary scene. Walter Höllerer, a leading exponent of the group, first published an extract of Weiss's *Der Schatten des Körpers des Kutschers* in the literary magazine *Akzente*. In 1962, Weiss participated for the first time in a meeting of the Gruppe 47 and almost won its literary prize. From then on, he was regularly invited to the group's annual meetings and he usually accepted these invitations. The discovery of Peter Weiss had to do with the group's overall change in attitude toward those writers who had emigrated during Nazism. These writers were initially excluded from the group, the members of which were mostly German soldiers returning from the war and sharing a wish for a radical new beginning.[8] As Helmut Peitsch shows, around 1960 the politicization of the Gruppe 47 and the new openness to East German literature—which had always been more inclined to integrate the heritage of exile literature—induced its members to change their view of exiled writers and to seek contact with exiles.[9] Moreover, emigration had become increasingly important for the self-definition of West German writers, a number of whom had moved out of West Germany by the end of the 1950s to express their political opposition to the reactionary politics of the Adenauer era. Figuring among the more liberal forces in German society, the Gruppe 47 after 1960 voiced strong appeals to resume the unfinished task of *Vergangenheitsbewältigung*. Around this time a new alliance formed between former refugees from Nazism and the Gruppe 47, an alliance that was based on an ever more fundamental condemnation of fascism and an increasing definition of exile as a site of resistance. A closer look at the integration of exiles, however, reveals that it was quite complex and contradictory. If Peitsch observes in the attitude of the Gruppe 47 toward exile literature a shift from rejection to identification, the structure of identification at the same time describes the limit of the group's understanding of exiled authors: it ended where identification was no longer possible, that is, when exile ceased to be a metaphor of political dissent and came to signify the unchosen position of those who were persecuted and expelled for racist and antisemitic reasons. A statement about the political inferiority of a "merely" Jewish exile, made privately by the group's patron Hans Werner Richter, illustrates this structure: "Please understand me correctly, I do not like those Jews who swagger politically and so magnanimously forgive, who fled Germany only because of their race and not for any political reasons. They have no right to offer political forgiveness."[10]

Weiss's encounters with the Gruppe 47, as scarce as the documentation on them is, indicate the chasm between him and the West German writers' collective. He records, for instance, his persecution fears during their meeting in Sigtuna: "Lurking in the streets, someone takes aim. I run. Barely in safety, I know that I'm already in his sights again—" (*Nb*, 293). The unpublished version of his notebooks has here even a short remark on "Ciacco's antisemitism."[11] Ciacco, a character taken from Dante's *Divine Comedy*, appears in Weiss's own unpublished adaptation of the epic as a childhood friend from Germany who has turned into a bystander to Nazism. Weiss's interpretation that the relation between West German and exile authors was still one of victims and perpetrators seems to be justified in view of the predisposition against exiles. He himself had to face this predisposition during the Gruppe 47 meeting at Princeton in 1966, where he intended to participate in a sit-in against the American politics in Vietnam but was rebuked by Günter Grass and Hans Werner Richter. These two hinted that, as an emigrant, he had no right to comment publicly on German political affairs or make political statements while attending the meeting. Such an argument implies that an exile cannot represent a German point of view, and Weiss was quite sensitive to this implication. He records in his notebooks: "Clash in the Hotel room. I ought not involve myself in American affairs. Abuse of hospitality. And anyway: what right do I have to give my political opinion like this? Haven't I already said far too much about German issues? And where had I been during the war?—20 years evaporated for them like rain water" (*Nb*, 491–92).[12]

At the same time, Weiss himself refused to represent German culture or politics and hardly ever joined into the collective activities of West Germany's critical intelligentsia. When he did, he resorted to a personal, "private" form like that of a letter submitted to Hans Werner Richter's *Plädoyer für eine neue Regierung* (1965), a collection of essays by writers and intellectuals supporting a change of government in West Germany in favor of the Social Democrats. Eager to integrate a variety of respected critical voices, Richter asked Weiss for a contribution, referring to him explicitly as an emigrant: "what do you expect from a change in the German government, or, more exactly, from a social-democratic victory, seen from Sweden, after your visit to Auschwitz, and from your position, that is, as an emigrant who is now a Swedish national but also a well-known German writer."[13] Weiss's response, which was published in the form of a letter, that is, with his salutation to Richter and his own signature, must have been quite a disappointment to the editors. Instead of supporting the book's general outlook, Weiss asserts that his political view originated in his emigration and subsequent distance to certain socio-psychological dispositions that are pervasive within German society, its forces of reform not excepted. This sense of a fundamental separation between him and German society as a collective deters him from returning to Germany—"This atmosphere of authority which is still found everywhere in Germany, in homes and work places—it is this threatening atmosphere which always forces me to leave"[14]—and also from assuming any political stance *within* the German political spectrum.

Ingo Breuer, after showing that the alleged Jewish identity of the revolutionary Marat played a key role for Weiss's fascination with this figure, has argued that Hannah Arendt's concept of the pariah furnished Weiss with a model for his own politicization and a means to restore some coherence to his own biography.[15] Yet the model of the pariah who accepts his or her own marginalization and becomes capable of acting in solidarity with other outsiders only partially describes

Weiss's sense of a Jewish identity. In his notebooks and some of his published writings, Weiss depicts Jews as vulnerable, ill, or paranoid in a way that makes it questionable whether these dispositions can be translated into a political program. As Breuer himself notes, Marat's Jewish identity disappeared as Weiss transformed him through successive stages of the text from a hypersensitive outsider into a powerful revolutionary. The Jewish dimension in Weiss thus resists universalization rather than facilitates it. In what follows now, I trace the ways in which the awareness of a particular, catastrophic Jewish exile provides impulses for Weiss's literary experiments.

REMNANTS OF COSMOPOLITANISM: WEISS'S AUTOBIOGRAPHICAL NOVELS

The first texts Weiss wrote after his sudden transformation into a German author were two semi-autobiographical novels, *Abschied von den Eltern* (1961) [*Leavetaking*] and *Fluchtpunkt* (1962) [*Vanishing Point*]. The autobiographical character of the first book—a dense, metaphorical, often esoteric text—may not be immediately evident, yet it was clearly assumed by its readership. The book was read as the autobiographical statement of an author who had just made a stunning, although belated, literary debut and had now set out to satisfy his audience's curiosity about his identity and past life. Thus one reviewer writes, as if mentioning a self-evident truth: "A second book, the autobiographical tale *Abschied von den Eltern*, now provides information on the origins and essence of this fascinating man."[16] The intrinsically political nature of Weiss's autobiographical novels lies in their recollection and representation of the forgotten victims to a largely indifferent German public. The refugees of National Socialism whose voice Weiss publicizes were widely ignored in favor of a public concern with the German *Ostflüchtlinge*. In fact, the expulsion of native Germans from former German regions in the East had come to occupy the German historical imagination soon after 1945, displacing the very memory of the refugees produced by National Socialism. Weiss's autobiographical texts relate critically to this repression of history, especially after his reception in Germany, through his progressive foregrounding of the theme of exile.[17] This political dimension is not immediately tangible in these novels. In accordance with Peter Weiss's own attitude during his emigration, their narrator never fully realizes the political situation or joins the antifascist resistance, embracing instead a cosmopolitanism devoid of

CHAPTER 2

any particular political commitment. Nevertheless, *Abschied von den Eltern* and *Fluchtpunkt* begin to elaborate the historical dimension of an exile previously understood in subjectivist and existentialist terms.

As the narrator of *Abschied von den Eltern* sets out to analyze his relationship to his parents and his own attempts at emancipation, he initially embraces a surprisingly apolitical perspective on his family's forced departure from their home country and subsequent odyssey through Europe when he was a young adolescent. "Exile" refers above all to the narrator's sense of alienation within a claustrophobic and suffocating *Heim* analyzed in terms of the distorted psyches and suppressed emotions of a bourgeois family. We learn that he has attempted, from his childhood on, to escape the unpleasant atmosphere at home, choosing the garden and the loft as his first exiles. The family's emigration is hardly seen to have a political dimension but instead to perpetuate a state of exile that originated within the family, more precisely, in the violent death of a daughter whose gracious presence had previously lent some warmth and sense of belonging to the family life. From then on, the narrator unsuccessfully attempts to escape the deadening family constellation, a constellation in which a powerful, castrating mother and a weak, absent father hamper the narrator's emotional, sexual, and artistic development. Under the veneer of this psychological narrative, however, a number of textual devices are at work that undermine a purely psychological interpretation of exile. The first of these devices is the juxtaposition of the *Heim,* with its connotations of familial intimacy, and the *Haus,* the spatial materialization of this intimacy, whose violent dismantling by the siblings after the parents' death triggers the narrator's stream of memory at the beginning of the novel. The narrator's description of his family's repeated and futile attempts to reestablish the *Heim* all over Europe makes us aware that their unhappiness derives not so much from their compulsive notion of domesticity but from their fate as refugees:

> Zwischen den silbergrünen Weidenbäumen einer englischen Landschaft wurde das Heim in einem roten Ziegelhaus errichtet, in der bösartigen Enge einer böhmischen Industriestadt wurde das Heim in einer schmutzgelben Villa errichtet, in dem großen, dunkelbraunen Holzhaus am Rand eines schwedischen Sees wurde das Heim zum letzten Mal errichtet. (*W,* 2:103)

> Among silver-green willow trees of an English landscape home was set up in a red brick house; in the mean-spirited narrowness of a Bohemian industrial city home was set up in a dirty yellow villa; the last time home was set up, it was in a large dark brown wooden house on the shores of a Swedish lake. (*Ex*, 49, trans. altered)

History enters the text not in the form of events localizable in time and space but as rhythmic noise and vague shadows that arise at traumatic moments of the oedipal drama. When the narrator shifts rather abruptly from the depiction of an erotic encounter and its interruption through the mother's return to the rise of National Socialism, his sudden sense of the abyss that separates him from his former self indicates the historical dimension of his trauma:

> Wie aus einem anderen Leben blicke ich in diese Zeit hinein, fremd vor dem Ich, aus dem ich hervorgegangen bin. Ich sehe die unendlichen Kolonnen, höre den einförmigen Marschtakt, das Scheppern der eisenbeschlagenen Stiefel, das Klirren der Dolche an den Gurten. Wieder und wieder kamen die Fahnen und Standarten, die ausgelöschten, anonymen Gesichter, die Münder im Gesang geöffnet, wieder und wieder kamen die Trommeln, und über der Stadt lag der Schein eines großen Feuers. (*W*, 2:97)

> I look at that time as if from another life, a stranger before the I from which I have emerged. I see the endless columns, hear the monotonous march beat, the clatter of nailed boots, the jingling of daggers on their belts. Again and again came the flags and the standards, the extinguished anonymous faces, the mouths opened in song, again and again came the drums, and above the city a vast fire seemed to glow. (*Ex*, 43, trans. altered)

In particular, the projection of images of the female body onto the city of Prague pushes the reader to an encounter with forces no longer mappable by means of psychological categories. In Prague the narrator attempts and fails to establish a personal and artistic existence of his own, and the juxtaposition of this failure and his sexual impotency suggests that both are due to the persistent oedipal fixation on his mother and sister. These passages dramatize the image of the female body whose penetration promises a sense of life, identity, and return to origins. However, this image transcends its stereotypical meaning in a scene that prefigures the historical catastrophe soon to happen, as the narrator witnesses a suicide together with Peter Kien, a friend of his who later perished in the Shoah. In this scene, the metaphor of the city as a womb pregnant with a suicide comes to evoke the helpless and paralyzed state of a city awaiting its destruction. The change of registers in this passage—the leap into apostrophe and exclamatory pathos—expresses an attempt to avert the apocalyptic vision by retrospectively warning the friend of the catastrophe to come. This shift also indicates the inadequacy of an interpretative mode that evolves exclusively around the psychic complexity of an individual protagonist:

> Der dunkle Fetzen hatte einen Kopf, und Blut umströmte den Kopf, und der Fetzen war ein Körper, der sich zusammenzog, der sich auf die Seite wälzte und die Knie dicht an den Bauch preßte, und der so liegen blieb, erstarrt, wie *ein Embryo in der großen Gebärmutter aus Stein*. Es kamen Menschen von allen Seiten hinzugelaufen, und wir hielten die brennende Stadt vor sie hin. Peter Kiens Atemzüge schluchzten. Fliehe, Peter Kien, bleibe nicht hier. Fliehe, verstecke dich, du mit deinem hilflos offenstehenden Gesicht, mit deinem fassungslos starrenden Blick hinter den dicken Prismen deiner Brille, fliehe, ehe es zu spät ist. Doch Peter Kien blieb zurück. Peter Kien wurde ermordet und verbrannt. Ich entkam. (*W*, 2:133, my emphasis)

> The dark rag had a head, and blood streamed around the head, and the rag was a body that huddled itself together, that rolled on its side and pressed its knees tightly against its belly, and then lay still, stiffened, *like an embryo in a great womb made of stone*. People came running from all sides and we held up the burning city to them. Peter Kien's breath came in sobs. Flee, Peter Kien, don't stay here. Flee, hide yourself, you with your hopelessly open face, with your disconcerted staring gaze behind the thick prisms of your glasses, flee before it is too late. But Peter Kien remained

behind. Peter Kien was murdered and burned. I escaped.
(*Ex*, 80, my emphasis, trans. altered)

While the historical-political interpretation of exile in *Abschied von den Eltern* remains largely hidden and manifests itself only in a failure to produce a self-contained psychological portrait, it becomes more explicit in Weiss's subsequent book *Fluchtpunkt*. This novel recounts the life of a refugee and artist in Stockholm from 1940 to 1947 and culminates in what is perhaps Weiss's most emphatic articulation of the cosmopolitan ideal. The text presents its subject in a clearly outlined spatial and temporal setting not previously used by Weiss, a fact that has induced most critics to read it as a more or less authentic representation of Weiss's own biography. In contrast to these readings, I suggest that the clear-cut topography in this text is indicative of a certain force that is necessary to transform the predicament of forced exile into freedom. The representation of rooms and houses as intact subjective spaces, for instance, is symptomatic of the narrator's rather desperate attempts at self-situating. After describing his move into a new room that exhibits traces of the numerous people who lived there before him, he continues:

> In diesem Raum würde ich umhergehen, mit Stühlen rücken, arbeiten, mich räuspern, husten, niesen, mit Besuchern sprechen. . . . Das Bücherregal, das Brett und die Stühle wurden hereingetragen, die Staffelei und der Zeichentisch wurden aufgeschlagen, die Koffer und Kisten geöffnet. Die Ausbreitung und Verteilung des Inventars war eine Tätigkeit, die ich oft, in meinen Zimmern im Elternhaus, in Hotelzimmern und Pensionszimmern, in gemieteten Zimmern in verschiedenen Städten, vorgenommen hatte. Im Überblicken meines Besitzes suchte ich nach einer Widerstandskraft gegen die Fremde, die außerhalb des Zimmers lag. Ich schlug ein Lager auf und befestigte das Lager mit meinem Eigentum. Selbst wenn der Raum in einer Wüste lag und der Vernichtung preisgegeben war, konnte ich die Dinge, die mir einen Wert bedeuteten, um mich aufstellen. (*W*, 2:182)

I would walk about in this room, move chairs around, work,

clear my throat, cough, sneeze, talk to visitors. . . . The bookcase, the bed and the chairs were carried in, the easel and the drawing board were set up, the cases and boxes opened. Spreading out and distributing this inventory was an activity I had often undertaken, in my rooms at my parents' houses, in hotel and rented rooms in various cities. Surveying my possessions I sought resistance against the strangeness outside. I set up a camp and fortified it with my property. Even if the room had been in a desert, abandoned to destruction, I could still set up around me the objects I prized. (*Ex*, 129, trans. altered)

Even though it is called a camp, this room still exhibits the features of a "room of one's own," a bourgeois interior space based on property. The narrator intensifies his appropriation of this space by indulging in a list of expressions of his own physical presence as he narrates the scene. Even if he will soon leave this specific room again, during his stay he takes entire possession of it. The protective house, characterized by Theodor W. Adorno in *Minima Moralia* as the spatial expression of a stable and secure self that has become obsolete in a world of mass destruction, is here erected as a shield against the disseminating forces of exile. Another topographical inscription affects the narrator's place of origin, to which he returns temporarily after the war is over:

Die Reise, die ich selbst ins Land meiner Herkunft unternahm, weckte in mir nicht den Wunsch, wieder dort ansässig zu werden. Die Fremde, mit der ich mich konfrontierte, war um so beunruhigender, als mir doch jedes Wort mit solcher Vertrautheit entgegenkam. Es war das Wiedersehn in einem Traum, in dem alles zu erkennen war, in dem alles offen und entblößt lag und doch von einer ungeheuerlichen Entstellung durchsetzt war. Was ich wiederfand, waren Ruinen von Häusern, in denen ich gewohnt hatte, und ein unversehrtes Haus in einem großen verfallenen Garten, doch was hier lag, war nicht wert, wieder angenommen zu werden, es ließ sich nur für Zeit und Ewigkeit verfluchen. (*W*, 2:267)

> The trip I took to the land of my birth awakened no wish in me to settle down there again. The strangeness that confronted me was all the more upsetting since every word I heard had such a familiar ring to me. It was a reunion in a dream, a dream in which everything was recognizable, in which everything lay open and bared to view, but which was shot through with a monstrous disfigurement. What I found was ruins of houses, in which I had lived, and one undamaged house in a big garden run wild, but what was there was not worth restoring to use again, it was fit only to be accursed now and forever. (*Ex*, 217, trans. altered)

The description of this landscape is reminiscent of the fear of touch characteristic of a taboo, which Freud related both to the psychological disposition of compulsory neurosis and to the religious structure of sacredness, and which he interpreted in terms of a need to express and contain deep emotional ambivalence. This is what seems to happen here with the sense of threat and uncanniness that accompanied the narrator's search for his origins in *Abschied von den Eltern* and that surfaces again in *Fluchtpunkt* when the narrator reminisces about his childhood.[18] In the previous chapter I suggested that Günther Anders attempts to counter a similar sense of uncanniness and forbiddenness during his return to Breslau by projecting moments of difference and heterogeneity into the German-dominated Eastern Europe of the past. In *Fluchtpunkt* such uncanniness is held at bay through a rather different gesture, namely the establishment of a taboo zone around the place of the narrator's childhood, a zone that both marks and banishes the unsettling force of this place. The taboo structure is also palpable in the narrator's avoidance of the proper name of this place throughout the book, and, if we accept Freud's analysis, it indicates that the narrator is full of ambivalence toward the country of his origin, torn between homesickness and rejection, desire and repulsion, feelings expressed by so many German Jews after the Holocaust. The taboo structure, in other words, refutes the narrator's attempts at self-interpretation at the beginning of the novel, where he claims never to have felt at home anywhere.

The cosmopolitan vision at the very end of *Fluchtpunkt* is predicated on a similar disavowal of the place of birth as place of origin. The

CHAPTER 2

sudden trip to Paris described in the last pages of the book initiates the narrator into an absolute freedom that he experiences first as threatening but then as redemptive as he gains a new sense of self and a cosmopolitan identity. In these scenes, the impact of an existentialism of Sartrian provenance is evident. The narrator's experience of nothingness, of an absolute rupture with his past that subsequently enables him to act freely, enacts the subject's emergence out of the unreflected *être-en-soi* into the *être-pour-soi*. One can see the attraction this model holds for a writer who struggles with his lack of home and roots, a lack that, from the perspective of existentialism, is a necessary freedom. Jean Paul Sartre's autobiography *Les Mots* shows that his own sense of exile arose from the early loss of his father and the natural rootedness that comes with being the successor to a father and an economic heritage. The freedom derived from this isolation, however, was contingent upon access to and legitimization in the cultural realm, as opposed to the more radical dislocation caused by physical exile. As Améry has keenly observed, the grand gesture of breaking away from one's origin is available only to those who have a choice between leaving home or remaining, which explains, perhaps, why in *Fluchtpunkt* the narrator's break with his past has to be introduced with a last forceful topographical inscription:

> Die Freiheit war noch vorhanden, doch ich hatte Boden in ihr gewonnen, sie war keine Leere mehr, in der ich im Alptraum der Anonymität lag und in der alle Bezeichnungen ihren Sinn verloren, es war eine Freiheit, in der ich jedem Ding einen Namen geben konnte. . . . Und die Sprache, die sich jetzt einstellte, war die Sprache, die ich am Anfang meines Lebens gelernt hatte, die natürliche Sprache, die mein Werkzeug war, die nur noch mir selbst gehörte, und mit dem Land, in dem ich aufgewachsen war, nichts mehr zu tun hatte. Diese Sprache war gegenwärtig, wann immer ich wollte und wo immer ich mich befand. Ich konnte in Paris leben oder in Stockholm, in London oder New York, und ich trug die Sprache bei mir, im leichtesten Gepäck. In diesem Augenblick war der Krieg überwunden, und die Jahre der Flucht waren überlebt. . . . An diesem Abend, im Frühjahr 1947, auf dem Seinedamm in Paris, im Alter von dreißig Jahren, sah ich, daß ich teilhaben konnte an einem

Austausch von Gedanken, der ringsum stattfand, an kein Land gebunden. (*W*, 2:293–94)

> The freedom was still there, but I had got a grip on it, it was no longer a vacuum where I lay in a nightmare of anonymity and where all designations lost their meaning: it was a freedom in which I could give everything a name. . . . And the language that now asserted itself was the language I had learned at the beginning of my life, the natural language that was my tool, that now belonged to me alone and had nothing more to do with the land where I had grown up. This language was present whenever I wanted it and wherever I was. I could live in Paris or in Stockholm, in London or New York, and I carried the language with me, however light I traveled. At this moment the war became a thing of the past and I had survived the years of flight. . . . That evening, in the spring of 1947, on the embankment in the Seine in Paris, at the age of thirty, I saw that it was possible to live and work in the world, and that I could participate in the exchange of ideas that was taking place all around, bound to no country. (*Ex*, 244, trans. altered)

This concluding vision of *Fluchtpunkt* resonates with traditional notions of cosmopolitanism, particularly the German Enlightenment tradition of *Weltbürgertum*, in that it links the cosmopolitan outlook to gestures of self-location.[19] Historically, cosmopolitanism has hardly been free of ethnocentrism, and that is still true for eighteenth-century conceptions of *Weltbürgertum*.[20] Though cosmopolitanism denotes a tolerant openness toward other cultures, a cosmopolitan lifestyle is usually contingent upon a secure position within a particular culture, or at least commensurable with the alignment to a particular culture. This safe anchoring in a native culture reverberates, for example, in Goethe's well-known concept of a future world literature, which would be a literature, "in which an honorable role is preserved for us Germans. All nations are paying attention to us, they praise and criticize, accept and reject, imitate and distort, understand or misunderstand us and open or close their hearts to our concerns."[21] And while cosmopolitanism figures as a regulative, never completely realized principle of human history in Kant's "Idea for a Universal History with a Cosmopolitan

Intent," its more pragmatic meaning in *Toward Perpetual Peace* betrays a similar centrist tendency. Cosmopolitan right is there defined as the stranger's right to fair treatment in a foreign country, a right Kant never fully disentangles from the rights of an individual within a national constitution.[22] Cosmopolitan and national identities are thus not mutually exclusive but rather interdependent: someone who has a safe place within a national constitution, or in a national culture, is also more likely to find a safe place anywhere else in the world. The tolerant, world-embracing view of the cosmopolitan emerges out of his being anchored somewhere.

In the concluding passages of *Fluchtpunkt*, the stabilization of the subject's position as a precondition for the expansion of its circle of concern transpires in a number of ways. Most important, it is a particular place name, Paris, that signifies cosmopolitan freedom and that tears down the barriers separating the narrator from the international community. Paris functions as a *Fluchtpunkt* in the technical sense of the word, a point that defines the perspective of a painting and thus renders it coherent, in this case, by giving a meaning to the narrator's erratic wanderings. Textually, this painting technique also translates into visual descriptions that fix and accentuate the narrator's location through the play of light against the cityscape, such as: "Ich stand auf dem Platz im Zentrum der Stadt, in einem scharf abgewinkelten, von der Sonne beleuchteten Feld in der Mitte des Schattenkraters" (*W,* 2:290). [I stood in a square in the center of the city, in a space sharply outlined by the sun in the midst of a crater of shadow (*Ex,* 241).] A similar doubleness of localization and de-localization marks the narrator's recuperation of his native language. The narrator's idea of an original language that belongs exclusively to himself depends on the detachment of this language from history and the disentangling of his biography from Germany's history. This is the deeper meaning of the strange rebirth fantasy preceding this scene, a fantasy in which the narrator, overwhelmed by feelings of nonbelonging, imagines himself as a baby who learns to speak, immersed in the noise of the street yet undisturbed by any other speaker of this language: "ich mußte wieder von vorn beginnen, radebrechend, lallend, in meinem Korb liegend, am dröhnenden Straßenrand" (*W,* 2:291–92). [I had again to start afresh, in broken speech, stuttering, lying in my wicker basket at the roaring edge of the street (*Ex,* 242, trans. altered).] The basket is also reminiscent of the Moses motif that serves in *Abschied von den Eltern* to depict

PETER WEISS'S SKEPTICAL COSMOPOLITANISM

the narrator's estrangement from his family. Stripped of its religious connotations, the Moses motif becomes here part of the narrator's gesture of distancing himself from a national collective.

It is significant that the site of this reinvention of self is Paris, not Berlin, the more plausible choice from what we know of Peter Weiss's biography. While he indeed spent the spring of 1947 in Paris, that summer he went to Berlin to write a series of articles on the defeated Germany for a Stockholm newspaper. These articles display a surprisingly sympathetic view of the people who had, after all, persecuted and expelled him. Weiss later turned the articles into a book, *Die Besiegten* [The Defeated], which diffuses the voice of the initially identifiable narrator into a series of different voices of both victims and perpetrators, thus dissolving any possible site for the narrator's identity and location. In Berlin, Weiss also met the publisher Peter Suhrkamp, who encouraged him to pursue his literary attempts in German more intensively. Weiss followed this advice and in 1949 submitted a manuscript that was, however, published by Suhrkamp only decades later under the title *Der Fremde* [The Stranger]. In short, Weiss's stay in Berlin in 1947 had a large impact on his development as a writer, and his overall attitude toward Germany and the German language and culture was far more ambivalent than the narrator's in *Fluchtpunkt*. Shifting the place of his retrieval of the German language from postwar Berlin to existentialist Paris in *Fluchtpunkt*, Weiss performs a gesture of distancing himself from Germany, paradoxically at the very moment when he was being reintegrated into German culture through the recent success of *Der Schatten des Körpers des Kutschers*. At the same time, the abrupt transitions in *Fluchtpunkt*, the sometimes stilted language, and the imposed teleology give this narrative a contrived character. These stylistic features express the simultaneous desire for and instability of a cosmopolitanism that grounds the self in a place of symbolic origin rather than in a place of birth.

Another indication of the instability of the narrator's self-chosen *Weltbürgertum* are the signs of persecution engraved upon the bodies of other Jewish refugees. The novel establishes the connection between Jewishness and exile, for instance, through the description of the narrator's gaze falling on an old Jewish cemetery at the moment when he becomes painfully aware of his own restlessness and inability to stay with a woman for any significant length of time (*W*, 2:174; *Ex*, 121). Most important, the narrator arrives at his vision of self-chosen exile

CHAPTER 2

only by separating himself from two other exiles who are associated with Jewishness. These are his father, whose self-hatred and fruitless pursuit of assimilation reveal deep-seated anxieties and ineluctable homelessness, and the painter Anatol, whose driven demeanor marks a similarly discomforting, unchosen exile. Anatol, who is at one point identified with the eternal Jewish wanderer Ahasveros, manages to transform his own exilic existence into political solidarity. Weiss's depiction of him as a pariah personality twists the old Christian stereotype around, casting Ahasveros not as the unredeemed wandering Jew but as a man who exposes himself to the suffering in an unredeemed world and who resists being blinded by false redemption.[23] At the same time, the highly theatrical staging of what looks like a mark of Cain on Anatol's forehead serves to distance him from the narrator, who chooses a different form of existence despite his sympathies for Anatol's art and politics: "Seine Stirn war bis zur Mitte des Schädels kahl, und auf ihrer Höhe zeichnete sich im scharfen Licht der Glühbirne, die von der Decke herabhing, eine kreisrunde Vertiefung ab" (*W,* 2:165). [He was bald from his forehead to the middle of his skull; in the harsh light of the bulb hanging from the ceiling, a circular depression was outlined at the top of the forehead (*Ex,* 112, trans. altered).][24] A similarly emphatic visualization of a physical marker of exile serves to distance the narrator from his father. At one point the narrator recounts, filled with horror, how he heard his father cursing one of his sons, named Gregor, with the words "Verfluchter Judenlümmel, verfluchter Judenlümmel!" (*W* 2:178). [You damned Jewish lout, you damned Jewish lout! (*Ex,* 125, trans. altered).] This scene is particularly powerful because it recalls a famous scene in Kafka's *Die Verwandlung* [*The Metamorphosis*] in which the father chases his son Gregor, who has been transformed into a giant vermin, in a similar fashion through the room. Weiss taps here into the cultural archive of images of the recently assimilated Jewish father venting his suppressed anger upon those of his children who display signs of nonassimilation. In *Fluchtpunkt,* the memory of this scene loses its horror as the narrator shortly thereafter becomes capable of understanding the father's problem. This understanding, however, is essentially an act of visualization in which the narrator's words render visible the otherwise hidden mark of forced exile, the father's circumcised penis:

Auch die verwirrten Worte meines Vaters wurden mir ver-

PETER WEISS'S SKEPTICAL COSMOPOLITANISM

ständlich, mit denen er das Unglück verfluchte, das ihn auf die Flucht und in die Heimatlosigkeit getrieben hatte. Ich *sah* ihn an einem Sonntagmorgen, als ich im Badezimmer stand und mich rasierte, und er nicht wagte, nackt in das eingelaufene Bad zu steigen, und deshalb die Hose seines Schlafanzuges anbehielt. Ich *sah* ihn im warmen Wasser liegen, von der Hose umflossen, *die mir sein Geschlecht verbarg, das beschnitten war,* und das er mir nie gezeigt hatte. (*W,* 2:181, my emphasis)

Now comprehensible were the confused words with which my father cursed the misfortune that had driven him into exile. I *saw* him on a Sunday morning as I stood in the bathroom shaving. He did not dare to step naked into the bath but kept on his pajama bottoms. I *saw* him lying in the warm water, the pants floating around him, and *hiding his sex from me; it was circumcised* and he had never shown it to me. (*Ex,* 128, my emphasis, trans. altered)

My reading of *Fluchtpunkt* has been largely symptomatic in its emphasis on the catastrophic leftovers that continue to undermine the cosmopolitan ideal the novel attempts to construct. In what follows I will focus on the new critical and creative possibilities that grow out of the tension the book is unable to resolve, including the construction of a diasporic community and the critique of the German rituals of *Vergangenheitsbewältigung*.

THE SEARCH FOR A DIASPORIC COMMUNITY: DAS GESPRÄCH DER DREI GEHENDEN

In the years following the publication of his autobiographical novels, Weiss was enormously productive, yet even more striking than this productivity is the variety of literary genres he engaged in and experimented with: various forms of drama, notebooks, and dense anti-narrative prose texts. As some critics have remarked, Weiss surprised his public with each new book and eluded every attempt to categorize his writing in terms of a certain genre or a literary school. One may argue with Paul Gilroy that a splintering into different textual registers and a subversion of genre conventions is in and by itself a feature of diasporic writing, a search for new forms of cultural participation.[25] Weiss constructs a range of diasporic perspectives in his literary experiments, which include the prose text from which he recited during his first attendance of a Gruppe 47 meeting in 1962, *Das Gespräch der drei Gehenden*. The text is usually subsumed under the same category as the earlier *Der Schatten des Körpers des Kutschers* and then, depending on the taste of the critic, regarded favorably as an avant-garde piece or rejected as a relapse into the apolitical perspective of Weiss's early works. In what follows, I will suggest a different kind of connection between experimental style and political impetus. A meta-reflection on the writing of autobiography, *Das Gespräch* revokes the teleology of self articulated in *Fluchtpunkt*, replacing the idea of an absolute freedom by the poetic license to fashion life stories. Such stories in turn become the tenuous ground of a new kind of community.

Formally, *Das Gespräch* is a montage of short descriptions and narratives, vaguely allocated in the introductory scene to the voices of "Abel, Babel und Cabel."[26] These three figures have met accidentally and are now telling each other various stories and incidents of their lives. "Sie gingen und sahen sich um und sahen was sich zeigte, und sie sprachen darüber und über anderes was sich früher gezeigt hatte" (*W*, 2:297). [They walked along and looked about them and watched what was happening, and they talked about it and about things which had happened earlier (*C*, 7).] And what "had happened earlier" consists for at least two of the speakers mostly of flight, persecution, and hiding. Frequently, their discourse starts with a deictic gesture, with one of them pointing to a place or an object and elaborating on the events associated with it. Or the rhythm of the walk itself dictates the stream of memories:

> Und wenn ich unsere Schritte im Kies höre, hier in dieser Stille hinter den Mauern, dann ist das andere wieder da, das nie zu einem Abschluß kam, und da liege ich immer noch, im Sand, vor einem offenen Schober, und kann ein Stück an Stacheldrähten entlangkriechen, in einer eng begrenzten, von Bäumen durchwachsenen Anlage. Wenn ich dort bin gibt es kein Herauskommen, ich kann es nur zeitweise vergessen, da sage ich mir, ich bin wach, ich lebe noch, und dann ist es wieder da, dann steht es wieder bevor, und ich zermartere mich mit Gedanken, auf welche Weise es

geschehen wird, mit dem Strick, dem Beil, den Geschossen. (*W*, 2:313)

And when I hear our footsteps on the gravel, here in the silence behind these walls, that other thing is there again, something which was never settled, and I find myself lying in the sand again, before an open barn, and I can crawl some way along the barbed wire, within a narrow enclosure full of trees. When I am there I know I cannot get out, I can only forget it at times, and say to myself, I am awake, I am still alive, and then it is there again, then it impends again, and I torture myself with thinking how it will happen, with the rope, by the axe, by shooting. (*C*, 34, trans. altered)

The experimental character of the text manifests itself in its spatial logic, a critical adaptation of the *nouveau roman* style. Like the *nouveau roman*, *Das Gespräch* is descriptive in a way that ultimately dissolves the temporal and spatial coherence of narrative. Certain scenes and places recur several times yet are cast into different times and circumstances, which makes their very existence questionable. The bridge where the three walkers initially meet, for example, figures as a variable in a number of different narratives, with one voice depicting it being built the night before and another voice claiming it as the site of a grotesque incident that happened long ago. This style, far from being an end in itself, mimetically reproduces the perspective of refugees who experience space as fragmented, as a net of hiding places and intersections on nomadic routes. The nomadic nature of the figures is first hinted at by the name of the second speaker, Babel, and becomes more evident in their various stories of flight and attempted return. The image of the harbor that underlies most of the text also suggests this kind of perspective. A nodal point of traffic and communication, but also a place of ongoing transformations where newly erected buildings stand next to ruins and piles of debris, the harbor in *Das Gespräch* is a site where different times and different places interconnect. One effect of the text's miming of the refugee's perspective is that narrated space fails to constitute a stable background for a set of events; the harbor, the bridge, and the street are transient effects of enunciation rather than chronotopes. As Mikhail Bakhtin defines them, chronotopes are categories of cultural systems that relate time and space in a narrative, thus establishing a realm of human action; they are relatively stable units that precede the individual literary text and prefigure its meaning.[27] In *Das Gespräch*, however, the lengthy topographical descriptions of the harbor continuously construct and deconstruct a spatio-temporal unit rather than organize the refugee's experience into a unity of signification.

The spatial logic of this text might be described, in Michel de Certeau's terms, as a continuous transformation of place into space, that is, as an infusion of human agency and movement into an otherwise stable configuration of positions. The distinction between place and space corresponds to that between the map, which is a static depiction of immobile objects, and the itinerary, which is a description of space traversed and "practiced" by human agents. The spatialization of place creates a multitude of possibilities while obfuscating geometrical order and spatial transparency. The multiple paths of pedestrians, who appropriate urban places through everyday activities such as walking and window-shopping, for example, transform the ordered space of architectural planning into the "*opaque and blind* mobility characteristic of the bustling city."[28] City walking thus presents a view from below, devoid of panoramic overview but in close proximity to concrete localities and events. Similarly, the speakers in *Das Gespräch* retrieve through walking what Weiss once called in his *Notizbücher* a topological memory, that is, a memory dispersed into the contingent particulars of a street without end or beginning: "Topological memory. The road. Recognizing the traveled path. Innumerable small marks, a scratch, a hole, a crack, this happened here, that there" (*Nb*, 108). In *Das Gespräch*, such a topological memory is relayed through the numerous deictic locutions, which disseminate memories while establishing tentative nodal points between past and present. It further becomes clear that the speakers' attendance to the concrete sites of experience reflects the fragmentation of this experience: "Als ich müde war legte ich mich hin, wo ich gerade war, in der Nähe des Wassers, auf eine glattgewalzte Straßenfläche, mit Bruchstellen, Speichelfladen, Pferdeäpfeln" (*W*, 2:311). [When I was tired I lay down wherever I happened to be, near the water, on the smooth-milled street, its surface cracked, and spotted with spittle and horsedroppings (*C*, 31, trans. altered).] The picaresque chronotope of the street could subsume these contingencies of the refugee's life once again under the logic of a sequence. But the particular, even contrasting, narrative uses each speaker makes of the spatial images of bridge, harbor, and street are analogous to the city walker's mobilization of localized objects for diverse, sometimes incommensurable, itineraries. Rather than containing the dispersion of time and space into formal coherence, the style of *Das Gespräch* redoubles dispersion.

What kind of conversation can take place in such a text, between these three walkers? It is a conversation that accommodates the experience of historical trauma as well as an irreducible distance between interlocutors. As we have seen previously, the bridge, the traditional metaphor for encounter and dialogue, becomes a variable in two different narratives contesting each other. Indeed, if the text relates a conversation, it is one in which mutual understanding is at best an effect of chance: "Wenn einer sprach schwiegen die beiden andern und hörten zu oder sahen sich um und hörten auf anderes, und wenn der eine zuende gesprochen hatte, sprach der zweite, und dann der dritte, und die beiden andern hörten zu oder dachten an anderes" (*W*, 2:297). [When one spoke the others were silent, listening or looking around and listening to other things, and when one had finished speaking the second spoke, and then the third, and the other two listened, or thought about other things (*C*, 7).] This casual indifference pointedly describes the character of the conversation in which a speaker would occasionally continue the speech of the previous speaker in an associative manner but more often would simply ignore it and relate something he sees or continue an earlier tale. The fictitious character of these tales is emphasized through the conspicuous use of the ferryman motif, which is associated with free-floating imagination in such German expressions as *Seemannsgarn spinnen*. Throughout *Das Gespräch*, speaker A relates anecdotes of a ferryman and his six sons whose fantastic physiques and lifestyles are reminiscent of tall tales. The speaker's implication that the ferryman's discourse is fuzzy and that he may not have understood him properly enhances the impression of stories constantly being made up, while the interspersed fairy tale motives emphasize the fantastic character of these stories. The dialogue that emerges in *Das Gespräch* is an indirect one: as the speakers tell their stories in an often grotesque manner in which lies and truths become inseparable, they sometimes merge, or affect each other, with one voice picking up the thread of another voice's tale, spinning it on and changing it.

One might be tempted to read *Das Gespräch* as a rather playful

CHAPTER 2

account of three travelers who improvise stories to deceive and outdo each other—*Seemannsgeschichten,* in short—were it not for some scenes in which the ordeal of exile surfaces with unexpected intensity. One of these reiterates the scene from the final pages of *Fluchtpunkt,* which depicts the exile's life as a drama of language lost and reclaimed. The exile who has been ousted from his native language, we recall, first regresses into a child's lallation and then reappropriates language in an act of self-empowerment that enables him to free language from its historical and geographical boundedness.[29] Earlier I suggested that the emphatic cosmopolitan vision in *Fluchtpunkt* functions as a screen memory that covers up the traumatic core of the refugee's experience. *Das Gespräch* approaches this traumatic core through a process of fictionalization and defictionalization and suspends trauma in a new form of collectivity. A series of three episodes in which someone hides under a pile of lumber near the railway bridge and observes the city culminates in a scene of language lost and reclaimed that recalls the narrator's experience in *Fluchtpunkt,* but it offers a decisively different view of that experience. The first of these scenes is narrated by speaker C, who relates personal experience; the second is told by speaker A, who renders the fantastic and possibly misremembered stories of the ferryman; and the third is again told by speaker C. While the first scene relates a relatively harmless episode in speaker C's life, the second one recounts how the fourth son of the ferryman, Jom, spent the latter part of his life under a pile of packing paper and corrugated board composing nonsense rhymes with a pencil discarded by a carpenter. These rhymes recall the lallation of the insane Hölderlin—Jom's odes and hymns and the carpenter's pencil evoke this figure—but also avant-garde artistic practices in which word sequences are generated through random letter variations. Jom seems to deploy here a modernist technique of writing, using chance and improvisation and foregrounding sound and rhythm at the expense of semantics: "Er, der des Sprechens nicht fähig ist, läßt diese Laute ertönen, sie klingen wie Salbe Malbe halbe kalbe balde Walde falte kalte halte Spalte, und so weiter, die Worte sind beliebig zu ersetzen" (*W,* 2:325). [He cannot speak, he intones sounds, like humper, dumper, thumper, pumper, lumber, number, punter, hunter, gunter, shunter, and so on, words at random (*C,* 54).] The fact that the speaker later states that he is not sure about the veracity of this scene, that Jom might rather be a successful writer sitting in an expensive apartment and composing polished sentences on a typewriter, underscores the hypothetical nature of the speaker's description.

The last time this scenario recurs, it is deprived of its playful grotesqueness and transformed into images of threat and horror. One of these images even evokes a mass grave. A few pages later, the wasting away of the speaker's speech gets metaphorically linked to the decomposition of bodies in the mass grave. In Weiss's *Rekonvaleszenz* [Convalescence], a similar metaphorical association is made, perhaps unwittingly, between the destruction of the exile writer's work and the burning of the Jews in the incinerators of the death camps.[30]

> Und da sah ich schon, daß dieser Raum angefüllt war mit Mengen von gleichartigen beweglichen Stücken, großen Füßen, Händen, Rümpfen oder Hälsen, alle behaart und verschorft, manche mit stumm aufklappenden Mündern, es waren auch Reihen von Zähnen mit Fleischfasern daran, und halbe Ohren, in deren Blutkruste es von Gold blinkte, und Finger, mit eingefaßten Steinen, und dies alles regte sich unter mir, und es war mir darum zu tun, herauszufinden, was dies für ein Tümpel, für eine Grube war. (*W*, 2:337)

> And then I saw that this space was filled with many similar moving objects, large feet, hands, torsos, or necks, all hairy and scabrous, some with mouths which opened noiselessly, also rows of teeth stuck with meat fibres, and halves of ears, in the encrusted blood a gleam of gold, and fingers with set stones, all this moved below me and I wanted to find out what sort of a hollow or pit it was. (*C*, 75, trans. altered)

> Und jetzt soll ich Zeugnis ablegen, Rechenschaft geben für ein Leben, mit all diesen zurückgelegten Wegen, diesen geöffneten und geschlossenen Türen, mit all diesen Bewegungen und Berührungen, mit diesen Worten, dieser Flut von Worten, die ausgesprochen und vernommen worden waren, zu keinem andern Nutzen, als zu versickern, zu verschwimmen, zu zerrinnen. (*W*, 2:338)

> And now I have to come forward and give evidence, to ren-

der an account of a life, of paths taken, doors opened and shut, with all that movement and those contacts, with all those words, that flood of words spoken and heard, to no other purpose than to dissolve, to vanish, to seep away. (*C,* 76–77)

In the third hiding scene of *Das Gespräch,* word cascades similar to those of Jom spring from the refugee's desire to bear witness to what he sees, a desire that is frustrated by his complete lack of understanding. In contrast to the babbling Jom, this speaker uses not only adjectives and nouns but also verbs, thus creating rudimentary propositional clauses. These are nonetheless still produced through a rather mechanical rhyming technique: "Mit ungeheurer Anstrengung versuchte ich, mir dies zu erklären, ich dachte mir dazu ein weißes Blatt Papier, dessen Leere sich völlig ausfüllen ließ mit Worten, und ich hörte mich lallen, lallen allen ballen fallen hallen schallen, Samen kamen Namen lahmen mahnen Bahnen, Lasten Masten faßten hasten tasten paßten" (*W,* 2:338). [I made a prodigious effort to sort it out, conjuring up in my mind a piece of blank paper to help me, and it completely filled up with words, and I heard myself stutter, splutter, mutter, utter, cutter, shutter, helter, skelter, shelter, delta, melter, pelter, sender, mender, tender, bender, gender, fender (*C,* 76).] If I am right in reading this scene as the expression of an exile's struggle with his language, we can say that he deploys here a mimetic mode of defense: overwhelmed by the hostility of language and unable to experience language as meaningful, he mimes the senseless spluttering of words in order not to be reduced to a mere object of linguistic violence. As the speaker imagines himself mechanically filling blank paper with words, the size of the sheet defines the measure of his speech. And yet, by organizing his linguistic material through the systematic deployment of chance, he also becomes, like a writer of concrete poetry, an agent in the automated production of words.[31]

In a way, this is a self-reflexive scene that discloses the principles of the text of *Das Gespräch* itself, whose main figures are alphabetical ciphers rather than psychologically developed characters. In fact, the names of the speakers as well as those of the ferryman's sons are generated through the systematic exchange of letters, respectively vowels: Abel, Babel, Cabel, and Jam, Jem, Jim, Jom, Jum, Jym. Whereas the names of the first two speakers relate mimetically to the themes of flight and persecution—Abel is an archetypal victim and Babel the most salient symbol of dispersion—the third name evinces the text's somewhat mindless adherence to the alphabetical sequence of letters. Even if we read the "Cabel" as a *Kabel* [cable], signifying interconnectedness in a world of electronic media, this letter substitution draws our attention to the ruling of the alphabet. Both speaker C and the author of the text surrender their linguistic creativity to an external order that ignores semantics but also provides a minimal form of resistance against the amorphous dispersal of the exile's writing. If this scene resolves the refugee's struggle with language, it arrives at a rather modest resolution, one that neither results from an act of self-empowerment nor entails a sovereign mastery over language. Rather, it is effected by the circulation and transmutation of speech fragments across the distances that never cease to separate the speakers from each other. A closer examination of the wording of the three segments shows how word sequences are repeated, conflated, and distorted while circulating among the speakers.[32] The text as a whole, then, presents a conversation between atomized exiles that is devoid of the grand gesture of the *Weltbürger* who speaks to the whole world owing to his stable position in one culture: from the experience of persecution and hiding, the possibility of meeting in transitory spaces and fashioning transitory life stories emerges.

Critique and Distance

Weiss finally directs his critique at West Germany in *Die Ermittlung*, but also in a rarely quoted pseudo-ethnographic report from 1963, "Bericht über Einrichtungen und Gebräuche in den Siedlungen der Grauhäute."[33] There is a hint in his notebooks that his encounters with the *Entschädigungsamt* [Compensation Office]—that is, with the West German administrative discourse on the plight of those persecuted under Nazism—were a possible inspiration for the "Bericht." During the early 1960s, Weiss and his brother sought compensation for the damages their father suffered because of war and emigration. The application process proved protracted and difficult, with the German administration demanding ever more medical evidence and legal opinions.[34] In the midst of excerpts from ethnographic works, we find in Weiss's notebooks observations on the ritualistic moments of this application procedure, which might have been in his mind when he wrote the "Bericht": "Office of Compensations, Insurances. How they try to bypass the survivors, to deceive them with magic spells—Medicine men are dispatched. Compensations Office" (*Nb*, 106). Furthermore, an unpublished note suggests that the traveler is Jewish and afraid of being found out as a Jew because of his physical difference:

> *With horror?*
> Again the idea of different looking clothes and—for example—of the nose—.
> As far as he can see it from the distance—foreskin.[35]

The "Bericht" mimics the perspective of a traveler who enters a Western industrialized city lacking the cultural knowledge that would enable him to recognize everyday objects and actions such as cars, cigarettes, shopping, reading the newspaper, and so on. Adopting an ethnographer's point of view, the traveler describes the observed incidents and actions in absurdly meticulous detail, using ethnographic terms to speculate on their ritualistic meaning. Gross misreadings of situations, for instance the interpretation of buses as "Ruhebetten" [daybeds],[36] emphasize the discrepancy between the traveler's horizon of interpretation and that of the culture he visits. The text as a whole harks back to the Enlightenment tradition of using the foreigner's perspective as a hermeneutic device to launch a critique of Western European societies.[37] Its depiction of commodities as fetishes that are guarded and protected by those who bought them, for example, reads like a satire of Western consumerism. Yet the text betrays a seriousness that indicates that more is at stake here. There is a pervasive sense of danger. The traveler has heard rumors about the cruelty and vindictiveness of the inhabitants and is constantly afraid of being discovered by them as a stranger. Simultaneously, he undergoes an uncanny process of assimilation, adopting a "Mimikry, die ihm das Dasein hier ermöglicht."[38] [Mimicry, which makes his existence here possible.] Walking through the cramped space of the city, the traveler is sucked into the rhythm of the masses and gradually loses his panoramic and distanced view. He discovers similarities between his own physiognomy and the species he researches, or more precisely, the differences between the two become blurred and indeterminable:

> Nur glaubt er, in der Hautfarbe das Grau zu erkennen, das den Bewohnern dieser Gegend bei uns ihren Namen gibt,

doch auch dies ist ungewiß, denn wenn er jetzt seine eigene Hand betrachtet, so erscheint sie ihm in derselben schmutzigen Bleichheit, die die Farbe des Himmels und des aufgetürmten Gesteins widerspiegelt, und die auch von dem glühenden Klumpen der Sonne nicht erwärmt werden kann.[39]

He believes he recognizes in their skin color the gray that gives the inhabitants of this area our name for them. But even this is uncertain, for when he takes a closer look at his own hand, he sees the same dingy paleness that is reflected in the color of the sky and in the piles of rocks, and that cannot be warmed even by the glowing clod of the sun.

What happens here, and what happens increasingly during the traveler's walk, is that his perceptive categories cease to keep his objects of research at a proper distance. He gradually loses his sense of orientation, as well as control over his steps, while following a tramp as if hypnotized. He moves underground and enters into a public restroom, which he perceives as the sacred center of this society. At this moment, the text breaks off, necessarily, for its very composition depends on distance, a distance that alone enables the traveler to write his report. Furthermore, it seems significant that the text breaks off at that very moment when the mark of the traveler's particularity—the circumcised penis—is in danger of becoming exposed. The "Bericht" epitomizes the difference between Weiss and the Enlightenment, which had used the stranger's perspective in order to confirm its premise that cultural differences ultimately dissolve—and should dissolve—in view of universal reason. In Weiss, the discovery of the unity underlying cultural difference does not lead to a redemptive universalism but to anxiety, thus making distance the elusive but necessary prerequisite for an encounter with this country.

The most unsettling effect of Weiss's "Bericht" derives from its radicalization of the monkey's perspective in Kafka's "Ein Bericht für eine Akademie" ["A Report to an Academy"]. Kafka's monkey tells a story of assimilation, the transformation of an African monkey first into a domesticated animal and then into an almost-human civilized European. The monkey-narrator presents his report to a scientific academy, that is, an institution that represents the society that captures monkeys

CHAPTER 2

to display them in zoos or to make them objects of scientific research. It thus brings to a head the double bind of the minority writer who is forced to explain herself to the very culture that denigrates her. Weiss's "Bericht" establishes a similar double bind. Throughout the text, the narrator invokes a collective "we" or "our" that establishes the horizon of interpretation for the strange incidents and habits the traveler observes and that simultaneously addresses a readership as the inscribed audience of the report. Aimed at a German-speaking audience, this text constructs a specific diasporic perspective, a perspective that draws its readership into the paradoxical situation of observing its own society as if from a distance.

> Gleichzeitig arbeitet sich, von vorn her kommend, eine Gestalt zwischen den Angesammelten hindurch, die ihren [*sic*] Ausdruck und ihren Gebärden nach dem Hüter entspricht, dem der Reisende bereits in den Höhlungen der festen Gebäude begegnet ist, und führt, im Zusammenwirken mit den Händen der Insassen, das schon bekannte Spiel des Tauschens aus, und diesmal scheint er den Sammlern den Genuß des eng aneinandergedrückten Dahingleitens zu geben, und dafür reichen ihm die Hände die kleinen Marken hin, die er in einem umgehängten rachenförmigen Gebilde verschwinden läßt, und er streckt den Händen die bereits angefertigten, in dicken Schichten zusammengehaltenen, schnell losgerissenen Bilder oder Beschreibungen hin, die ihrem neuen Besitzer das Recht zur Teilnahme an diesem Zusammensein verbürgen.[40]

> A figure, whose expressions and gesticulations correspond to those of the guard whom the traveler encountered in the hollows of the solid buildings, simultaneously works his way back through the crowd and performs, in collaboration with the hands of the passengers, the same ritual of exchange observed before; this time he seems to give the collectors the pleasure of gliding along pressed tightly together, and in exchange for this pleasure the hands pass him the small coupons, which he hides away in a thing shaped like mouth and hanging around his neck. He then quickly rips pre-fash-

ioned pictures or descriptions from a many-layered, bound stack, and extends them to the hands. These articles now authenticate their new owner's right to take part in this collectivity.

This bureaucratic, pseudo-scientific language is reminiscent of Kafka's "Bericht an eine Akademie." However, Kafka emphasizes the monkey's mimicry of gestures it does not understand to alienate the readers from their own behavior. Weiss instead creates the sense of distance and lack of comprehension entirely through his peculiar use of language. The use of ethnographic terms to produce exacting technical descriptions of the most common and recognizable events makes the reader thoroughly aware of the force being used to tear her away from habitual, familiar language. Through such long-winded circumlocution, Weiss makes the German language alien to itself.

In 1964, shortly after composing the "Bericht," Weiss left for Frankfurt to observe the Auschwitz trial, which became the subject of one of his best known and most controversial works, *Die Ermittlung*.[41] Situating this play with a number of other, partially unpublished texts, I argue that Weiss's diasporic perspective shaped his representation of the trial and of its particular form of historical discourse, that is, the pursuit of historical truth via pieces of evidence and oral testimonies that are verified and evaluated by a codified system of juridical rules. Weiss's specific angle on the trial expresses and intensifies the crisis of witnessing brought about by the Shoah, the difficulty of testifying to events that shatter human forms of perception and comprehension. Shoshana Felman and Dori Laub, who have theorized on this crisis, emphasize the performative aspect of testimony, seeing it as a mode of narration in which the witness does not possess but instead embodies a truth that constantly eludes him or her. Felman and Laub draw attention to the situational context of testimony, which is essentially a dialogic event between a witness and an addressable other, an empathetic listener. The effect of such dialogicity can be recognized in the interviews with survivors that are currently being conducted and collected in the Fortunoff Archive for Holocaust Testimonies at Yale University. During these interviews, the stories the survivor tells frequently break down, as traumatizing memories interrupt the flow of his or her speech. The interviewer then helps the survivor to resume speech by listening attentively and empathetically or by asking questions, so that the interview proceeds like a psychoanalytic session, providing a dialogic situation appropriate to the recollection of traumatic experience. Felman and Laub emphasize that testimony does not aim at an "objective" historical truth but that it creates a meaning for the past, a meaning that emerges from and reflects upon the community that is formed in the act of giving testimony. Not only the individual sessions but also the larger context of the Video Archive, which was founded to preserve the survivors' testimonies and to learn from them, encourages survivors to tell their life stories and thus to break "the frame of death."[42] Weiss's texts on and around the Auschwitz trial reflect on the possibilities and the limits of testimony in the case of witnesses who, in contrast to the interviewed survivors, lack a sympathetic audience or, worse, who speak in front of a decidedly unsympathetic audience. Originally, Weiss had planned to incorporate the material from the Auschwitz trial into a modern adaptation of Dante's *Divine Comedy*.[43] Weiss's fascination with Dante's world theater was related to his own attempts to universalize the meaning of the Holocaust by linking it to other forms of violence and exploitation—and the metaphor of Dante's inferno was widely used in connection with Auschwitz. However, as Martin Walser observed, the sensationalistic use of this metaphor by the media led to a highly problematic shift of meaning: Dante's inferno, originally the site where sinners suffer brutal punishments, came to depict the suffering of innocent Holocaust victims.[44] Weiss evidently planned to return the focus to the sinners, namely the complacent former perpetrators in contemporary Germany, rather than highlighting the drastic images of suffering itself.[45] However, Weiss intended to adopt the *Divine Comedy* not as a structuring framework to depict the reality of contemporary Germany but as a subjective perspective. In fact, his notebooks show almost more concern with the figure of Dante than with the imagery of the inferno, and it is clear that Weiss endows his Dante with features that he identified in himself: Dante knows no "homeland" (*Nb*, 253), suffers from phobias (*Nb*, 284), is Jewish (*Nb*, 258), ill (*Nb*, 276), persecuted (*Nb*, 289), and emotionally attached to a dead woman (*Nb*, 254).

 Several unpublished texts pertaining to Weiss's *Divine Comedy* project similarly portray Dante as a half-Jewish exile returning to the inferno of postwar West Germany. Although Weiss seems to suggest in his "Vorübung zum dreiteiligen Drama divina commedia" [Preparatory

Exercise for the Three-Part Drama Divina Commedia] that his visit to Frankfurt inspired reflection on his own faults, especially his historical blindness and failure to act, these sketches betray a different preoccupation in their depiction of the returning exile as instrumentalized and silenced by the German public. The first version, for example, transforms the allegories of human vices, which appear at the beginning of Dante's journey, into three deceptively friendly beings. Drawing an idealized picture of a modern country that has come to terms with its past, they try to persuade the exile to return.[46] The next scenes, then, show how the phraseology of peace and harmony serves to cover up the continuity with the past. An all-pervasive philosemitism barely conceals the underlying antisemitism, and the returning exile is treated in a friendly manner only to improve the public image of the country. As soon as he resists conforming to the role that is imposed on him, he is silenced, sometimes by rebukes, sometimes by violence. And while this modern Dante does not face a homogeneously hostile front—there are hints that he has some genuine allies on the Left of this country[47]—the sketches foreground the loneliness and the vulnerability of the exile who, in contrast to the original Dante, cannot even rely on the support of his Virgil. This does not mean that Weiss fashions Dante exclusively as a victim. The self-criticism hinted at in the *Vorübung* is also evident in the preliminary sketches, for example in Giotto's reproach of Dante's narcissism.[48] Yet the figure of Dante, in all its ambiguity and faultiness, continues to embody the only voice of testimony in these sketches. Dante's exilic biography and his inability to comply with the alleged demands of the present are all that is left of the past.

Why did Weiss abandon this focus on the subjective perspective of the returning exile? Why did he choose instead a form of representation that claims the utmost objectivity, the documentary theater of *Die Ermittlung*? As is well known, the play is based on documentary material from the Auschwitz trial, on testimonies of both victims and perpetrators, that Weiss compiled, condensed, and rearranged without radically altering the wording. It has not gone unnoticed that the play nonetheless conveys a distinct interpretation of the Shoah, one that has drawn criticism from the very beginning. James Young has formulated a compelling critique of *Die Ermittlung*, contending that Weiss uses the alleged objectivity of documents—their "rhetoric of fact"—to conceal his own particular reconstruction of the Holocaust, a reconstruction undertaken from a reductive, economistic Marxist point of view.

According to Young, this point of view effaces the Jewish identity of the victims and subordinates the specific role antisemitism played in National Socialism to a universal critique of capitalism and fascism.[49] It is certainly true that Weiss intended to show both that German industry collaborated with and profited from National Socialism, and that the continuity of the German administrative and economic elite after 1945—at least in the Western part of the country—prevented a deeper confrontation with the past, fostering a latent continuity of National Socialism itself. By focusing exclusively on questions of representation, however, Young overlooks the play's reflection on what I would call the location of testimony. Weiss certainly does not use the courtroom motif to establish an objective framework and a discursive authority, nor does he pretend to present the documents from the trial in an entirely unmediated fashion. Rather, by drawing attention to the particular constellation of motivations and relations between witnesses, defendants, and juridical authorities, he unmasks the hidden bias of juridical discourse.

Weiss had noted the difficult position of the witnesses in the trial early on and had drawn an analogy between their situation and that of the returning exile, who is subject to the same discursive strategies of scrutiny and denial: *"Paradiso:* The witnesses are continually confronted with the (almost indifferent, mechanical) rejections and denials of the defendants—Students may discuss "emigration" with him— completely ignorant (and fundamentally uninterested)" (*Nb,* 275). In *Die Ermittlung,* it becomes evident that the juridical categories for verifiable enunciations do not match the witnesses' forms of memory. In the name of these categories, the defense claims that the emotions that surface as the witnesses have to face their persecutors once again renders their testimony unreliable:

Zeuge 7   Herr Vorsitzender
es ist lange her
daß ich ihnen gegenüber stand und es
  fällt mir schwer
ihnen in die Gesichter zu sehn
Dieser hat Ähnlichkeit mit ihm
er könnte es sein
Er heißt Bischof
Richter   Sind Sie sicher

	oder zweifeln Sie
Zeuge	Herr Vorsitzender
	ich war diese Nacht schlaflos
Verteidiger	Wir stellen die Glaubwürdigkeit des Zeugen infrage

. . . .

Die Übermüdung des Zeugen
kann keine Grundlage bilden
für beweiskräftige Aussagen (*W*, 5:22)

7th Witness:	Your Honor
	it has been many years
	since I last stood in front of them
	and I find it hard
	to look them in the face
	That one looks like him
	That could be him
	His name is Bischof
Judge:	Are you sure
	or do you have any doubts
7th Witness:	Your Honor
	I could not sleep at all last night
Counsel for the Defense:	We question the credibility of the witness

. . . .

Certainly the exhaustion of the witness
does not inspire confidence
in the validity of his testimony(*I*, 130)

This devaluation of the victims' voices continues in the utterances of the defendants. Whereas the witnesses relate their experiences in a highly impersonal, descriptive language devoid of affect,[50] the defendants oscillate between abstract, passive, euphemistic forms when referring to what they did in Auschwitz and emotionalized, personalized forms of speech when defending themselves. They exhibit friendliness when facing a witness they know, anger when they feel wrongly accused, and most important, they repeatedly break out into a collective, ritualistic laughter. "*Die Angeklagten lachen*" [the defendants laugh] reads the soon monotonous line that is almost the only stage direction Weiss uses in this play, all the more astonishing if one considers the wide range of theatrical forms he employed in his previous play, *Marat/Sade*.[51] Given the scarcity of expressive moments in the rest of the play, the collective laughter of the defendants is extremely effective. It recalls the musical form of an oratorio (which is in the subtitle of *Die Ermittlung*), functioning as the chorus, while the individual, whiny vindications correspond to the arias.[52] Considering that the original function of the chorus in drama was to represent the public and common reaction to the dramatic events, *Die Ermittlung* implies a sharp criticism of the Auschwitz trial as a form of public discourse: the alleged objectivity of the trial proves to be contingent upon a public consensus that allows the subjectivity of the defendants to resonate within a collective, while it excludes the subjectivity of the witnesses.[53] In other words, Weiss has transformed the theme of the *Divine Comedy* project—the exile's loneliness within the German public sphere—into a critique of the discourse established in the Auschwitz trial.

This critique is all the more important since the publicity of trial procedures in court was, according to Jürgen Habermas, an important element of the emerging bourgeois public sphere, a means of controlling the application of the laws through public opinion. Although Habermas believes that this critical function has faded in the twentieth century, when trial reports are broadcasted by the mass media primarily to entertain and manipulate a consuming public, Martin Walser referred to this function in his analysis of the Auschwitz trial and demanded a more responsible media coverage of the trial. Walser observed that the West German media tended to depict particularly sadistic scenes of torture in a way that invited the audience to indulge in a fascination with horror. Through the same strategy, the audience was able to distance itself from the obviously sadistic perpetrators and to forget about its own agency in the history of National Socialism. Whereas Weiss's desensationalizing representation in *Die Ermittlung,* which prevents the audience from consuming the trials like a horror movie, complies with Walser's notion of responsible public discussion, the form of Weiss's contribution to the debate reveals the difference between the two writers. In appealing to his audience, Walser uses the inclusive "we," suggesting that he himself is part of the collective he is addressing, that he is speaking as an equal to equals. Weiss, in contrast, emphasizes the exclusion of the witnesses from public discourse, thus questioning the residual Enlightenment notion that public debate can generate a set of shared values and thus contribute to the regulation of politics.

What kind of speech is available for the witnesses in this situation? As a point of interest, Weiss originally planned to use the material from the Auschwitz trial for the *Paradiso* part of his *Divine Comedy* project, and his notes suggest that topographical precision and a factual, detailed language were to mark the witnesses' discourse. "The Investigation (Paradiso)—ask with extreme exactness about every single detail, again and again—Did they come from the right? Where was the door? What did it look like?" (*Nb*, 282); "above all in Paradiso: very simple, short sentences; extreme austerity; crucial, concrete details" (*Nb*, 255). Another note reinforces the idea that heaven and hell were to represent two different discursive spaces, allowing for two different modes of speech: lies, evasions, and rationalizations in hell, contrasted with clear exactness in heaven (*Nb*, 216). Given that Weiss intended to rewrite Dante's *Divine Comedy* from a radically secular perspective, rejecting the possibility of otherworldly compensation for earthly suffering, it seems consistent that the victims' testimonies figure as the sole substitute for paradisiacal redemption. The sober, largely descriptive language of the witnesses in *Die Ermittlung* still betrays Weiss's original intention of setting a straightforward recounting of facts against the distortions of the defendants.[54] The problem, however, is that such a purely descriptive language tends to reproduce the system of persecution. Weiss intensifies this linguistic predicament by depersonalizing the witnesses in *Die Ermittlung* to a degree that they are nothing but megaphones (*Sprachrohre*, [*W*, 5:9]) for a language that in and by itself testifies to the crimes of Nazism. This is testimony in a modest, nonemphatic sense, far from the means of resistance and healing that Felman and Laub envision it to be. Yet it is, perhaps, the only adequate form of testimony in a situation in which the witnesses lack both an empathetic audience and a language able to express their memories.

This aporetic position of the witness shapes *Die Ermittlung* as a whole. The play constructs a specific author persona, that is, the figure of a distant observer, a non-persona whose essential characteristic is to remain unaffected by the trial he witnesses. Just like the witnesses within the Auschwitz trial, Weiss functions as a medium of a discourse detached from himself as he travels to Germany to attend the Auschwitz trial, to compile the documents, and to present them to the

CHAPTER 2

German public. The shift from the *Divine Comedy* project to documentary theater transforms the vulnerable subjectivity of the returning exile into a hyper-objectivity that may be regarded as a protective mechanism on Weiss's part but that was also likely to produce an unsettling effect on its audience. As other critics have noted, *Die Ermittlung* was meant to have an impact on its (German) audience beyond its rational insight. Huyssen characterizes the effect of the play as numbing, devised "to affect the consciousness rather than emotions of sadism or horrified empathy."[55] Söllner argues that the cold-shock technique employed by the play potentially induced a kind of collective psychoanalysis in the German audience.[56] We may add that the chorus of the defendants functions as a distorting mirror of the theater audience. Laughing exactly at those moments when one of them makes an appeal either to emotions or to common sense, the chorus represents the human reaction that results from a collective identification with the accused. By ascribing emotionality and personhood exclusively to the defendants, Weiss makes the spectator uneasily aware of his or her own inclination to identify with the accused as long as they appear as human beings rather than sadistic perpetrators.

I have attempted to show that the critical force of the drama derives from a continuous, experimental reconfiguration of the diasporic perspective. This reading is also supported by Weiss's short essay "Meine Ortschaft" [My Place], which describes his visit to the Auschwitz death camp in 1964 as the collapse of an empathetic understanding of history. Walking over the camp and registering meticulously the material remnants of the Holocaust—the barracks, the crematoria, the prison cells, but also the piles of hair, clothes, and shoes—the narrator is incapable of relating to the events that happened here. Filled with an anesthetic indifference, he cannot empathize with the victims or identify with them or mourn them. Although designed as a memorial space, the camp utterly fails to function as a *lieu de mémoire* that would enable its visitor to create in his imagination a connection among history, memory, and the individual. According to Pierre Nora, *lieux de mémoire*, including museums, archives, and festivals, emerged at a moment when memory ceased to be an integral part of everyday life and became confined to places exclusively devoted to it.[57] The problem of the memorial site in *Meine Ortschaft* is not only that it lacks the symbolic excess necessary to conjoin individual and collective memory, but also that it depletes both forms of memory in a single stroke.

Knowing that he himself was meant to perish there, the narrator calls Auschwitz the only fixed point in the topography of his life, and in another scene he is reminded of the elusiveness of his own birthplace: "[Auschwitz] also bears a Polish name, like my birthplace, which was perhaps pointed out to me in passing once, through the window of a train heading elsewhere."[58] Just as Auschwitz lies outside of experience, memory, and narration, such a place of birth fails to be an imaginative point of departure from which to recollect the fragments of one's life.

The lengthy topographical descriptions in *Die Ermittlung* reproduce just such a sense of overproximity to a place of death that nonetheless remains withdrawn from the imagination. The structure of *Die Ermittlung* parallels that of the *Inferno* in that it moves gradually toward the center of horror: from the ramp, to the inmates' barracks, the examination and torture rooms, the "black wall" where people were shot, the hospital where medical experiments were conducted, the bunker cells, the gas chambers, and finally to the ovens. This structure forces the audience progressively deeper into the camp while it stares at a stage that, according to Weiss's own instructions, is stripped of any props or decoration, anything that would make it a place. This lack of a set, and therefore of a setting, thus reproduces the incommensurability of place, narration, and subjectivity that I have shown to be a central moment in Weiss's rewriting of exile. With any optimistic vision of cosmopolitanism finally gone, *Die Ermittlung* suggests that catastrophic exile cannot be converted into freedom but that the fissure between the subject and its place of origin, which returns as the fissure between the subject and its language, can be performed upon an audience with a radically different historical perspective.

3
Nelly Sachs and the Myth of the "German-Jewish Symbiosis"

Of the authors discussed in this study, Nelly Sachs is the one who most explicitly and unequivocally drew on Jewish religious concepts as an interpretative frame of her own dislocation. Coming from an assimilated German Jewish background, Sachs was suddenly forced to confront a Jewish label as a result of Nazi persecution. After her last-minute escape from Germany to Sweden in May 1940, she turned this imposed Jewish identity into a deliberate one, first by empathetically identifying with the victims of the Holocaust, then also by reconnecting to Jewish cultural and religious traditions, particularly to its mystical strains as mediated by Martin Buber and Gershom Scholem. Sachs, who stayed for the rest of her life in Sweden, is best known for her early Holocaust poetry, written in the first postwar years and collected in a volume titled *In den Wohnungen des Todes* [*In the Habitations of Death*]. In 1966, she received the Nobel Prize for Literature together with the Hebrew writer Shmuel Yosef Agnon, an award that treated both of them, due to the inevitable political subtext of the Nobel Prize awards, as representatives of the Jewish people. The fact that the Israeli author in this constellation is male and the diaspora author female is itself noteworthy. There is some irony in the fact that despite, or rather because of, her Jewish identification, Sachs was appropriated by sectors of the West

CHAPTER 3

German public as a symbol of reconciliation between Germans and Jews after the Holocaust. This reception reached its first climax in May 1960 when she returned to Germany for the first time after the war to receive the *Annette von Droste-Hülshoff-Preis für Dichterinnen* in Meersburg. The fact that Sachs suffered from persecution fears leading to a nervous breakdown and repeated hospitalization after this visit, however, indicates that she was ultimately unable to inhabit the position assigned to her by the German public. In fact, she experienced the events related to her reception in Germany as a return of history. An outbreak of persecution fears, recorded in 1962 shortly after a delegation from the city of Dortmund visited Sachs in Stockholm to discuss plans to establish a Nelly Sachs prize hints at this connection:

> In the past week, the climax approached; the moment when the German men from Dortmund arrived. Everywhere I encountered the red Hieronymus Bosch color: blood, blood, every car, every motorcycle, garden tools. . . everything red.
> . . . I ask you one thing: It can't be that these were all bloodthirsty avengers for Eichmann who made the day red (and before and after)—why this lynch-mob atmosphere against me? Must I leave this country? But where can I go? Can I still be saved?[1]

In this chapter I analyze the way in which Sachs's personal crisis reveals her discomfort with the public persona created by and for a German audience, and I take this discomfort as the point of departure for an analysis of the relation between diaspora and cultural mediation. More precisely, I confront Sachs's reception as a conciliatory figure in Germany with her own complicated attempt to locate an interstitial space for Jews in postwar German culture. I first offer a critique of the mechanisms at work in Sachs's initial reception in West Germany, such as the use of gender stereotypes and Christian religious language, and the invocation of continuity between the historic "German-Jewish symbiosis" and post-Holocaust German-Jewish relations. Sachs's own definition of exile as a privileged place of mediation is in some ways compatible with such readings. In her early Holocaust poems words like *heimatlos* come to describe the state of the world after the Holocaust, projecting the suffering of the survivors onto landscapes of mourning. In her poetry of the 1950s, Sachs transforms exile into a metaphor for a special metaphysical disposition, an interpretation that is consistent with her overall aspiration to recuperate hope in the midst of destruction. One of her most frequently discussed poems, "In der Flucht" ["Fleeing"], uses images from the Bible and Jewish legends to depict the drivenness and restlessness of a refugee, and yet dissociates these images from their original context to describe a human predicament beyond cultural and ethnic particularities. The final line suggests that the shelter of home might be replaced by a special sensibility for transformative processes: "An Stelle von Heimat / halte ich die Verwandlungen der Welt—"[2] [I hold instead of a homeland / the metamorphoses of the world— (*OTC*, 145)].

By tracing the genealogy of Sachs's crisis of the 1960s, I seek to complicate the view of her as a poet of exile in search of transcendence. I show that Sachs's conception of the Jewish diaspora is attuned to philosophical and theological ideas that interpret cultural mediation as conflicting juxtaposition rather than harmonious fusion. Akin to the philosophy of Franz Rosenzweig, but also to more recent theoretical reflections by Dan Diner, this conception includes a temporal dimension, that is, the idea that diaspora Jews remain separated from their surroundings by different memories. To be sure, Sachs's work demonstrates the difficulty of transposing Rosenzweig's model into the post-Holocaust era. Her idea that diaspora Jews are endowed with the task of giving testimony to their non-Jewish neighbors tends to sacralize violence rather than mobilize the concept of revelation for new visions of communal life. Yet the textual crises that undermine the idea of mediation—most fully in her poem on the Eichmann trial, "Überall Jerusalem" ["Everywhere Jerusalem"]—indicate her resistance to a concept of reconciliation that obscures both history and cultural difference.

THE CONSTRUCTION OF JEWISH WOMEN AS CONCILIATORY FIGURES IN POSTWAR WEST GERMANY

Nelly Sachs's work started to attract attention in West Germany beginning with the 1957 publication of *Und niemand weiß weiter* by a West German publishing house. As in the case of Peter Weiss, a few critical intellectuals, often associated with the Gruppe 47, were engaged in introducing her to the German public: Alfred Andersch supervised the first German broadcasting of her Holocaust drama *Eli* as a radio play in 1958, and Hans Magnus Enzensberger published Sachs's collected poems for the Suhrkamp publishing house in 1961. Enzensberger's earlier, very influential article on Sachs introduced the redeemer topos that soon came to occupy a central place in her reception, a representation that was sustained by the critics' focus on her early Holocaust poetry and on her efforts at healing and recuperation. Quoting Adorno's by-now famous verdict about the impossibility of poetry after Auschwitz, Enzensberger states: "If we want to continue living, then this claim must be refuted. Few are capable of this. One of them is Nelly Sachs. Her language holds salvation. When she speaks, she gives us back, sentence after sentence, what we were in danger of losing: language."[3] Sachs's public impact, however, immediately extended beyond her literary readership. She was courted, for example, by the *Gesellschaften für Christlich-Jüdische Zusammenarbeit* and the organizers of the *Woche der Brüderlichkeit,* both of which were established to foster a Christian-Jewish dialogue in postwar West Germany.[4] These institutions became crucial in promoting the public image of Sachs as a missionary of reconciliation. When *Eli* premièred in 1961 in Dortmund during the course of the annual *Woche der Brüderlichkeit,* the reviews almost uniformly celebrated the supposedly conciliatory message of the play.[5] The attendance of the president of the Federal Republic of Germany, Heinrich Lübke, certainly enhanced the publicity of the play.

One explanation for the cult around Sachs is the fact that her work, in spite of its promotion by liberal intellectuals, fit into the peculiar fusion of Christian religious language and political idiom that characterized the conservative Adenauer era. In the first postwar years, the churches as well as the Christian Democratic government attributed the rise of Nazism mostly to the erosion of the Western Christian value system and, accordingly, cast Christian belief and morality as the principal antidotes to Nazism. The turn toward religion as a remedy for social and political malaise not only transformed the Holocaust from a political-historical into a religious-universal event, but it also delegated the task of remembering the Holocaust to the Jews as a *religious* community. According to Y. Michal Bodemann, the Jewish communities in Germany and institutions such as the *Gesellschaften für christlich-jüdische Zusammenarbeit* and the annual *Woche der Brüderlichkeit* functioned as sites of a religiously inspired, ritualistic remembrance that hampered a political analysis of National Socialism.[6] It would be inaccurate, however, to blame Christian theological discourse as a whole for the ideological uses that some made of it. In fact, it has been argued that in the early 1960s a genuine critical inquiry into the origins of

Christian anti-Judaism and Christian complicity with Nazism arose for the first time. Theologians and laymen began to question the apologetic myth of Christian victimhood under Nazism propagated by both Catholic and Protestant churches during the first postwar years.[7] The case of Nelly Sachs, however, shows that the infusion of religious tropes into political discourse for apologetic ends persisted throughout the 1960s. The most blatant example of this is Heinrich Lübke's speech on the occasion of Sachs's reception of the *Friedenspreis des Deutschen Buchhandels* in 1965. Even Lübke's appearance at this event, which generally celebrated the reconciliation between Germans and Jews allegedly exemplified by Sachs's poetry, is somewhat paradoxical. As a former deputy building supervisor of concentration camp barracks, Lübke embodied the continuity between the Third Reich and postwar West Germany that threatened such a reconciliation. Lübke's speech is a model of exculpation:

> In her art Ms. Nelly Sachs has created images and visions of an unsettling power of expression which represent and interpret the martyrdom of the Jewish people and the suffering of all innocent victims of persecution. . . . Her work also proclaims the redeeming power of understanding, reconciliation and charity. . . . This message is honored in the city of Goethe, where more than a century ago the National Assembly struggled for the democratic foundations of a unified Germany, and most recently a trial attested to the memory of gruesome crimes committed in the name of Germany. This message finds renewed recognition at a moment when, two decades after the end of a terrible war, the commitment to reconciliation between the German and Israeli people has been affirmed by the exchange of ambassadors.[8]

In this speech, Frankfurt comes to symbolize German high culture and a democratic political tradition. Although Lübke mentions the Holocaust in association with the Auschwitz trial that had just taken place in Frankfurt, he diminishes its significance by speaking of "crimes committed in the name of Germany," a euphemism implying that Germans were not the actual perpetrators of the Holocaust and that the name of Germany was simply abused for an ideology. Furthermore, Lübke takes the (Christian) topoi of reconciliation and love for one's neighbor from

CHAPTER 3

Sachs's poetry and translates them into the current political relations between Germany and Israel. Particularly disturbing is his rhetoric of war and peace, as if the slaughter of six million unarmed civilians who had never declared war against the German nation, some of whom belonged to the German nation, could at all be compared to a war. The speech not only amalgamates Jewish and Israeli identity but it also attaches a redemptive aura to the political relations between Germany and Israel, suggesting that the exchange of ambassadors could rescind the horrors of the Holocaust. The president of the *Börsenverein des Deutschen Buchhandels,* Friedrich Wittig, presented a somewhat subtler, but by no means less effective, rhetorical appropriation of Sachs's religious discourse:

> For is it self-evident, is it in accord with human nature, to respond to menace and humiliation, to suffering and cruelty, with forgiving love? Don't we learn daily that it goes the other way, that he who sows wind reaps storm, that hate is repaid with sevenfold hate? For my generation in any case, which knowingly or unknowingly, actively or negligently, tangled itself in the 12-year web of guilt, it is not self-evident that where hate was planted, we should meet reconciliation. . . . Quite certainly, the answer that Nelly Sachs found is a miracle. What was heavy in the world becomes light as air, horror becomes a verse, what was wild is subdued and, contrary to every experience, reconciliation and peace come to us.[9]

The rhetorical power of this passage derives from a slippage between religious tropes and their secular, political equivalents. In the religious atmosphere of the Adenauer era, the theme of "reconciliation" carried distinctively Christian connotations, and its evocation easily reproduced the stereotypical dichotomy between the Christian God of Mercy and the Jewish God of Revenge. The speaker evokes these connotations through his use of quotations from the Old Testament—"They sow wind, / And they shall reap whirlwind" (Hosea 8:7)—which associate revenge with the Jews even while he alleges to speak of vengefulness as a general human disposition. The religious stereotype resonates with a socio-psychological disposition on the part of many Germans, recognized by Dan Diner, to translate repressed guilt feelings into a fear of punishment that was projected onto the victims, leading to the charge that the Jews were unwilling, or unable, to forgive the Germans for the Holocaust and were seeking revenge.[10] Wittig's celebration of Sachs as an exceptional voice, even as a miracle, underscores this charge through its implication that the vast majority of Jews are incapable of her Christian gesture of reconciliation.

Gender played an important role in this reception of Sachs, which occurred at the time when the film on Anne Frank's diaries was widely seen in Germany, and when the German Jewish writer Else Lasker-Schüler was being reintegrated into the German literary canon. All three women came in remarkably similar ways to emblematize the victims of Nazi persecution. Highlighting the innocence and the purity of the victim, as well as its closeness to Christian ideals, representations of them drew on older stereotypes of the "good Jewess."[11] Frances Goodrich and Albert Hackett's play *The Diary of Anne Frank*, first staged in Germany in 1956 and the first representation of Jewish victimhood under Nazism to meet with great popular success in West Germany, illuminates the receptive mechanisms that were also at work in Sachs's reception.[12] The play universalizes the victim of the Holocaust by individualizing her. As for its formal aspects, it builds on the symbol of the house; the hidden rooms of the rear building in which the Frank family lives activate the comforting connotation of home with only a slight claustrophobic twist. Though the diary itself, the play, and the film (directed by George Stevens, 1959) do not lack compelling moments in which the sense of danger undercuts any protective feeling the house may convey, the symbolism still functions by providing the familiar backdrop for a young girl's inner journey toward adolescence. *The Diary of Anne Frank* tends to diminish the horror of genocide by allowing the reader to enter into a narrative of privacy, of domestic conflicts and budding love, a narrative that ends before the brutal reality of the death camp sets in. Bruno Bettelheim criticized the Frank family's decision to go into hiding rather than emigrating or taking up arms as an individual, and thus inadequate, political response to mass persecution and destruction.[13] Such a critique, while an inadequate description of the possible means of escape or defense, nonetheless indicates something crucial about the attitude of a post-Holocaust German audience. Although aware of the full horror of the Holocaust, they nonetheless preferred to view it through the naive consciousness of a girl whose belief in humanity remained uncontested by the experience of persecution. The concluding line of the drama emphasizes Anne's youthful idealism: "I still believe, in spite of everything, that people are really good at heart."[14] Furthermore, the film version at times takes on a Christian tone, notably through the sound of a church clock featured at crucial moments of the narrative. The strokes of the church clock counterbalance other sounds from the outside, such as the marching steps and the police sirens associated with the German occupation. In conjunction with a camera focus on the sky visible through the window of the attic chamber, the bell becomes a metaphor of the longing for freedom.

The universalization and Christianization of Anne Frank were two factors that made *The Diary of Anne Frank* appealing to non-Jewish audiences. Its portrayal of Gentile courage and support of Jews might have been a third factor, especially in view of a reality in which such support had too often been absent. Both the play and the film emphasize that Krahler and Miep, the non-Jewish employees of Otto Frank whose help made the family's hiding possible, might suffer the same fate as the family if they were detected. The reviews and portraits of Nelly Sachs inscribed her into a similar narrative, fostering her positive reception by feeding into a preexisting pattern. Almost every review retold the story of how the famous Swedish novelist Selma Lagerlöf and a Swedish prince intervened to obtain an entry visa for Sachs, although it is quite unclear what Lagerlöf's role in this matter really was.[15] This image of sotereologic non-Jews who are invested with a great deal of symbolic meaning delivered a hopeful message regarding Jewish-Gentile relationships.

Jewish women generally came to be associated with the historical German-Jewish cultural "symbiosis." This tendency is most obvious in the case of Else Lasker-Schüler, who was being reintegrated into the German literary canon around the time when Nelly Sachs's reception reached its first climax. The reviews of the 1960s stereotypically repeated set pieces of Gottfried Benn's 1952 speech on Lasker-Schüler, which first introduced the topos of symbiosis: "A poem such as the poem "My People" from *Hebrew Ballads* presents in its perfection such a total fusion of the Jewish and the German, and offers an expression of a genuine community of being, that it could have had political consequences on both sides as well, if art made any difference to us at all."[16] In his famous polemics of the 1960s, Gershom Scholem has attacked just such an idealized notion of German culture as conducive to cultural symbiosis. He argued that the "German-Jewish symbiosis" had always been chimerical, nothing but a delusion of assimilated Jews who failed to realize that their own desire for dialogue and integration lacked a German counterpart.[17] We do not need to accept this as a historically complete analysis to appreciate its critical thrust within the context of the 1960s. Scholem's essay developed from a letter he wrote in response to Manfred Schlösser, who solicited contributions for a *Festschrift* for Margarete Susman, an eminent figure among German Jews both of the Weimar and of the post-1945 period. Scholem refused to contribute to this volume because he objected to its purpose of paying homage to "a German-Jewish dialogue, the core of which is indestructible."[18] By analyzing the historic German-Jewish relations, he thus launches a critique of the public commemoration of the "German-Jewish symbiosis" in West Germany during the 1960s, which, as he keenly observed, was part of an ongoing attempt to reduce National Socialism to a short deviation within the course of German history.

The collective desire for a historical continuity that would bracket the Holocaust explains why the symbolization of Jewish women as retrospective proofs of the "German-Jewish symbiosis" coincided with their factual absence from Germany. Anne Frank and Else Lasker-Schüler were dead, and Nelly Sachs's few, short visits to Germany were immersed in an aura of distance and foreignness.[19] Indeed, the Jews living in Germany during the 1950s and 1960s could hardly have fulfilled the role bestowed on Lasker-Schüler and Sachs through the cultural spectacles of the *Woche der Brüderlichkeit*. The Jewish minority of postwar Germany may have, as Bodemann argues, performed the "ideological labor" of restoring Germany's reputation abroad by demonstrating that Jews could live there, but it could not symbolize continuity, simply because most of its members were not of German descent. They were Jews of Eastern European origin who were stranded in Germany after liberation, or American or Israeli Jews who stayed in Germany for limited periods. Jewish writers of German extraction who lived in Germany, such as Hilde Domin and Wolfgang Hildesheimer (before 1957), furthermore, tended to downplay their Jewish identity in the public sphere. Sachs's orientation toward the past, her closeness to German Romanticism, and her self-identification as a Jew were more suited to conjure up an imaginary continuity between the pre-Holocaust "German-Jewish symbiosis" and post-Holocaust German-Jewish relations.

Sachs herself contributed to her public image without being able

CHAPTER 3

to fully live up to it. In her mind, her conciliatory function was predicated on the preservation of clearly demarcated boundaries, such as that between herself and her published work. When her mentor Walter Berendsohn sought to accompany his essays and reviews with some biographical information, for instance, she strongly objected to his plans and beseeched him to stop asking about her personal life and making such information public.[20] She further betrayed anxiety, even self-censorship, when it came to presenting her early Holocaust poetry and dramas to German audiences, works which she saw as expressions of her Jewish identity.[21] At the same time, Sachs's letters evince attempts to create alternative kinds of public, such as the personalized and private circle of those German critics, authors, and friends who were to receive a free copy of her book, "my German family."[22] A letter, I would suggest, is always a means of mapping space, connecting distant places and creating a route along which the mind wanders. Sachs enhances this intrinsic feature of the letter through her strategies of citation, quoting frequently in her letters from other letters she has received. The quotes often involve her own poetry, conveying to her mentor Walter Berendsohn, for example, the praise of the young West German poet Peter Hamm: "This morning happiness arrived: a letter from a despairing youth in Germany who ascribed his salvation to my works."[23] Believing that her words have rescued the young German poet, just as Lagerlöf's intervention had obtained the lifesaving visa for her, Sachs recuperates an agency that was to lost to her as a victim. In addition to her own correspondence with Germans, Sachs tried to establish contacts between Germans and Israelis—for instance, between the poets Peter Hamm and David Rokeah—and the cultural mediation she brought about was clearly meant to have a conciliatory effect.[24]

The Germany to which Sachs relates is largely an ahistorical construct that ignores geographical borders, including the postwar division of Germany into two different states. Harking back to a preferred slogan among German exiles between 1933 and 1945, she speaks of the "Other Germany" to designate those elements within German culture and society from whom she expects, or actually receives signs of, a positive attitude toward the victims of Nazism. After describing in a letter her disappointments with German publishers, she refers to a favorable review of her poetry in a journal of the *Gesellschaft für Christlich-Jüdische Zusammenarbeit* in Hamburg: "Today I received, like a response from the "Other Germany," a German journal, a page of which I enclose for you."[25] This epithet of Germany sounds particularly anachronistic because by the 1950s attributes like the "other," "better," or "new" Germany had already been claimed by the GDR—whose most important (party) newspaper was named *Neues Deutschland*—to mark its difference from the Federal Republic of Germany. But Sachs seems to be unaware of such overtones. The "Other Germany" means for her, as it did for many exiles during National Socialism, a community of like-minded, anti-fascist people, an alliance consisting mostly of public intellectuals and artists such as Peter Hamm who "belongs to the cultural circle around Alfred Andersch and other important figures of a new, better Germany."[26] Exile authors can be easily imagined as members of such a German cultural community. Sachs identifies Paul Celan as the leading poet among young German writers and rhetorically adjoins him to the "Other Germany" in phrases like "the glowing efforts of the Andersch and Celan circle."[27] It is not difficult to imagine how this idealization of the "Other Germany" collapsed once the spatial distance between Sachs and the real Germany diminished.

Memory, Myth, Mediation

While Sachs herself contributed to the public image of herself as a conciliatory figure, her conception of Jewish diaspora points the way to a more critical notion of cultural mediation, one that offers an alternative to a reconciliation that would obscure both history and cultural difference. In letters from the mid-1940s, Sachs repeatedly indicates that life in the diaspora may help to preserve memories that other nations forget. Though she primarily refers to Holocaust remembrance, the concrete content of these memories frequently seems unclear, and at the same time they carry a sacred aura. In a letter to her mentor Walter A. Berendsohn, she invokes the task of remembrance beyond issues of territorial settlement and cycles of agriculture, commenting on the efforts to establish a Jewish state in Palestine:

> That this country means far more than seed and harvest, war and peace, science and art, planted in this soil, that its people are not just a people like others. This is meekly felt as a burdensome task never anything else. . . . It is this readiness to access something stored above and beneath the local seeds and harvests, that I ask the youth not to forget. It is

CHAPTER 3

this that I believe we Jews must hold in memory for all people of the earth, for all those who forget.[28]

Sachs's emphasis on a special Jewish mandate resonates with a longstanding strain of Jewish thought and belief that, in effect, sought to justify life in the diaspora by attributing it to a divine intention. Jewish tradition beginning with the Bible has recognized a political as well as a metaphysical dimension of exile; both the land of Israel and the absence from it came to express symbolically states of being that were suffered or desired by Jews. Most pertinent among them was the concept of exile as a divine punishment for idolatry or other deviations from the path of the Torah, a sense of punishment that was mitigated by the hope for a future restoration to the land of Israel. As early as during the period of the second temple, the doctrine of divine punishment was complemented by a more positive interpretation of exile, according to which the dispersion of the Jews served a deeper purpose: "to spread the knowledge of the true Teaching throughout the world."[29] The concrete content of the purpose has been interpreted differently in the course of Jewish history, but as a general conception, the idea of divine intentionality continued to lend meaning to diasporic existence. This conception has to be distinguished from the idea of voluntary exile as the consequence of individual decision and in the pursuit of a better life. It has further been argued that the symbolic and spiritual interpretations of the land and of exile tended to proliferate at times when the social and political situation of the Jews in exile worsened. After the 1492 expulsion of the Jews from Spain, for example, the Lurianic Kabbalah located exile at the very core of creation, thus transforming the experience of forced migration into a symbol of the inner deficiency of everything that exists.[30] During the nineteenth century, the Enlightenment ideal of rational religion produced a new variant of the conception of exile as ordained by a higher authority, the idea "that the dispersion of the Jews had a mission to set the Gentiles an example of pure rational, prophetic, monotheistic faith."[31] This idea of a Jewish mission resonates in the letter by Sachs in which she ascribes to the Jews the task of preserving memory for the Gentiles. Sachs reformulates this task as that of addressing Jews and Gentiles alike with testimony of the Shoah, a task that is aided by her position in the diaspora. She thus translates the divine intentionality of exile into an ethical mandate that she hopes to realize in her own poetry. Her early collection of Holocaust poems, *In den Wohnungen des Todes,* whose individual poems bear titles such as "Chor der Toten" ["Chorus of the Dead"], betrays just such an effort to diminish her individual voice in favor of a metaindividual voice calling upon humanity to mourn.[32]

Sachs's valorization of the diaspora as a site of remembrance is also tangible in a series of poems on the land of Israel that appeared in her *Sternverdunklung,* published in 1949. Though commonly read as expressions of her Zionism, these poems tend to interrupt visions of Jewish homecoming through strategies including the metaphorization of place, the narrative suspension of arrival, and the use of symbols from other cultures. The poem "Land Israel" ["Land of Israel"] first depicts original Israel's biblical sanctification and then the survivors of the Holocaust, who return to the land and reconnect to its sacred traditions. This part is shaped by agricultural images and imbued with a sense of completion encapsulated in a word prominent in the Sabbath prayer, *Vollbracht* [finished].[33] In the last stanza, however, the evocation of Ruth, the biblical figure whose Jewishness was a matter of becoming rather than of being—the first convert to Judaism—suspends the scene of homecoming.[34]

> Land Israel,
> nun wo dein Volk
> aus den Weltenecken verweint heimkommt
> um die Psalmen Davids neu zu schreiben in deinen Sand
> und das Feierabendwort *Vollbracht*
> am Abend seiner Ernte singt—
>
> steht vielleicht schon eine neue Ruth
> in Armut ihre Lese haltend
> am Scheidewege ihrer Wanderschaft.
>   (*S*, 127, emphasis by Sachs)

> Land of Israel,
> now when your people
> come home from the corners of the world with tear-stained eyes
> to write the psalms of David anew in your sand
> and that afterwork word *Finished*
> sings on the evening of its harvest—

> there stands perhaps already a new Ruth
> in poverty holding her gleanings
> at the crossroad of her wandering.
> (*TS*, 115–17, emphasis by Sachs, trans. altered)

The poem's shift from the center to the periphery, from completion to deferment, and from consolation to hope is one of the poetic gestures with which Sachs revalidates the diaspora despite her sympathies for what was soon to become the state of Israel. Picturing the new Ruth at a moment when she has not yet joined the Jewish people and when the direction of her wandering is still unclear, the poem foregrounds Ruth's difference from the collective that is gathering in the land of Israel. The difference is accentuated through the opposition between harvest and poverty, and between writing and reading, the latter of which is evoked in the German word for gleaning, *Lese*. The fact that the poem represents Ruth as an emblematic diasporic figure, whose wandering has not yet ended, illustrates how Sachs relates space and cultural position. Yet even more than wandering, the poem accentuates a moment of arrested movement. This pause is most palpable in the emphatic beginning of the third stanza, "*steht* vielleicht schon eine neue Ruth," [*there stands* perhaps already a new Ruth] and in the line that begins with "am Scheidewege" [at the crossroad], locutions that interrupt the progress of time and suspend narrative closure.

The suspension of homecoming in Sachs's Israel poems is compounded by poetic strategies that establish the land as a metahistorical site of hope rather than a concrete dwelling place. The poem "Aber deine Brunnen" ["But Your Wells"] provides an example of how Sachs's celebration of return metaphorizes the land in a manner that detaches memory from concrete places and, following in the vein of earlier symbolizations of Zion, ultimately validates life in the diaspora:

> ABER DEINE BRUNNEN
> sind deine Tagebücher
> o Israel!
>
> Wieviel Münder hast du geöffnet
> im vertrockneten Sand,
> die Scheibe des Todes abgeschnitten
> vom lebenden Leben.
> . . . .

Deine Tagebücher
sind in die leuchtenden Augen
der Wüsten geschrieben
o Israel!

Schlagrutenhaft
dein Herz zuckt
wo die Schalen der Nacht
eine Brunnentiefe halten,
darunter die Landschaften Gottes
zu blühen beginnen,
die du, Erinnernder unter den Völkern,
hinaufhebst
mit dem Krug deines Herzens—
hinaufhebst
in die brunnenlosen Räume
der Vergessenheit!
   (S, 98–99)

BUT YOUR WELLS
are your diaries
O Israel!

How many mouths have you opened
in the parched sand,
the slice death cut off
from living life.
. . . .

Your diaries
are written into the shining eyes
of the deserts
O Israel!

As if struck by a rod
your heart quivers
where the bowls of night
hold the depths of a well
beneath which the landscapes of God

CHAPTER 3

> begin to bloom,
> which you, rememberer among the nations,
> lift up
> with the vessel of your heart—
> lift up
> into the spaces of forgetfulness
> where no wells are!
>   (*TS,* 91–93, trans. altered)

The comparison between the first two and the last two stanzas of this poem shows how the concreteness of the landscape gradually diminishes as it is being transformed into a metaphor of writing and memory. Whereas the initial stanza establishes the connection between wells and diaries through emphatic predication, this connection is simply assumed in the second to last stanza, which further substitutes "eyes" for "wells." And whereas the image of the mouth in the second stanza evokes the ideas of speaking and drinking equally strongly, the image of the jug in the last stanza is largely a metaphor for the faculty of memory. Two other elements of the land have become mere attributes—"schlagrutenhaft," "Brunnentiefe"—of the moment of poetic inspiration and the Romantic cipher of poetic creation, the night, respectively. What is ultimately left of the landscape is the idea of a memory whose deepest layers the Jewish people brings back to the surface through an act of remembrance that is imagined as purely internal and spiritual and therefore can take place anywhere.[35] The production of a metaphorical surplus out of rural images in this poem transforms the land of Israel into what Alain Finkielkraut has called an imaginary center, a strategy that generally enabled Jews to live in the European diaspora after 1945 in an otherwise traumatic temporal and spatial proximity to the Holocaust. By creating a set of images that refute common antisemitic stereotypes, Finkielkraut writes, the state of Israel has continually undone the ideological basis of antisemitism in the eyes of European Jews, who, thanks to increasing globalization and media saturation, have received and ritualistically consumed these images: "The farmer of the Negev erased the image of the lender, the flowering desert erased the image of the parasite, and the Israeli soldier served as proof that *Jew* and *coward,* or *Jew* and *victim,* are not synonymous terms."[36] Though Sachs's Israel portraits contest the post-Holocaust image of Israel as a modern state based on a powerful army and an agricultural economy, it functions as an imaginary center for her, one that guarantees the possibility of remembrance in poetry.

The nexus Sachs establishes between diaspora, memory, and interaction with non-Jews harks back to the philosophy of Franz Rosenzweig. Sachs knew some writings by Rosenzweig, and she learned more about him through Shmuel Hugo Bergmann, a philosophy professor at Hebrew University in Jerusalem who lectured in Stockholm during the winter of 1947–48.[37] Rosenzweig's major work, *The Star of Redemption*, presents primarily a critique of German idealism but also a new vision of how Jewish particularity could be realized within modern German culture; it proposes an alternative to assimilation, Zionism, and separatist religious Orthodoxy alike. In the course of the book, Rosenzweig makes a powerful argument in favor of Jewish diaspora existence. The basis for his revaluation of diaspora is the assumption that the Jews fulfill a specific role in the divine economy, that is, the role of anticipating messianic redemption on earth. Briefly summarized, the Jews realize this role through genealogical continuity— through an emphasis on familial rather than political relations—and through their liturgical tradition. Because their liturgical practice structures everyday life as a cycle of prayers and holidays, the Jews live a rhythm that runs counter to historical time, a time that is cyclical but not organic, a series of repetitions rather than a cycle of growth and decay. The Jews' being always already there, namely, close to God, makes them an "eternal people" and creates a kind of static present through which eternity breaks into historical time. The model of this rupture in history that anticipates redemption is the revelation at Sinai, reinterpreted by Rosenzweig as a structure rather than an event.

According to Rosenzweig, the geographic dispersal of the Jews guarantees that they are divested of all exterior means of identification, such as language, customs, or territory, all of which would make them subject to the historical process in the course of which nations appear and disappear again. As Paul Mendes-Flohr has shown, Rosenzweig's valorization of the Jews' intermediate position between history and redemption also reflects his experience of the First World War, in which he served as a soldier in the German army.[38] The war left Rosenzweig with the conviction that history is a violent, man-made struggle for power rather than the unfolding of a divine principle, or any other kind of consistent movement toward a telos. In Rosenzweig's philosophy of

CHAPTER 3

history, which implies a critique of Hegel on the one hand and of nineteenth-century historicism on the other hand, history ultimately amounts to acts of often arbitrary violence. His claim that the Jews live withdrawn from history establishes them as a metahistorical point of reference that restores a redemptive perspective to a history that has no intrinsic meaning. The location of the Jews in the diaspora further entails a specific relationship between them and the nations they live in, a kind of absence-presence in their cultures. While sharing space and culture with another nation, they nonetheless remain separate and therefore are able to function as a reminder of something beyond history and nations. Rosenzweig's ideas resonate here with contemporary, politicized models of diaspora, such as Homi Bhabha's theory that the other temporality of postcolonial migratory experience subverts national narratives. In fact, one could claim that Rosenzweig anticipates this politicization. Although he employs a religious rather than a sociopolitical vocabulary in *The Star of Redemption*, Rosenzweig identifies the Jews' special position vis-à-vis history as a countermodel to the logic of war that follows from the struggles for national self-determination.

Similar figures of thought operate in what has become by now a classic essay on post-Holocaust German-Jewish relations, Dan Diner's "Negative Symbiose: Deutsche und Juden nach Auschwitz." The essay was first published in 1986 in the journal *Babylon* and belongs to the new Jewish public voice that has emerged in Germany during the last two decades. Although Diner does not seem to be particularly concerned with questions of place or displacement, he legitimizes, in effect, a new kind of diaspora, namely that of Jews living in postwar Germany. While sharing Gershom Scholem's critique of the idealized historic "German-Jewish symbiosis," Diner claims that the Holocaust has created a real interdependency of German and Jewish cultures, but a negative one. This is so because German and Jewish identities after 1945 are largely constituted in relation to the Holocaust and the naturally opposed traumas it has inflicted on the collectives of the perpetrators and of the victims. As a result both collectives tend to form "screen memories," which is a psychoanalytic term for narratives that relate to a trauma yet cover up its traumatic core. Diner further suggests that Jews living in postwar Germany might prevent through their sheer presence the formation of German screen memories. Although he never speaks of diaspora, he emphasizes that most of today's German Jews are descendants of the so-called DPs, or "displaced persons," who came to Germany during the first postwar years, mostly from Eastern Europe. Diner not only shares with Rosenzweig the idea that the diaspora fulfills a positive, or at least necessary, role, but he also uses some of the same rhetoric. Because they continue to embody the trauma of the Holocaust, Jews in Germany function as a reminder, as the "guardians of memory,"[39] as Diner puts it. Of course, Rosenzweig and Diner not only write at very different historical moments but also differ with regard to their concepts of history. Whereas Rosenzweig's philosophy establishes redemption as the other of history, Diner's critical historiography is concerned with the Shoah as the limit of existing historiographical or other explanatory narratives. According to him, the Jews in Germany remind their contemporaries not of something beyond historical violence but of a specific historical violence that has remained unfathomed, unexplained, and—on the part of many Germans—unacknowledged. Nonetheless, in Diner's account, the acts of remembrance necessitated by the void left after the destruction of European Jewry seem to perform a function analogous to that of liturgy in Rosenzweig: they infuse another rhythm into the time of a nation inclined to move progressively away from the Holocaust.

The term "negative symbiosis" also means that the presence of Jews in Germany prevents the formation of what Diner perceives to be specific Jewish screen memories. Such screen memories of the victims tend to restore meaning to an utterly meaningless industrial genocide, or they provide explanations—for example, by reading the Holocaust as a kind of oversized pogrom—that prematurely close the inquiry into the nature of the Holocaust and the challenges it poses to Western concepts of civilization and rationality. And here I would criticize Diner's use of the term symbiosis, even though negated. Implying that the traumas are symmetrical and the relations reciprocal, the term conceals the fact that the victim's trauma is of a different psychological and moral order than the perpetrator's trauma, a confusion that points to the limits of the very discourse of trauma. As Dominick LaCapra reminds us, "victim" and "perpetrator" are not psychological but political, social, or ethical categories that describe a position within a structure of power rather than a psychical state. The discussion of perpetrator trauma must therefore include a greater consideration of an individual's agency, responsibility, and moral choices.[40] To the extent that it blurs this distinction, Diner's use of "symbiosis" undercuts his critical intention. The term symbiosis, a biological metaphor transposed into the domain of

CHAPTER 3

cultural and social relations, not only implies that cultures are organic entities at the cost of neglecting human consciousness but also tends to bracket questions of power and conflict. In his book on the medieval Jewish-Muslim "symbiosis," Steven Wasserstrom proposes to reconceptualize the term as the creative tension between culturally and religiously distinct groups.[41] However, in view of the ideological uses that were made of the term symbiosis in postwar West Germany in an attempt to elide tension, the recuperation of the term for German-Jewish relations after the Holocaust would mean taking away the edge from what Diner demands: the prolongation of necessarily painful memories.

I have dwelt on Rosenzweig and Diner because they allow us to perceive a connection between trauma and revelation that is more fully elaborated in the work of Nelly Sachs, whose self-understanding as a guardian of memory in the diaspora is attuned to the ideas of both these thinkers. The connection between trauma and revelation is, in principle, not far-fetched. Both have been understood acts of interpellation so powerful that they elude the addressee's cognitive and emotional registers and propel her into the future and contact with others. One of Sachs's early plays, *Abram im Salz* [Abram in the Salt], shows, however, the inevitable doubleness of this analogy, the fact that the invocation of the divine in conjunction with historical trauma can produce either uncanny effects or a sacralization of violence. The play, begun in 1946 and completed in 1956, retells the legend of Abraham's struggle with the violent and idolatrous Nimrod, which led to Abraham's departure from his Chaldean hometown Ur for the Promised Land. Sachs's preoccupation with the figure of Abraham is itself an indication of her privileging of diasporic, unsettled forms of existence. In contrast to other biblical paradigms of exile, Abraham's story is one of a departure without return and without genuine arrival at a new home, for, as the Bible tells us, he keeps roaming around at the margins of the Promised Land. Rosenzweig, for instance, cites Abraham's departure as the first and founding example of the Jews' tenuous relationship to territory.[42]

One of the main effects of *Abram im Salz* is the conflation between the origins of monotheism and the experience of flight and persecution, which derives from two alterations of the biblical and legendary material. First, when the voice (of God) calls upon Abraham in the desert, the destination it indicates to Abraham is the mountain Moriah rather than the Promised Land. Moreover, Moriah, the mountain where Abraham was supposed to sacrifice Isaac and which traditionally symbolizes Abraham's absolute trust and belief in God, comes in Sachs's play to signify suffering depicted in real physical terms: "Ich will den Augenblick dir zeigen / wo Er dich greifen wird / M o r i a h / heißt er / da wird der Weg mit Flammen dir vom Leib gerissen werden / . . . / Dies ist der höchste Leidensberg der Erde— / Du trägst schon sein Gewicht in dir."[43] [I want to show you the moment / when He will grasp you / M o r i a h / it is called / there the path will be torn from your body by flames / . . . / This is the highest mountain of suffering on earth— / You already carry its weight within you.] The replacement of the Promised Land by the mountain Moriah, however, does not retract the redemptive perspective, for after Abraham accepts his vocation, the hunters' shouts turn into the sounding of the shofar, which traditionally both recalls the binding of Isaac and heralds the messianic age. Second, the play intertwines Abraham's departure with a very different kind of flight, that of his parents, who are expelled from Ur because they are held responsible for their son. Wandering through the desert and searching for Abraham, the parents are utterly indifferent to Abraham's religious fervor but lament the loss of their everyday duties and pleasures.[44] In the very end, the parents and the voice (of God) call upon Abraham almost simultaneously, and it remains undecidable to whom Abraham's repeated response "Ich komme"[45] [I am coming] is addressed. In contrast to its biblical and exegetical sources, the play leaves open the question of whether Abraham ever separates himself from his parents, thus associating their fate with Abraham's and, ultimately, monotheistic revelation with the sheer human plight of refugees.

This narrative link between revelation, persecution, and flight can be regarded as a screen memory. It endows an expulsion that is quite unequivocally associated with the Holocaust with a religious meaning and integrates it into a mythic structure that generalizes Jewish suffering instead of, as Diner demands, interrogating a particular historical suffering that still awaits its full understanding. The Abraham narrative, however, is itself destabilized by the framing scenes of the play that rather than containing trauma produce a bottomless depth. These scenes depict an archeological site in Ur where one of the excavators falls asleep and experiences Abraham's struggle and departure as a kind of vision from which he awakes in the end. On the one hand, this is a scene of remembrance. Excavation is a traditional metaphor for the retrieval of memories, a connotation that is supported by the fact that "Ur" also designates a special kind of sand, often cemented into rock, that lies below the earth's surface. Sachs possibly alludes to this meaning in the play's prologue when speaking of the "Erinnerungsstein"[46] [memory stone] in Ur. On the other hand, the excavator seems to awake from a dream filled with a feeling that something entirely new has begun: "Es fiel etwas aus mir fort— / Es hat etwas begonnen in mir—."[47] [Something fell away from within me— / Something began in me—.] The indeterminate status of the excavator's experience makes it questionable when, or even if, Abraham's story has happened. This structure is analogous to revelation in Rosenzweig, which cannot be placed in historical time, because it is a possibility rather than a reality, or, in a more paradoxical formulation, a memory of the future. The fact that the play also presents a quintessential scene of remembering violence shows that Sachs merges, indeed, the two points of reference, the two others of history as usual, which despite some analogous argumentation in Rosenzweig and Diner are radically opposed: revelation and the Holocaust. This conflation accounts for Sachs's uncertainty regarding the nature of the memories that the Jews in the diaspora have to preserve, an uncertainty that we observed in her letters but that in fact pervades her whole work, in which even poems explicitly referring to the Holocaust endow the idea of remembrance with a sacred aura.

As for the critical thrust of Sachs's work, the structure of an event that has always-already and yet never really happened inevitably contains an uncanny doubleness. Sachs enhances this doubleness by dramatizing the semantics of Ur across two languages: the German prefix *Ur* is a privileged signifier for that which is withdrawn from history. Since the eighteenth century, it has occurred primarily in compounds referring to the primordial, original, or pure, like *Urbild, Ursprung,* and *Urgeschichte*. Because of its double connotation of origin and ideal, it has predominantly positive connotations.[48] The Hebrew place name Ur, on the other hand, has the same root as the word *or*—light—and means "flame" or "fire," probably alluding to the fiery furnace into which Abraham was thrown by Nimrod after he had smashed his idols.[49] One effect of Sachs's rereading of Abraham and his departure from Ur, then, is that she inscribes the violence associated with the Hebrew place name into the German prefix, thus creating a conflictual cipher, an overdetermined signifier. Sachs's poems intensify this overdetermination through further linguistic relations, such as the phonetic assonance and graphic difference between *Ur* and *Uhr* [clock]: "O Abraham, / die Uhren aller Zeiten, / die sonnen- und monddurchleuchteten / hast du auf Ewigkeit gestellt—" (*S*, 89) [O Abraham / you have set at eternity / the clocks of all the ages, / lit by sun and moon— (*TS*, 83)]. The graphic difference parallels the transformation of Abraham's name, which was originally Abram and to which the "h" was only added after he entered into the covenant with God (Gen. 17:5). Just as *Abram* represents the other of *Ur*, so does *Abraham* embody the other of *Uhr*, which in Sachs's work generally symbolizes measurable, historical time, often associated with the brutal rhythm of persecution.[50]

The potentially unsettling effect of overlaying the German connotations with the Hebrew, however, is counterbalanced by Sachs's projection of the German meaning of Ur onto the literary image of Abram's departure from Ur. Abraham's departure becomes the hypostasized moment of pure origin and part of a rhetoric that, at its most problematic moments, even deploys the antisemitic stereotype of the deracinated Jew who becomes morally corrupt. This is most apparent in Sachs's early play *Eli* (written in 1944–45), her most explicit dramatic treatment of the Holocaust. The play is set in a Polish Jewish village "After Martyrdom." Michael, one of the thirty-six righteous who according to Hasidic legends are God's hidden servants in the world, leaves the village to seek the soldier who has murdered the boy Eli. After passing through the ghostly landscape of the concentration camps, he crosses the border and tracks down the murderer, who dies from a strange vision after he catches sight of Michael. Michael professes at one point:

> Seit Abraham aus Ur auswanderte,
> haben wir uns bemüht,
> unsere Wohnung zu Ihm hinzubauen,
> wie andere nach der Sonnenseite bauen—
> Freilich, manche schlossen sich der entgegengesetzten Richtung
>   an—
> Alte Hirten ließen die Sternenuhren schlagen
> und schliefen wie Isidor der Pfandleiher mit gekrümmten Fin-
>   gern—
> (*E*, 80)

CHAPTER 3

> Since Abraham wandered forth from Ur
> we have worked hard
> to build our house toward Him
> as others build facing the sun—
> True, many turned themselves in the opposite direction—
> Old shepherds let the star clocks strike
> and slept like Isidor the pawnbroker with crooked fingers—
> (*OTC*, 376, trans. altered)

The insistence on this clear-cut dichotomy between the primordial Jew and his historical deviations is analogous to the German Jewish idealization of the "authentic" East European Jew at the beginning of the twentieth century. This idealization reversed the earlier negative stereotyping of Eastern Jews while fulfilling a similar function. It split "the identity of the Jew into polar opposites,"[51] the authentic Eastern Jew and the cosmopolitan Western Jew. This mechanism enabled German Jews to redirect stereotypes, projecting them onto Jews who fit neither type and who were labeled as superficially assimilated, inauthentic Jews. Similarly, Sachs's play creates a Jewish ideal, Abraham, and its opposite: Isidor is the only contemporary Jewish figure depicted with negative undertones, with his "crooked fingers" metaphorically referring to greediness. Being a pawnbroker and carrying a name that became almost an antisemitic invective during the latter half of the nineteenth century, Isidor recalls the worst antisemitic stereotypes.[52]

The evocation of Jewish origins serves in *Eli* to ameliorate the emotional effect of antisemitism. The judge, for example, uses imagery to link several victims of anti-Jewish hatred to their biblical origins while his emphatic language bestows on these origins the meaning of the German *Ur*, thus creating archetypes that restore dignity to the victims:

> Ich sehe,
> sehe den Anfang deiner schlenkrigen Schultern, Schimon—
> als du grubst mit Abraham den Brunnen der Sieben Schwüre
> in Ber Scheba—
> Ich sehe,
> ich sehe den Anfang deines Lächelns, Aman—
> am Horeb eingepflanzt den siebzig Alten,
> daß es keimt.
> (*E*, 40)

> I see,
> see the beginning of your jerking shoulders, Simon—
> when with Abraham you dug the well of the "Seven Oaths"
> in Beersheba—
> I see,
> I see the beginning of your smile, Aman—
> on Horeb planted in the seventy elders,
> to sprout again
>   (*OTC*, 342)

This rhetoric of origin that seeks to counteract the effects of anti-semitism by establishing a set of positive archetypes has a visual counterpart in the stage settings of the play. In the midst of an almost completely ruined Polish Jewish village, we see a number of craftsmen and workers engaged in rebuilding the town. Withdrawn from the world of destruction, however, stands the tabernacle ("das Gebetszelt," [*E*, 14, 37]). Set in the back of the stage, at the end of a narrow lane, it appears like a vanishing point at the horizon. The tabernacle, the portable sanctuary from the Exodus, replaces here the post-biblical synagogue ("das Bethaus" [*E*, 14]) that was destroyed during the war. One may perceive here a deeper affinity between Sachs's textual strategies and her problematic reception in West Germany. By establishing the Bible as a metahistorical frame of reference, Sachs reformulates unfathomable difference as distinct cultural tradition. This strategy is not incompatible with a reception that, by celebrating her work as a successful expression of Jewish themes in the German language, first disentangles German and Jewish cultures in order to then imagine their reconciliation.

Sachs's Melusine cycle from her poetry collection *Und niemand weiß weiter* furnishes further examples of how the conflict between German and Jewish origins materializes in signifiers from the different cultural traditions. If the cipher "Ur" contains rather than exposes the tension inherent in Sachs's negotiation between a German Christian-Romantic heritage and her post-Holocaust rediscovery of Jewish traditions, in the Melusine cycle such a tension repeatedly surfaces in a displaced word, a blurred metaphor, or a fragmented sentence. Coming from a Medieval French legend, the figure of Melusine has inspired many literary variants in poetry and prose, particularly during Romanticism.[53] Melusine, a native of the water world, sets out to find the love of a

CHAPTER 3

human and to receive a soul only to be pulled back into the water after her human husband Raimund discovers her true identity. Sachs's adaptations of the legend eliminate most of its epic content and single out the moment after Melusine's separation from Raimund, a moment that evokes the double exile of German Jews after the Holocaust. Associated with Melusine is a contrast between land and water that reflects the division of the world into a sphere of human action and a sphere of numinous otherness inhabited by females who are, like Melusine, banished from the human world. This sphere of otherness also represents a special sensibility shared by the poem's speaker and a collective invoked through the use of the first-person plural possessive pronoun: "Melusine, / dein landloser Teil / ist in unserer Träne geborgen—" (*N*, 193) [Melusine, / your landless part / is preserved in our tear (*OTC*, 121)]. One of the poems of this cycle conflates a number of female figures of exile from different cultural traditions, a process out of which the poem's speaker, herself an exile, emerges.

IMMER HINTER den Rändern der Welt
die ausgesetzte Seele Genoveva wartet
mit dem Kinde Schmerzensreich
im Heimwehgestrahl.

Auch *Schechina* kannst du sagen,
die Staubgekrönte,
die durch Israel Schluchzende

Und die heilige Tierfrau
mit den sehenden Wunden im Kopf,
die heilen nicht
aus Gotteserinnerung.

In ihren Regenbogenpupillen
alle Jäger haben
die gelben Scheiterhaufen der Angst entzündet.

Auch mein Fuß
hier auf der Straße
stößt an den Aschenhorizont—

ein Granatsplitter,
nachtbehaustes Fragezeichen,
liegt in der Fahrtrichtung.

Aus der Kriegerpyramide,
blitzverkleidet,
erschießt wehrlose Sehnsucht
die Liebe
im letzten Schwanenschrei—
  (N, 194, emphasis by Sachs)

ALWAYS BEYOND the edges of the world
the abandoned soul of Genoneva waits
with the child Woeful
in the radiance of homesickness.

You can also say *skekhinah,*
the dust-crowned,
the one sobbing through Israel.

And the holy animal-woman
with seeing wounds in her head,
they do not heal
because of the memory of God.

In her rainbow pupils
all hunters have
enflamed the yellow stakes of fear.

My foot, too,
here on the street
hits against the ashen horizon—
a shell splinter,
night-housed question mark,
lies on the way.

Out of the warriors' pyramid,
disguised as lightning,
defenseless yearning shoots down

CHAPTER 3

the love
in the last swan's cry—

This poem both invokes and questions the idea of exile as a privileged site of cultural mediation, a tension that emerges out of the conflicting strategies of poetic fusion on the one hand and linguistic disintegration on the other hand. Fusion is the dominant logic of the first four stanzas, which stage a process of cultural translation as they transpose figures of exile from Christian and Romantic German traditions into Jewish mysticism. Genoveva, the saintly figure from a medieval legend and German folktales who is expelled from her castle after an unjustified charge of adultery, is identified with the *skekhinah*.[54] Originally a Judaic theological concept referring to the Divine Presence on earth, the *skekhinah* was later feminized and became a symbol of exile in Jewish mysticism. The poem conflates these figures by foregrounding the points of convergence between the narratives associated with them, such as their endless crying and their separation from a beloved man, who in the case of the *skekhinah* is God. While the italics in the line "Auch *Schechina* kannst du sagen" [You can also say *skekhinah*] highlight the foreignness of the Judaic concept within the German language, this differential moment is immediately reabsorbed by the reassuring phrase that translation between different cultural traditions is possible, that one can simply substitute the *skekhinah* for the Christian-Romantic Genoveva. The logic of fusion culminates in the third stanza, which effaces any tangible work of translation while conflating Melusine, the fishwoman who was violently banished from the world, with the exiled people of Israel, which Sachs frequently depicts as a deer with gleaming or rainbow eyes.[55] By seizing upon the various iconographies of exile in a way that reduces them to a set of common elements, poetic imagination creates here a site of cultural synthesis, a site where German and Jewish traditions become compatible. We may discern here an instance of unconscious hypridity in the Bakhtinian sense, that is, a merging of different cultural, social, or national registers of language that lacks a critical dimension, an orientation that is underscored by the narratives of redemption Sachs evokes despite her emphasis on suffering.[56]

However, the feasibility of cultural synthesis through marginalization is called into question by the last two stanzas, which exhibit a shift from mythological and theological paradigms of exile to the narrator's experience of her everyday space. Formally, this transition entails a shift from metaphor to metonymy, reflected in the localization "hier auf der Straße" [here on the street] and in the synecdoche that represents the poem's speaker by her foot. While the speaker appears to call the violent and exclusionary principles of the world into question from behind its margins, here representation itself becomes violent, as it metonymically disfigures the speaker's body. The locution "stößt an" [hits against], furthermore, contrasts with the "immer" [always] of the first stanza, connoting a sudden change, a moment of contingency that undermines the attempt to create a speaking self in the image of mythological models. The failure to merge the various mythological figures into a cohesive poetic vision also manifests itself in the self-reflective attitude of the poem about its own speech, which is associated with violence: the bomb splinter that is compared to a question mark threatens not only the speaker's movement on the street but also calls into question her very speaking. The question mark rescinds, or at least problematizes, the translating moves made in the first stanzas of the poem, effecting a sudden instability of speech and a change of poetic expression in the last stanza.

Whereas the opacity of the previous stanzas stems from condensation and disappears if the reader is familiar with the figures and their context, the last stanza, with its sudden leap into diffuse allegorical personification, defies any attempt to tie down its meaning, even syntactically. In cases of inverted word order such as in the line "erschießt wehrlose Sehnsucht / die Liebe," the first noun is normally the subject, but such a reading is here rendered unlikely by the qualification of "Sehnsucht" [longing] as "wehrlos" [defenseless], which leaves the reader pondering over subject and object. The swan's cry, finally, evokes the swan song, the traditional metaphor for a dying poet's last words and for the ability of poetry to transcend death. However, the song here turns into a scream and, perhaps more significant, is said to be the last one. This violent, abrupt, and absolute end mutes all positive teleology, thus invalidating the promise of redemption held out by the figures of exile in the first stanzas. The inner split of the poem "Immer hinter" signals the demise of what Roman Jakobson has defined as the basic principle of poetry, that is, the projection of paradigmatic (metaphoric) relations into syntagmatic (metonymic) chains of words.[57] Whereas this principle functions as the vehicle of cultural translation in the first half of the poem, it fails to do so in the second half. Instead, the poem issues in a scene of senseless, irredeemable violence.

CHAPTER 3

THE EICHMANN TRIAL AND THE RETURN OF HISTORY

The insight that Sachs's attempts at cultural mediation were undermined by textual crises throughout the 1950s also sheds new light on her nervous breakdown some years later. In September 1960, shortly after her return from Germany, Sachs was hospitalized in a psychiatric clinic with the diagnosis of paranoid psychosis after she had been vexed for months by the sound of knockings on the wall, anonymous telephone calls, and radio signals that she heard in her apartment and believed to emanate from monitoring devices installed by invisible Nazi neighbors.[58] While such sensations of influencing machines are part of the symptoms of paranoia, they have in this case an undeniably real, historical core. The total constriction of space Sachs experienced, and the lack of boundaries protecting the private sphere, reiterated the experience of Jews living in Germany during the late 1930s, who were subject to an elaborate system of anti-Jewish laws and regulations intended to completely segregate "Jews" and "Aryans."[59] Ruth Dinesen has further attributed Sachs's breakdown to an identity crisis following a series of events that threatened her tenuous double identity as a German and a Jew. The crisis was precipitated by the fact that Walter Berendsohn had, against Sachs's wishes, emphasized her Jewish identity in his publications on her and that the opera version of her drama *Eli* had by some reviewers been interpreted as a call for revenge against Germany, an interpretation that Sachs desperately contested.[60] Both these incidents positioned Sachs vis-à-vis German audiences. Berendsohn was crucial in introducing Sachs to a German public, and the theme of revenge around which the reviews of *Eli* circled was a neuralgic point of postwar German-Jewish relations.

The public dimension of Sachs's crisis suggests that her paranoia can be understood in terms of what Eric Santner has called a "crisis of symbolic investiture," which occurs when a person fails to metabolize a new title, social role, or symbolic mandate.[61] In his reading of the memoirs of Daniel Schreber, a famous modernist document of paranoia, Santner argues that such a failure has less to do with individual dispositions than with the rites of investiture themselves. Paranoics have particularly fine antennas for the inconsistencies and contradictions of such rites. Indeed, Nelly Sachs's crisis can be understood as a response to the doubleness inherent in the reintegration of exile writers into the German public sphere analyzed earlier, the fact that their incorporation into the canon of German literature was based on a new set of exclusions. However, Sachs's breakdown was also accompanied by a crisis of her construal of an imaginary center. Earlier I suggested that Sachs's symbolic recovery of the land of Israel during the first postwar years was a survival strategy that contained the trauma of expulsion and genocide. The poem "Überall Jerusalem," which was written in a psychiatric clinic and relates to the Eichmann trial, shows how this strategy falters as historical reality invades the center of her imaginary map, the land of Israel. In 1960 Adolf Eichmann was kidnapped in Buenos Aires by Israeli agents, and he was brought to trial in Jerusalem on April 11, 1961. Attended by extensive media coverage, the Eichmann trial brought the horrible details of the Holocaust back to public consciousness. Sachs's encounter with the actuality of genocide had an effect similar to that of the Auschwitz trial on Peter Weiss, reviving in her mind the confrontation between victims and perpetrators.[62] "Überall Jerusalem" starts with the opening date of the Eichmann trial. The only poem in Sachs's entire oeuvre that is dated, it creates a tension between the real and the symbolic, the local and the universal, the political and the metaphysical dimension of Jerusalem, a tension that is never resolved and that ultimately undermines the metaphorization of Israel as a sacred center.

ÜBERALL JERUSALEM

Am 11. April 1961
In der Trauer

Verborgen ist es im Köcher
und nicht abgeschossen mit dem Pfeil
und die Sonne immer schwarz um das Geheimnis
und gebückt die Sechsunddreißig im Leidenswerk

Aber hier
augenblicklich
ist das Ende—
Alles gespart für das reißende Feuer
Seiner Abwesenheit—

CHAPTER 3

Da
in der Krankheit
gegoren zur Hellsicht
die Prophetin mit dem Stab stößt
auf den Reichtum der Seele

Da ist in der Irre Gold versteckt—
   (*T*, 381)

> *On April 11, 1961*
> *In mourning*

EVERYWHERE JERUSALEM

It is hidden in the quiver
and not shot down with the arrow
and the sun always black around the secret
and the Thirty-Six bent in the work of suffering

But here
momentarily
is the end—
Everything saved for the devouring fire
of His absence—

There
in sickness
in a fermented clairvoyance
the prophetess strikes with her staff
the riches of the soul.

There in confusion gold is hidden—
   (*TS*, 377, trans. altered)

    The first two lines of this poem function like the date in a letter, establishing the pragmatic frame of speech and marking the singularity of the words that are to follow. The date's implication that these words are bound to a specific time and place forms a curious contrast to the title, which evokes the idea of a spiritual Jerusalem that signifies God's presence throughout the world. More than any other place in Israel, Jerusalem has engaged the eschatological imagination of both Jews and

Christians and become the source of symbolic meanings that are attached to, but ultimately independent from, the earthly city, thus allowing for the metaphysical interpretations of exile I traced in Sachs's early poetry. However, such an interpretation is here undermined by the political dimension emblematized by the Eichmann trial. Before the trial opened, critical voices were raised suggesting that the Israeli government should call for the establishment of an international tribunal to prosecute Eichmann. The decision of the Israeli government to conduct the trial nonetheless in its own court was a gesture of national sovereignty. Just as the various countries occupied by the Germans during World War II had conducted trials to convict the perpetrators of the crimes committed against their people, the existence of the state of Israel enabled the Jews to finally sit in judgment of a person responsible for the genocide against their people. The Eichmann trial in Jerusalem thus demonstrated Israel's status as a political entity with a juridical executive of its own.[63]

Sachs's letter to the Israeli prime minister David Ben-Gurion shows that she attempted to diminish this political dimension—or was unaware of it in the first place—and to restore a religious framework to the Eichmann trial. Alluding to the idea of the thirty-six hidden righteous who, according to a Jewish mystical legend, sustain the world and halt its destruction, Sachs pleads to Ben-Gurion that he should intercept Eichmann's execution because of the righteous who lived in Germany.[64] Accordingly, the first stanza of "Überall Jerusalem" uses arrow and quiver imagery, which in the book of Isaiah pertains to the prophet's role in bringing about redemption not only for the people of Israel but also for the nations of the world (Isa. 49:2, 6), to allude to the symbolic dimension of Jerusalem. However, the poem's date suggests that universalization means something quite different here, pointing not to a promise extended to the whole world but to the all-pervasiveness of the confrontation between victims and perpetrators reactivated by the Eichmann trial. The first stanza already somewhat retracts the messianic perspective characteristic of Isaiah. Some undefinable "it" remains in God's quiver even after the arrow has been shot, and the black sun, one of the biblical images announcing the advent of the day of God's judgment, hovers "always" over the earth, endlessly deferring the actual moment of judgment. The end described in the second stanza, then, mutes any form of teleology, culminating in nothing but the absence of God. The mention of the fire should not be read

CHAPTER 3

as a conflation of the Holocaust with a burnt sacrifice. Such an interpretation, which takes the Greek meaning of "Holocaust" literally, would presuppose a separation between God and the fire, so that the sacrifice could establish a relationship between the human and the divine—yet in this stanza everything collapses into something else: the end, the fire, the absence of God.[65]

The disruption of the symbolic continues in the last two stanzas of the poem. The move from "here" to "there" and the gold recovered in the soul (which possibly refers to one of the divine sparks of light scattered over the earth) suggest that the hope for messianic redemption may be rediscovered in the subject's interiority. However, the representation of mental and emotional states throughout the poem counteracts such a restoration of symbolic meaning. These states not only become increasingly intense, turning from mourning to illness into confusion or madness, but also acquire a curiously spatial character. "In der Trauer" [in mourning] follows the date of an inscription, thus replacing the indication of place that conventionally would follow the date. The "da" [there] preceding "In der Krankheit" [in sickness] has a deictic effect, and although it could also be a temporal or causal conjunction, one is more inclined to read it as the localizing "there." Finally, "in der Irre" [in confusion] conflates the image of a madwoman (which, however, does not make grammatical sense here) with idiomatic expressions like "in die Irre führen," or "in die Irre gehen," which generally connote errancy and disorientation, making confusion, or madness, appear like a place.[66] The word "Irre" also evokes the biblical wilderness through which Israel wandered before entering Canaan and the desolation brought to biblical Jerusalem by foreign armies. These sites signify states of suspension, and it is consonant with Sachs's poetics of exile that she can locate hope only in places like these. However, even this minimal hope is diminished by the concreteness, almost brutality of the prophetess suddenly striking gold with her stick, which calls into question the transformation of this reified form of hope into redemption. Instead of using place to symbolize something ultimately independent from place, the last line concretizes the meaning of Jerusalem, thus reversing the signification process of Sachs's early poetry on the land of Israel, which posited a symbolic center meant to empower the dispersed and marginalized. Rather than recuperating the promise of redemption, "Überall Jerusalem" illustrates that trauma cannot be contained through reference to such a metahistorical site of hope.[67]

In my reading of Nelly Sachs's lyrical and dramatic work of the 1950s, I have suggested that her breakdown of 1960 is related to structural impasses arising from her revival of pre-Holocaust concepts of diaspora, in a faltering attempt to reconcile her own conflict between German and Jewish origins. Unlike Peter Weiss's crisis, Sachs's breakdown did not usher in an entire reconceptualization of diaspora. In her late poems, many of which are collected in the collection *Glühende Rätsel* [*Glowing Enigmas*], she makes relatively few allusions to exile, and when she does, her images do not depart far from the earlier ones. Even the condensed ambivalence of *Ur* persists in poems such as "Der Jäger" [The Hunter].[68] However, we observe in Sachs's late poetry interesting stylistic changes, the development of a kind of "old-age avant-gardism"[69] that is marked by minimalism in the form reductions, ellipses, quotations, and simplified syntax. To be sure, Sachs's late poetry does not abandon the mystical-romantic motives but rather reduces them to ciphers and evocative signals whose reception by the reader is contingent upon his or her familiarity with her earlier poems.[70] The laconism of her late poetry, however, points to a contemporary trend never fully embraced by Sachs. It recalls the sobriety of some postwar German poetry, a style that Paul Celan has interpreted as a reaction to the inflation and abuse of aesthetic forms during Nazism:

> German poetry, I believe, is going in a very different direction from French poetry. No matter how alive its traditions, with most sinister events in its memory, most questionable developments around it, it can no longer speak the language which many willing ears still seem to expect. Its language has become more sober, more factual. It distrusts "beauty." It tries to be truthful. . . . This language, notwithstanding its inalienable complexity of expression, is concerned with precision. It does not transfigure or render "poetical"; it names, it posits, it tries to measure the area of the given and the possible. True, this is never the working of language itself, language as such, but always of an "I" who speaks from the particular angle of reflection which is his existence and who is concerned with outlines and orientation. Reality is not simply there, it must be searched and won.[71]

CHAPTER 3

Some of the poems in *Glühende Rätsel* evince just such an attempt at orientation in their attendance to everyday spaces and slight gestures and movements. Marked by deictic tendencies similar to those of "Überall Jerusalem," these late poems sometimes express a traumatizing claustrophobia, yet their mapping of space also serves to reestablish boundaries between inside and outside and to create protected interior spaces. Sachs's use of laconic descriptions of domestic interiors to carve out protected spaces is evident, for instance, in a poem in which a Jewish mystical motif is preceded by a sober list of pieces of furniture: "In meiner Kammer / wo mein Bett steht / ein Tisch ein Stuhl / der Küchenherd / kniet das Universum wie überall / um erlöst zu werden / von der Unsichtbarkeit—" (*SNL,* 63) [In my room / where my bed stands / a table a chair / the kitchen stove / the universe kneels as everywhere / to be redeemed / from invisibility (*OTC,* 289)]. Though the poem continues with an apocalyptic vision of destruction and salvation reminiscent of Sachs's earlier poetry, this vision is now contingent upon the creation of an everyday place. In another poem, Sachs reduces some of her mystical ciphers (*Tür, Seil, Quelle, spiegeln*) to the image of a bathroom, thereby creating a site for an intimate mourning scene: "Hinter der Tür / ziehst du an dem Sehnsuchtsseil / bis Tränen kommen / In dieser Quelle spiegelst du dich—" (*SNL,* 14) [Behind the door / you pull on the rope of longing / till tears come / In this wellspring you're mirrored (*OTC,* 247)]. This contraction of the poetic self into a closed interior space mirrors Sachs's own retreat from the outside world during her last years. It also presents, perhaps, a minimal solution to a situation in which an imaginary center has become unavailable and reconciliation unimaginable.

4
Paul Celan's Revisiting of Eastern Europe

The Plagiarism Charge

When in 1960 Claire Goll, the widow of the French Jewish poet Yvan Goll, charged Celan in an open letter with plagiarizing her late husband's poetry, the ensuing debate in West Germany about the validity of this accusation cast Celan into a major crisis during the course of which he was temporarily hospitalized in a psychiatric clinic. Goll's charges concerned a number of metaphors in Celan's poems, among them the famous "Todesfuge" ["Deathfugue"], which by then had been canonized and reprinted in German high school textbooks.[1] In Western aesthetic culture, which regards originality as the most important quality of art, and especially of poetry, the public charge of imitating another poet's work would challenge any poet's self-legitimization. This is even more true for a writer such as Celan, whose postwar work developed in the absence of a German-speaking environment and relied on the ability of poetry to free language from its historical boundedness, especially its implication in German Nazism. Left by the Holocaust "searching for a self and a voice by which to describe [his] own obliteration,"[2] Celan had espoused a notion of the text as the proper place of the Jew. Yet the plagiarism charge annulled even this last home, his own language: "you know what it means for an author

CHAPTER 4

of the German tongue, who survived the Nazi terror, to be severed a second time from his language. For *among other things,* they have managed—perfectly well—to create a vacuum around me."[3]

Growing up in the Bukovina, a historically multiethnic and multilingual region in today's Romania, Paul Celan spoke German as his mother tongue. After the Second World War, during which both of his parents perished in a concentration camp while he himself was temporarily incarcerated in a labor camp, he went first to Bucharest, then to Vienna, and finally to Paris, where he continued to write and publish in German. He never ceased to write in German, a choice he sometimes explained in terms of the specific demands and possibilities of poetic language. In the immediate postwar years, he "answered everyone who reproached him for writing in the language of his parents' murderers: 'Only in the mother tongue can one speak one's own truth. In a foreign tongue a poet lies,'"[4] and later he emphasized, as a friend recalls, "how much his linguistic isolation served to refine his poetic language."[5] Celan's emphatic affirmation of German was, however, accompanied by an uneasiness regarding the public dimension of this language, a language that exposed him to an audience from which he felt separated both geographically and historically. During the late 1950s, Celan grew concerned about the political climate in West Germany. He was alarmed by the resurgence of Nazi groups in West Germany and by a series of desecrations of Jewish cemeteries in 1959. As a result of such public displays of antisemitism, he grew more aware of his own Jewish identity and regarded the resonance his poetry found in Germany with some suspicion: "Every now and then I am invited to Germany for readings. Even the antisemites have discovered me."[6]

Celan's vehement reaction to the plagiarism charge shortly thereafter is not surprising, given the tenacity of the antisemitic stereotypes of unproductive, thieving, or parasitic Jews in German culture. Some comments in his letters, one of which he signed with "Old-Metaphors Dealer,"[7] show that Celan heard the reverberations of these stereotypes in the accusations against him. Less comprehensible, at first glance, is the paranoia he developed during the course of the plagiarism affair. He suspected behind the charge a conspiracy comprising not only his assailants but also a number of prominent German writers who immediately came to his defense, including Hans Magnus Enzensberger and Marie Luise Kaschnitz, and critics such as Reinhard Döhl, who dismissed the plagiarism charge on philological and chronological grounds.[8] Thus he wrote in a letter "that the defamation campaign instigated against me continues in the so-called Federal Republic. . . . What is new in this Nazi-Renaissance is that nowadays one can discover how one—in contrast to Hitler—can do things 'better': namely through the *double game*. . . . My 'defenders' are those who collaborated against me."[9] Celan's suspicions seemed to have objective grounds; he had a keen sense, for instance, for the discursive violence we saw at work in Nelly Sachs's reception. Indeed, he indicated in a conversation with Sachs in May 1960 that the public homages to Jewish writers in West Germany, such as the Droste prize that was about to be awarded to Sachs in Meersburg, were examples of how postwar German philosemitism exploited Jews as part of a rhetoric of reconciliation.[10]

Regarding his own case, Celan interpreted the patronizing attitude of his defenders as a means to assimilate—and thus to annihilate—difference, a liberal equivalent to the open anti-Jewish violence of right-wing antisemites. The fact that he simultaneously objected to his public presentation as a Jew first appears as a contradiction, but it is quite consistent given his analysis of such public interest. He perceived in it a tendency to reduce a potentially unsettling Jewish otherness to a set of attributes that could be circulated in a discourse devoid of any real concern with Jews: "After I have been 'nullified' [aufgehoben] as a person, as a subject, I am permitted to live on, perverted to an object, as a 'theme': mostly as an Steppenwolf with no place of origin, with features recognizable as Jewish from a distance. What comes from me achieves redistribution—my Jewishness recently included."[11] This sense of being objectified and handed over to his critics for distribution reflects, as Jean Bollack suggests, Celan's belief that any positive manifestation of Jewish difference in West German culture is self-destructive because it is inevitably either stigmatized or absorbed.[12]

In 1963 Celan published a collection of poetry called *Die Niemandsrose* [*The No-One's Rose*], which is often considered the beginning of a shift toward the highly elliptic, minimalist, and recalcitrant style of his late work. In this chapter I read the *Die Niemandsrose* in the context of the plagiarism crisis, which Celan experienced as a return of exile and persecution. In so doing, I expand on recent criticism that focuses on the question of how his poetry reconstitutes a place in face of the radical destruction of place by the Shoah. In her study of geological terminology in Celan, Uta Werner identifies at the core of Celan's poetry the problem of the annihilation of death itself through

CHAPTER 4

industrial genocide.[13] Because the Holocaust destroyed every trace of the dead and refused them any form of proper burial, no place exists that could form the ground of remembrance. In Celan's poetry, the dead of the Shoah appear as revenants, ghosts whose uncompleted and unmemorializable existence haunts the poet. Werner argues that the semantic wealth and depth of his language creates a complex interior structure that enables him to perform a kind of textual burial, a procedure comparable to geological sedimentation. By allowing the dead to return and find a burial place in his poems, Celan rescinds the irreversibility of the Final Solution. In a more explicit reference to psychoanalytic trauma theory, Ulrich Baer examines Celan's appropriation of the tradition of landscape poetry to create a place for traumatic memories that elude placement on cognitive and affective maps. Against Peter Szondi's influential reading of Celan's poems as textual "landscapes," Baer argues that only "terrains"—that is, places radically depleted of setting—can be found in these poems, which might be best understood as "proleptic sketches" of memorials yet to be built.[14]

There is another facet to Celan's reflections on place and mourning that has so far been underexplored: his renewed interest in Eastern Europe in the wake of the Goll affair. The poetry collected in *Die Niemandsrose* is replete with references to places and people in Eastern Europe. And in letters written during the early 1960s to Jewish friends from the Bukovina, Celan expressed his increased sense of exile while reminiscing about his lost home or projecting hope onto a generalized image of the "East" (whose political dimensions include Eastern European socialism): "My hope lies in the East—*yes, there,* Pierrot!"[15] Celan's friend Jean Bollack, who also published studies of his poetry, has argued that the East functioned for Celan as a cipher of exteriority and of his radical otherness in German culture: "The East, where his origins lie and where he situates them, takes on the value of a rupture, a non-belonging. It is *his* East, the Bukovina, and behind it other Easts there emerge, even more "oriental" vis-à-vis the West, which are comprised of exteriority and freedom."[16] But if Celan's East is a cipher of difference, he never fails to acknowledge that it emerged from a devastating loss of concrete places. Toward the end of his 1960 "Meridian" speech, he attempts to locate the landscape of his origin on an imaginary map, yet instead he ends up with what would become his central poetological term: "I am seeking all of that with an inexact because uneasy finger on the map—on a children's map, I must admit. None of these places is to be found, they do not exist, but I know where, especially now, they would have to exist, and . . . I find something! . . . I find . . . a *meridian*."[17] The hope to recover the lost places in the connection between places that is the meridian does not undo the logic of destruction and abstraction that governs this scene: the landscape of Celan's childhood is so absolutely destroyed that no visual representation of it is imaginable, except for a children's map. Two years earlier, he had spoken of the Bukovina as a landscape "now fallen into historylessness" (*SP*, 395).

I propose to examine Celan's revisiting of Eastern Europe in *Die Niemandsrose* in terms of the dilemmas laid out in the second chapter of this study: how can one commemorate a historic diaspora, German-speaking Jewry in Eastern Europe, that was destroyed by the Holocaust not only physically but also symbolically? Like Günther Anders, Celan revisits the landscape of his youth at a moment when the Holocaust has retrospectively rendered the German cultural and/or political hegemony in this region problematic, and when the past participation of Jews in this hegemony appears now as suicidal. Yet where Anders tends to fall into narrative backshadowing, Celan's poetry offers a way beyond fixed concepts of historical necessity, allowing for alternative visions of mourning and resistance. His deployment of sideshadowing strategies in "Eine Gauner- und Ganovenweise" allows for a revisionist reading of the Bukovina as a culturally heterogeneous space, thus locating symbolic resources for a resistance against what he perceived to be a resurgent fascism in Western Europe. Furthermore, the elegies in the last part of *Die Niemandsrose,* which relate to a number of places in Eastern Europe, hover in traumatic ambivalence and fail to arrive at unequivocally consoling signs. Simultaneously evoking and corroding utopian ciphers, Celan translates the eschatological hope for an ingathering of the exiles into a provocative intertextuality that creates momentary alliances across spatial, temporal, and textual borders. In the final section of this chapter, I argue that such connective strategies potentially extend to Celan's readership through his peculiar use of place names. Building on Jacques Derrida's concept of the shibboleth, I suggest that place names may serve in Celan to inscribe historical events into the poems as wounds, a strategy that reflects the experience of radical contingency and addresses the readers of poetry as *Spurensucher*. In that sense, Celan's poetry is an example of diasporic discourse traveling tenuously across unknown distances.

CHAPTER 4

REMAPPING THE BUKOVINA

The poem "Eine Gauner- und Ganovenweise / gesungen zu Paris emprès Pontoise / von Paul Celan / aus Czernowitz bei Sadagora" ["A Rogues' and Gonifs' Ditty / sung at Paris emprès Pontoise / by Paul Celan / from Czernowitz near Sadagora"] is an example of Celan's use of sideshadowing strategies to locate moments of difference and resistance in his place of origin.[18] This poem occupies a special place in Celan's work, as one perhaps guesses when reading the author's name and birthplace in the title. Czernowitz, the capital of the Bukovina, was during his time home to a thoroughly assimilated and mostly middle class Jewish population living in an ethnically diverse environment. Karl Emil Franzos's representation, in *Aus Halb-Asien Kulturbilder* (1876), of the Bukovina as a region in which different ethnic and religious groups coexisted peacefully under the sign of German cultural hegemony was after World War II revived by Czernowitz-born writers such as Rose Ausländer. As Winfried Menninghaus argues, Czernowitz has since become an "emblem of successful multiculturalism and creative multilingualism" of mythic dimensions.[19] The image of Czernowitz as the site of a vibrant cosmopolitan culture tends to produce a certain nostalgia about the purported "German-Jewish symbiosis" in these Eastern parts of the Habsburg empire.

A comparison of different versions of "Eine Gauner- und Ganovenweise" shows that Celan reworked the poem almost obsessively in the course of the plagiarism affair. In particular, he continuously changed its title and epigraph, affiliating himself in various ways with Germany, Russia, and France while always emphasizing his own somewhat secondary role as a singer, that is, as the one who does not create but performs a song.[20] The curious place designation in the title of the poem's final version echoes a quatrain that the fifteenth-century French poet François Villon wrote on the walls of a prison cell at a moment when he believed that he was about to be hanged. This quatrain —"I am François, no source of cheer, / Parisian born (Pontoise is near), / And from the six-foot rope, I fear / My neck will know the weight of my rear"—reverses the importance of Paris, the nation's capital, and Pontoise, an insignificant small town on the periphery of Paris.[21] Through a similar inversion of center and periphery, Celan's poem debunks the myth of a culturally homogeneous Bukovina in which all Jews were Westernized and spoke German, and he destabilizes the traditionally perceived hierarchy between Eastern and Western Jewish cultures. Sadagora, a village next to Czernowitz and the birthplace of Celan's mother, was not only known for its traditional, Hasidic Jewish culture but was also despised in Czernowitz as a refuge for rogues and crooks, a connotation that resonates in the poem.[22] Rather than positing Sadagora as the locus of another, idealized culture, Celan's unapologetic imitation of Villon's gesture offers a provocative affirmation of the stigma Eastern European Jews traditionally carry in Germany. Indicating in its title the singer's move from Czernowitz to Paris, the poem goes on to connect elliptical reminiscences of a nomadic and ostracized existence to the poetic traditions of bandit ballads and gallows songs.

EINE GAUNER- UND GANOVENWEISE
GESUNGEN ZU PARIS EMPRÈS PONTOISE
VON PAUL CELAN
AUS CZERNOWITZ BEI SADAGORA

Manchmal nur, in dunkeln Zeiten,
Heinrich Heine, An Edom

Damals, als es noch Galgen gab,
da, nicht wahr, gab es
ein Oben.

Wo bleibt mein Bart, Wind, wo
mein Judenfleck, wo
mein Bart, den du raufst?

Krumm war der Weg, den ich ging,
krumm war er, ja,
denn, ja,
er war gerade.

Heia.

Krumm, so wird meine Nase.
Nase.

Und wir zogen auch nach *Friaul.*
Da hätten wir, da hätten wir.

CHAPTER 4

Denn es blühte der Mandelbaum.
Mandelbaum, Bandelmaum.

Mandelbaum, Trandelmaum.
Und auch der Machandelbaum.
Chandelbaum.

Heia.
Aum.

Envoi

Aber,
aber er bäumt sich, der Baum. Er,
auch er
steht gegen
die Pest.
  (*Nr*, 41)

A ROGUES' AND GONIFS' DITTY
SUNG AT PARIS EMPRÈS PONTOISE
BY PAUL CELAN
FROM CZERNOWITZ NEAR SADAGORA

Only now and then, in dark times,
    Heinrich Heine, "To Edom"

Back then, when they still had gallows,
then—right?—they had
an On High.

Wind, where's my beard, where's
my Jew's-patch, where's
my beard you tear at?

Crooked, the path I took was
crooked, yes,
because yes,
it was straight.

Hey-ho.

Crooked, so goes my nose.
Nose.

And we made for *Friuli*.
There we would have, there we would have.
For the almond tree was blossoming.
Almond tree, Talmundree.

Almonddream, Dralmondream.
And the Allemandtree.
Lemandtree.

Hey-ho.
Hum.

Envoi

Yet,
yet it shoots up, that tree. It,
it too
stands against
the plague.
 (*SP*, 161)

The motto is taken from the dedicatory poem to Heinrich Heine's fragment of a novel, *Der Rabbi von Bacharach* [*The Rabbi of Bacharach*]. The Edom of the poem's title refers to the descendants of Esau, who in the Bible are both neighbors and enemies of Israel. The poem itself evokes centuries of a troubled coexistence between Jews and Christians, during which the Jews were time and again subject to violence, concluding with the vague prospect that emancipation and assimilation will end this one-sided violence.[23] Isolating from this poem the recurrence of dark times—"Manchmal nur, in dunkeln Zeiten" [Only now and then, in dark times]—Celan retracts any kind of promise of progress in history, even the highly ironic one of Heine's poem. The first stanzas of "Eine Gauner- und Ganovenweise" dramatize the return of the past. After initially stressing his own distance from a past of gallows and "ein Oben" [an On High]—of religious transcendence and social hierarchy—the speaker in Celan's poem invokes two markers of Jewish identity in premodern times, "Bart" [beard] and "Judenfleck" [Jew's-patch], while indicating through the locution "wo bleibt" [where's] that he is awaiting the recuperation of these markers. The invocation of recent history emphasizes the threat of persecution: during the Second World War, German soldiers humiliated Orthodox Eastern Jews by shearing their beards before they deported and killed them. The stanza following the first refrain, then, describes the singer's assimilation to the past. With his nose becoming as crooked as his exilic paths have been, he acquires the physiognomic trait that in modern antisemitic imagination replaced the Jew's spot and beard as external markers of Jewish identity.

In this context, it is important to remember that parts of *Der Rabbi von Bacharach* were written at a moment when history seemed to be uncannily repeating itself. Heine began the novel in 1824, left it unfinished, and resumed work on it in 1840 after a blood libel charge was leveled against Jews in Lebanon, an incident that recalled the notorious pretext for anti-Jewish pogroms during the Middle Ages. The fragment, which is set in medieval times and relates the escape of the rabbi of Bacharach and his wife from a pogrom after being framed for blood libel, invites the reader to reflect upon the fragility of Jewish emancipation. It invokes the golden age of Spanish Jewry at the very moment when the Muslim-Jewish "symbiosis" was established as a model for the nineteenth-century emancipation of the Jews in Germany. As the rabbi and his wife arrive in the Jewish ghetto of Frankfurt, they meet a former friend of the rabbi, an emancipated Jew from Spain who has cut his religious ties with Judaism but still returns occasionally to the Jewish community to revel in its food and familial atmosphere. After several lengthy monologues that reveal this man to be a double of the modern German Jew, the text breaks suddenly off on the note: "The conclusion and the chapters which follow are lost, not from any fault of the author."[24] By publishing the text as a fragment, Heine creates an effect Bernstein helps us to identify as sideshadowing.[25] The story takes place just a few years before the expulsion of the Jews from Spain in 1492, which marks the end of the peaceful coexistence and mutual influence of different religious groups, that is, to the "symbiosis" symbolized by the Spanish Jew. Breaking off conspicuously before the catastrophe, Heine invites his readers to construct later developments on the basis of their historical knowledge, yet at the same time leaves room to imagine alternative courses of history or, at least, alternative fates for the story's characters.

Unlike Anders, who subsumes signs of Jewish difference immediately under the rubric of catastrophic history, Celan, much like Heine before him, finds a way to restore a sense of possibility to history. In order to accomplish this, however, Celan must first dismantle the notion of a telos in history by shifting the implications of what it means to end somewhere. If the epigraph and the first four stanzas of "Eine Gauner- und Ganovenweise" present historical time as open-ended repetition, the decomposition of the word "Mandelbaum" [almond tree] in an echolike wordplay threatens to lead into a dead end, into silence. The almond tree, which Celan interpolates with the fragments of a sixteenth-century German lansquenet song to which I will return below, is an eschatological symbol introducing the idea of an end of time. In Jeremiah, the almond rod is a symbol of the certainty that God's promises will come to pass, and in Ecclesiastes the blossoming almond tree serves to illustrate the approach of death.[26] The almond tree further figures as a symbol of Jewish strength in "Hashkeidia Porachat" ["The Almond Tree is Blooming"], a Zionist song sung on the Jewish holiday of trees, Tu B'shvat. In "Eine Gauner- und Ganovenweise," however, the tree is subject to a series of transformations into the dreamt fulfillment of eschatological hopes ("Mandeltraum") and into nonsense words created through the exchange of letters. The "Machandelbaum," finally, evokes a gruesome fairy tale related by the Grimm brothers in which an evil stepmother kills her stepson, cooks him, and serves him to his father for dinner. The son's sister, however, collects his bones and buries them under the "Machandelboom," a North German dialect word for the juniper tree. The brother's bones are transmuted into a bird that sings a song about the crime until the evil stepmother is punished and the murder avenged. The tree in the fairy tale, in other words, embodies continuity and anticipates the advent of justice. In "Eine Gauner- und Ganovenweise," however, the tree is drawn into an echolike wordplay that first transforms the "Mandelbaum" through a series of intermediate stages into "Machandelbaum" and then gradually reduces it to the onomatopoetic evocation of pain, "Aum." This wordplay corrodes any positive eschatological vision associated with the tree, an effect that is particularly tangible in the word "Chandelbaum." For

CHAPTER 4

"Chandel" means in *Rotwelsch*—the secret language of thieves and vagabonds that contains numerous Yiddish expressions—"candle" or "light," and the "Chandelbaum" thus evokes a menorah, which indeed looks like a tree. The fact that this Jewish symbol appears here as a mere echo effect, a mutilated form of the German "Machandelbaum," indicates how the poem mimetically reproduces the violence about which it speaks. The mesmerizing, even lullaby-like tone of the "Mandelbaum" passages lulls the reader into complacency to awaken her all the more brutally.

The concluding *envoi* relates one of Celan's central poetological concepts, *Atemwende*, or "turn of breath," to the idea of resistance. In Celan's famous "Meridian" speech, *Atemwende* denotes the moment when language falls silent and is about to turn into something new, which remains, however, unarticulated and unarticulable. Such a turning point is here marked by the conjunction "aber" [yet]. The "aber," pure signifier of linguistic inversion, replaces the poetic address that in the traditional *envoi*, for instance in Villon's ballads, opens up the poem's interior by literally "sending" it to a reader—*envoyer* means in French "to send." And it is indeed through intralinguistic movements that Celan's poem issues in a form of resistance: the tree's transformation from a noun into a reflexive verb evokes and concretizes a conventional metaphor for "to resist"—*sich aufbäumen*—which at the same time preserves a sense of pain. This concrete resistance is also tangible in another variation of a German idiom: the use of "steht gegen" emphasizes bodily posture and action rather than the more passive form of resistance associated with *widerstehen*. Yet what resistance is Celan depicting here? He experienced, we recall, the plagiarism charge as a replay of historical violence on the level of public discourse. By incorporating the terms of this charge into the very form of his poem, which seems to generate words by having them bounce back and forth between the walls of an echo, Celan refutes the charge through ironic affirmation. This possibility of resistance, however, involves not only figures of inversion but also a fragmentation of sentences that creates an effect akin to sideshadowing. While this is a narratological concept that refers to the disruption of causal relations between narrated events, sideshadowing has its equivalents in poetry, in which the disruption of chains of predication might similarly restore a sense of possibility, the possibility that unspoken words might have been spoken, or spoken words might have been spoken differently. And that is what Celan's technique of citation accomplishes as well. By incorporating fragments from a sixteenth-century German lansquenet song into "Eine Gauner- und Ganovenweise," Celan stakes his own claim on an already ambiguous German folk tradition rendered even more problematic by Nazi appropriation.[27] On the one hand, the lansquenets, poor foot soldiers whom the song depicts on their way into hunger, plague, and death, may be regarded as victims of history. On the other hand, however, they were also mercenaries who fought wars of conquest in the army of Maximilian I, the Habsburg head who made his family dominant in sixteenth-century Europe. Friuli in Northern Italy, to which Celan specifically refers, was one of the decisive battlegrounds.

Whether the lansquenets are perceived as victims or perpetrators, Celan's repetition of the *"Da hätten wir"* [*There we would have*], which deviates from the original, disrupts the flow of their quoted sentence and its deadly predication. Furthermore, in assimilating the line to modern High German, Celan transposes the verb into the subjunctive mood; he was surely aware of the fact that the Middle High German in the two versions of the song that can be found in his library—"do het wir" and "do hätt'n wir"—are in the indicative mood. Celan makes the subjunctive stand out even more by continuing it with a causal "denn" [for], creating a discrepancy between the factual and the hypothetical, the actual and the possible. In shifting moods, finally, Celan prepares the poem's most radical alteration of the song, its fragmentation and rearrangement that turn *"die Pest"* [the plague] into an object of resistance. Despite the emphasis Celan places here, though, there is little of the heroic in this gesture. The concluding line curiously focuses the reader's attention on the italicized words *"die Pest."* Whether read as a hint toward a classic pretext for pogroms in medieval times or as an allusion to Albert Camus's famous novel *La Peste,* which makes the plague a symbol of fascism, the weight that the word attains in its own rejection indicates just how fragile is the possibility of resistance, but how necessary its attempt.

This observation about the ambiguity of the final line, which highlights the plague even while resisting it, may serve as a point of entry into the long elegiac poems in the final sections of *Die Niemandsrose*. As my reading has shown, "Eine Gauner- und Ganovenweise," which begins with a reclamation of Eastern European origins ("Paul Celan / aus Czernowitz bei Sadagora") uncovers the heterogeneity of pre-Holocaust Eastern Europe rather than producing idealized images of origins.

I have further argued that the cultural fragmentation of the Bukovina is accompanied by a temporal fragmentation enacted through Celan's manipulation of intertextual references. However, if his intervening just before the catastrophic moment opens up the dynamic relationship to the past that is the precondition of all mourning, I do not want to suggest that the mourning process is ever, or could ever be, or should ever be, completed in Celan's poems. The concluding elegies in the poetry collection *Die Niemandsrose*, which are the most vivid expression of Celan's new concern with the East, often end emphatically in a place, such as a geographical location, a house, or a deictic expression. These places, however, are marked by splittings or signify dispersion in a way that undermines the poems' promise of ingathering through memory. Whereas traditional elegies achieve consolation and renewal after lament, Celan's elegies lead to uncanny sites that remain haunted, as in a line of the concluding poem "In der Luft" ["In the Air"], by an excommunicating curse: "heimgekehrt in / den unheimlichen Bannstrahl" (*Nr*, 147) [gone home again to / uncanny anathema (*SP*, 211)]. In what follows now, I will argue that this uncanniness also affects the imagination of the East as a future site of messianic redemption.

Unsettling Tradition:
Celan and Jewish Mysticism

The representation, in some of Celan's elegies, of the East as both origin of dispersal and utopian point of recovery resonates with the nostalgic reminiscences in Celan's letters as well as with Jewish mysticism. More precisely, it reflects an image of Eastern Europe that was transmitted to a German-speaking audience primarily through the works of Martin Buber and Gershom Scholem. Since the beginning of the twentieth century, Buber's widely read German translations of Hasidic stories have associated Eastern European Jewry with mystical practices at the expense of the more rationalist streams of thought that also flourished in Eastern Europe, such as Haskalah and Zionism. Scholem consolidated this association, for instance, by concluding his historical survey *Major Trends of Jewish Mysticism* with an analysis of Eastern European Hasidism. Celan, however, avoids resurrecting the Jewish mystical tradition as a protective shield against the memory of destruction. He both invokes and dismantles the idea of the East's redemptive power and he references this idea in a way that unhinges it from a recognizable tradition. In so doing, Celan corrodes not only the messianic promise traditionally associated with the East but also its post-Holocaust analogue: the hope that the commemoration of Eastern European Jewish life could in some way compensate for its destruction.

One example of Celan's eclectic and unsettling use of Jewish mystical motives is "Hinausgekrönt" (*Nr*, 109–11) ["Crowned Out" (*SP*, 191–93)]. The poem starts out with an act of expulsion—"HINAUSGEKRÖNT, / hinausgespien in die Nacht" [CROWNED OUT, / spewed out into the night]—and goes on to relate multiple exiles and acts of ingathering, resulting in a resolution to stay away from the very symbol of dispersion, "Babel." The third and fourth stanzas of the poem recall the kabbalistic (Lurianic) motif of the collection of divine sparks that were scattered into earthly exile after the cosmic catastrophe of the breaking of the vessels:

> Blauschlucht, in dich
> treib ich das Gold. Auch mit ihm, dem
> bei Huren und Dirnen vertanen,
> komm ich und komm ich. Zu dir,
> Geliebte.
>
> Auch mit Fluch und Gebet. Auch mit jeder
> der über mich hin-
> schwirrenden Keulen: auch sie in eins
> geschmolzen, auch sie
> phallisch gebündelt zu dir,
> Garbe-und-Wort.
>   (*Nr*, 105)

> Blue chasm, I drive
> gold into you. With that too
> wasted on whores and wenches,
> I come and I come. To you,
> beloved.
>
> With curse and prayer too. And with
> each of the cudgels whirring
> over me: they too melted
> into one, they too
> phallically bundled towards you,
> sheaf-and-word.
>   (*SP*, 151)

CHAPTER 4

The "Keulen" [cudgels] possibly refer to a passage in Scholem's *Major Trends in Jewish Mysticism* concerning a bold reinterpretation of the psalms after the expulsion of the Jews from Spain. According to this passage, which is underlined in Celan's French copy of the book, the psalms will become in apocalyptic times "swords in Israel's hand and deadly weapons."[28] This reading of "Keulen" as prayers that have turned into weapons is supported by the expressions "mit Fluch und Gebet" [with curse and prayer] and "Garbe-und-Wort" [sheaf-and-word]. *Garbe* means both "burst of fire" and "sheaf," thus encoding the Hebrew *shibboleth*, which originally denoted an ear of grain before it came to signify the password that, as we will see below, is central to Celan's poetic creation of political alliances. The stanzas just quoted further evoke the kabbalistic motif of the unification between the seventh and the tenth *sefiroth*, as the ten divine emanations are called in the Kabbalah. The two *sefiroth* here in question, the *sefirah* justice and the *shekhinah*, are also associated with East-West and male-female oppositions. According to Scholem's account of this Kabbalistic motif, the seventh *sefirah* is seen as the East of the world and origin of the seed of Israel, and described in a distinctively phallic symbolism.[29] However, although they are intrinsic to the Jewish mystical tradition, the sexual and martial metaphors in "Hinausgekrönt" profane and brutalize the ingathering to an extent far beyond that in the source text. If Celan uses such texts, he isolates remarkably disturbing, implacable images from the mystical tradition rather than establishing this tradition as a stable frame of reference.

A look at Celan's poem "Hüttenfenster" (*Nr*, 121–23) ["Tabernacle Window" (*SP*, 197–99)] brings into sharper focus the subversive effect of his use of Jewish mysticism. This poem combines allusions to the Kabbalah, including the idea of a future return to the mystical East, with hidden references to another discourse on the East. "Hüttenfenster" reflects Celan's complex relationship with Johannes Bobrowski, an East German writer who was born and raised in Tilsit in East Prussia and who served as a German soldier in the Second World War.[30] In his poetry Bobrowski commemorated the cultural and ethnic heterogeneity of the historic Eastern Europe while highlighting the devastating consequences of German hegemony in this region: "A long history of unhappiness and wrong-doings since the days of the Teutonic Order."[31] Though Celan was initially well disposed toward Bobrowski, he grew increasingly critical of what he perceived to be a tendency to subsume the Jews to the other ethnic groups of Eastern Europe and to blur distinctions between victims and perpetrators. In a letter to a friend he polemicized against Bobrowski's "Pruzzische Elegie" [Prussian Elegy], which laments the downfall of the Old Prussians, as a mystifying celebration of German ethnic particularity.[32] In another letter he indicted in more general terms the tendency among German liberals to appropriate Jews and Judaism: "The 'Left' includes a certain 'liberal' anti-Semitism that, this time (this time too!) not without assistance from Jews, or 'Jews,' has aimed to brush aside that which is Jewish—i.e., *one* of the forms [Gestalten] that humanity takes, but *a form* [Gestalt] nevertheless—through isolation, paternalism, etc. It is in the end—the word is not too strong—a disguised Aryanization process."[33]

"Hüttenfenster" first describes the ingathering of the destroyed Eastern European Jewish world by an eye, probably alluding to the paintings of Vitebsk-born Marc Chagall, who has preserved a distinct image of Eastern European Jewry as inhabiting a mystical atmosphere, hovering between earth and sky. The hut or tabernacle window mentioned in the poem's second line simultaneously evokes Gottfried Keller's famous poem "Abendlied" ["Evening Song"] and the opening left in the roofs of Sukkhot huts. The poem goes on to depict a desolate landscape over which a wounded figure wanders, endowed with the features of Hermes, the gods' messenger who is said to accompany the dead into the Hades. This wounded figure of death is a first indication of the poem's shattering of traditional elegiac forms. Weighed down by something invisible, it evokes the angel of Rilke's *Duineser Elegien* [*Duino Elegies*] that, according to a famous letter by its author, signals the transformation of the visible into the invisible.[34] In Celan's poem such transcendence gives way to another form of invisibility, the result of a process of destruction so absolute that no visible traces remain:

> Das Aug, dunkel:
> als Hüttenfenster. Es sammelt,
> was Welt war, Welt bleibt: den Wander-
> Osten, die
> Schwebenden, die
> Menschen-und-Juden,
> das Volk-vom-Gewölk, magnetisch
> ziehts, mit Herzfingern, an
> dir, Erde:

du kommst, du kommst,
wohnen werden wir, wohnen, etwas

—ein Atem? ein Name?—

geht im Verwaisten umher,
tänzerisch, klobig,
die Engels-
schwinge, schwer von Unsichtbarem, am
wundgeschundenen Fuß, kopf-
lastig getrimmt
vom Schwarzhagel, der
auch dort fiel, in Witebsk,
   (*Nr,* 121)

The eye, dark:
as a tabernacle window. It gathers
what was a world and still is a world: the wander-
East, the
hovering ones, the
humans-and-Jews,
the cloud crowd, it pulls
magnetically on you, earth, with
heart fingers:
you come and you come,
dwell, we shall dwell, something

—a breath? a name?—

goes about over orphaned ground,
dancerish, cloddish,
the angel's
wing, heavy with what's invisible, on
the foot rubbed sore, trimmed top-
heavy with
the black hail that
fell there too, in Vitebsk,
   (*SP,* 197)

Of particular interest in the context of Celan's critique of the effacement of Jewish particularity is the expression "Volk-vom-Gewölk" [cloud crowd]. It recalls the apostrophe, in Bobrowski's "Pruzzische Elegie," of the Old Prussians as "Volk / der schwelenden Haine, / der brennenden Hütten, zerstampfter / Saaten, geröteter Ströme—/ Volk, / geopfert dem sengenden / Blitzschlag; dein Schreien verhängt vom / Flammengewölke—"[35] [People / of the smoldering groves, / of the burning huts, of crushed / crops, of reddened streams— / people, / sacrificed to the scorching / stroke of lightning; your screaming, veiled by / clouds of flames—]. Bobrowski's poem "Die Heimat des Malers Chagall" [The Homeland of the Painter Chagall] similarly ends on an apocalyptic vision that recalls both the destruction of Vitebsk in World War II and the hope for a future messianic redemption. This amalgamation of different kinds of destruction in the image of fiery clouds exemplifies the identification of perpetrators and victims Celan indicted. He also criticized the reduction of Jewishness to a set of positive attributes that, precisely because they were so readily identifiable, could be either ignored or assimilated. His own contraction of Bobrowski's words into "Volk-vom-Gewölk," then, restores a formless, uncanny, unsettling Jewish *Gestalt*. The expression has multiple associations with Jews and Judaism, emphasizing their nomadic character, which contrasts with Old Prussians' rootedness in a native soil. "Volk-vom-Gewölk" simultaneously evokes the cloud column that led the people of Israel during their Exodus, the epithet *Luftmenschen* for poor Eastern European Jews, and the corpses of the death camp victims whose smoke vanished into the sky. On a formal level, "Volk-vom-Gewölk" counteracts the hierarchical tendency of Bobrowski's genitive constructions in "Pruzzische Elegie," which both ground the Old Prussian *Volk* in a landscape and reduce the landscape to a series of grammatical attributes: "Volk / der schwarzen Wälder, / schwer andringender Flüsse, / kahler Haffe, des Meers!"[36] [People / of black forests, / of rushing rivers, / of bleak haffs, of the sea!]. In contrast, Celan's paratactic and paranomastic construction entwines the Jewish people and the clouds in a way that precludes the reduction of either to a set of generic markers. The hyphenated expression "Menschen-und-Juden" [humans-and-Jews] similarly demarcates the transition from the universal to the particular without subsuming one to the other.

CHAPTER 4

The logic of juxtaposition also informs Celan's invocations of Jewish mysticism in the second half of the poem. This part describes a process of ingathering that culminates in the Hebrew word *beit* [house] and two lights on a table, signaling, perhaps, the advent of Sabbath, the day when the return to the mystical East is said to take place: "Beth,— das ist / das Haus, wo der Tisch steht mit // dem Licht und dem Licht" [Beit,—this is / the house where the table stands with // the light and the light]. The dwelling that has been made possible once more, one of the leitmotifs of the poem, may also refer to a proper burial, particularly since the Hebrew expressions for cemetery are *beit olam* [house of eternity] or *beit chayim* [house for life]. However, despite the promise in these last lines that the burial will be performed and the earth made inhabitable again, destruction continues to haunt the poem and fragment its language. The incompleteness of ingathering manifests itself in structural principles that split up phrases. The initially announced ingathering, for instance, is immediately dispersed again by a series of enjambments and hyphenations that splinter the object of the ingathering. The serial arrangement of these designations creates a sense of difference in the same: "den Wander- / Osten, die / Schwebenden, die / Menschen-und-Juden, / das Volk-vom-Gewölk" [the wander- / East, the / hovering ones, the / humans-and-Jews, / the cloud crowd]. In the last expression, the replacement of "Luft" by "Gewölk" produces an assonance that, while unifying the hyphenated word, also emphasizes its irreducible doubleness. Interpolation produces a similar splitting effect: "geht, geht umher, / sucht, / sucht unten, / sucht droben, fern, sucht / mit dem Auge" [goes, goes around, / searches, / searches below, / searches above, far, searches / with the eye]. The poem's continuous elaboration and commentary through the repetition and variation of phrases do not come to a standstill but rather culminate in the last line of the poem, in which the identity of the two juxtaposed lights foregrounds the very structure of juxtaposition or duality: "mit dem Licht und dem Licht" [with the light and the light]. To be sure, this line can be unpacked via recourse to extratextual knowledge, for instance, of the two Sabbath candles or the kabbalistic distinction between the primordial light, or ether, and the light that emanated from it.[37] Yet even if such references are divined by the initiated reader, it is crucial that they do not find expression in language. Whereas the difference in "Menschen-und-Juden" [humans-

and-Jews] materializes in different words, the difference between the first and the second light eludes any form of linguistic registration.

The dense set of images and allusions in the last stanzas shows that for Celan, Jewish mysticism itself becomes affected by trauma rather than furnishes a means of recuperation. *Beit* is also the second letter of the Hebrew alphabet, which traditionally signifies duality and is associated with the kabbalistic doctrine of creational dualism.[38] A few lines earlier, the poem describes a mystical contemplation of letters that parallels the unfolding of the alphabet by which, according to the Kabbalah, the world was created: "schreitet / die Buchstaben ab und der Buchstaben sterblich- / unsterbliche Seele, / geht zu Aleph und Jud und geht weiter" ["paces off / the letters and the letters' mortal- / immortal soul, / goes to Aleph and Yud and goes farther"].[39] Interspersed among these kabbalistic images is, once more, an image of destruction and subsequent return of the dead: "baut ihn, den Davidsschild, läßt ihn / aufflammen, einmal // läßt ihn erlöschen—da steht er, / unsichtbar" [builds it, the Star of David, lets it / flare up, once // lets it die down—it stands there / invisible].[40] Read upon the backdrop of the simultaneously evoked creational drama, we can say that the invisible presence of the destroyed Eastern European Jewish world inscribes a fissure into creation. This reinterpretation of Jewish mysticism is more than a comment on the untenability of religious belief after Auschwitz. Celan's refusal to reference this Jewish tradition in a way that can be readily identified and absorbed is an ethical and political gesture as well. In what follows, I will further elaborate on textual strategies that aid this gesture, including cryptic intertextual allusions and a peculiar use of place names.

No Sense of an Ending

Intertextuality in Celan is best understood as a conscious and signaled reference to other texts, however cryptic, rather than as a property of texts per se, that is, the irreducible openness, fragmentation, and non-originality highlighted by poststructural criticism.[41] Conceived in this way, intertextual strategies can effect the destabilization and dissemination of meaning elaborated by poststructuralist readings, but they are also ways of relating, both constructively and deconstructively, to a larger cultural space. As we have seen in "Eine Gauner- und Ganovenweise," Celan's incorporation of other texts into his own poem fragments both the quotations and the cultural heritage from which they are derived, while working to construct a space in which resistance can be conceived; the gallows humor of the texts to which the poem refers is one source of such resistance.

"Und mit dem Buch aus Tarussa" (*Nr*, 139–43) ["And with the Book from Tarussa"[42]] similarly demarcates its emergence from and continuous dialogue with other texts, while encrypting these reference texts more strongly than "Eine Gauner- und Ganovenweise." The poem's title evokes a collection of works by Russian writers published in 1961, *Tarusskie stranitsy* [Pages from Tarussa], an important document against Moscow censorship. Its epigraph, a quote in Cyrillic letters from a poem by the Russian poet Marina Tsvetaeva, links poets and Jews while highlighting the social ostracism of both: "Vse poety zhidy" [All poets are Yids].[43] This epigraph indicates the foreign code as foreign; it signals the presence of another text through the Latin-lettered name of the author while rendering the text itself illegible for most of its German-speaking readers. Similarly, the title suggests through the use of a definite article and a place name that a particular book is being referred to while withholding any further information that would give the reader a hint regarding the book's content and meaning. The impression of a missing reference text is enhanced by the fact that the title begins with a connective "und" [and], as if continuing a previous text, and that each of the poem's eleven stanzas, except for the last, begins with a "von," the precise reference of which remains unclear. It can be read as either "of" or "about," in which case it would relate to a missing locution like "(I will tell you) about," a reading that is also suggested by the poem's original title "September Bericht" (*Nr*, 139) [September Report].

Like several of the long elegiac poems in the concluding section of the collection *Die Niemandsrose*, "Und mit dem Buch aus Tarussa" evokes the idea of a journey, or rather of several journeys from East to West, while traversing an uncanny landscape of death. The poem is structured around the opposition of Tarussa and Paris, of the Oka (the Russian river at which Tarussa is located) and the Seine, evoking Marina Tsvetaeva's as well as Celan's own exile in Paris. Other East-West passages in the poem are Jacob's pilgrimage to the West, the blind Orion's journey to the East, and the vacation trip Celan's friend Erich Einhorn planned to undertake to Colchis. The "von" that introduces each stanza therefore may also be read as a spatial preposition, one that answers to the question "from where?" and which indicates a departure, or rather a series of departures. The destination of these movements could be "Kolchis," the final word of the poem and the most conspicuous deviation from its principal structure. The last stanzas read:

> Von einem Brief, von ihm.
> Vom Ein-Brief, vom Ost-Brief. Vom harten,
> winzigen Worthaufen, vom
> unbewaffneten Auge, das er
> den drei
> Gürtelsternen Orions—Jakobs-
> stab, du,
> abermals kommst du gegangen!—
> zuführt auf der
> Himmelskarte, die sich ihm aufschlug.
>
> Vom Tisch, wo das geschah.
>
> Von einem Wort, aus dem Haufen,
> an dem er, der Tisch,
> zur Ruderbank wurde, vom Oka-Fluß her
> und den Wassern.
>
> Vom Nebenwort, das
> ein Ruderknecht nachknirscht, ins Spätsommerohr
> seiner hell-
> hörigen Dolle:
>
> Kolchis.
>   (*Nr*, 141–43)
>
> Of a letter, of it.
> Of the one-letter, of the East-letter. Of the hard,
> tiny word-heap, of the
> unarmed eye that it
> leads to
> the three
> belt-stars of Orion—Jacob's

CHAPTER 4

staff, you,
once again you come walking!—
on the
celestial chart that opened for it.

Of the table where this happened.

Of a word, from the heap
on which it, the table
became a galley-seat, from the Oka River
and the waters.

Of the other word that
a galley-slave gnash-echoes, into the late-summer ear
of his keen-
eared tholepin:

Colchis.
   (SG, 211)

Situated at the Eastern periphery of the world of antiquity and home to the ancient, nomadic people of the Scythians, Colchis is also close to the area where Ovid lived in exile, vexed by his absence from Rome—and the place of Ovid's exile, Ponto, might be encoded in the "Pont Mirabeau" of the seventh stanza. The associations of the mythological Colchis are mostly positive. It is best known from the myth of the Argonauts who went to Colchis in a rowboat to recover the Golden Fleece. Colchis is also the place where Orion, after having been blinded by Oinopion, went to regain his eyesight from Helios, who is said to dwell there. The rise of the Orion constellation on the Eastern horizon at the end of September or beginning of October is mythologically understood as the return of the healed Orion from Colchis, a meaning hinted at in "Und mit dem Buch aus Tarussa." In Celan's poem, the name Colchis indicates the utopian quest of reading as it transforms the table, the site where the sky map and letter are being read, into a rowboat. The utopian impetus, however, is undermined by the poem's qualification of Colchis as a "Nebenwort," a condensation of "Nebenbedeutung" [secondary meaning] and "Beiwort" [adjective] that suggests that the transposition of the place name into another grammatical category produces a second meaning. And indeed, the Latin adjective derived from Colchis, "colchicum," designates a flower, the *Herbstzeitlose,* or meadow saffron, which sometimes symbolizes eschatological hopes but is also known for its treacherous poisonous effect.[44] The latter connotation is evoked in Apollinaire's poem "Les Colchiques," which Celan translated into German. In other words, rather than defining a utopian point of ingathering, the name Colchis is itself split up into contrasting meanings in different languages. In fact, the word is presented in the poem as the product of a curiously mechanic and belated speech act: "Nebenwort, das / ein Ruderknecht nachknirscht" [other word that / a galley-slave gnash-echoes]. The verb *knirschen* signalizes the disarticulation of human language into the sound of a machine or of grinding teeth, a sign of shame or suppressed anger. Furthermore, the combination with the prefix "nach" endows the verb with the connotations of imitation (as in *nachsprechen*) and deferment, inserting a gap between destruction and redemption that makes it doubtful whether the latter can ever redeem this landscape of death.[45]

The dismantling of the utopian cipher Colchis does not invalidate the poem's quest for solidarity and resistance but suggests that the political possibility of poetry for Celan lies in the creation of momentary intertextual and intersubjective alliances rather than in the reestablishment of a utopian telos that has lost its credit. Celan's tendency to end his elegies on an ambiguous, if not entirely hopeless, note expresses his refusal to restore a redemptive meaning to the East. If elegies traditionally arrive, by means of troping and substitution, at "a consoling sign that carries in itself the reminder of the loss on which it has been founded,"[46]—a sign that accommodates unfulfilled desire while directing it to new objects—Celan's elegies are stuck with a loss that thwarts any redemptive vision; they exhibit an inability or unwillingness to fashion substitutes for a destroyed world. Read against the backdrop previously sketched out, the West German public's instrumentalization of conciliatory voices of self-identified Jewish writers, Celan's insistence on the unfinished, perhaps unfinishable, task of mourning is a political gesture that works against the public endorsement of his texts as if they could comprise alibis.

"Es ist alles anders" (*Nr,* 135–37) ["It's All Different" (*SP,* 205–9)], a

CHAPTER 4

poem replete with personal reminiscences as well as names of Eastern European towns, landscapes, and rivers, lends further substance to the idea of a resistance arising from incomplete mourning. At first sight, this poem seems more hopeful than some other poems of *Die Niemandsrose*, which refer more openly to unredeemable violence, death, and destruction in Eastern Europe. Yet the Hades motif and the reference to Jewish memorial practices indicate that this poem, too, wrestles with the difficulties of memory and mourning. Combining the work of mourning with elliptical evocations of messianic thought, the poem dwells in the transitional space of a mourning ritual while gesturing, in its first line, toward the "otherland" of Sergei Esenin's poem "Ioniia."[47] Esenin's poem, which Celan translated into German, rejects Christian yearning for transcendence and calls for the realization of utopian ideals on earth, a redirection of energies that also occurs in "Es ist alles anders," where it ushers in a mnemonic process that locates resources of resistance in the memory of the past.

The first stanzas of "Es ist alles anders" superimpose images of an—imagined—journey to Eastern Europe with invocations of the process of translation and the resurrection of the dead. The image of a silver coin melting on the tongue invokes the custom of placing an obolos into the mouth of the dead to pay for the ferry trip across the Styx on their way to Hades, suggesting that the journey to the East leads indeed to the land of the (unburied) dead. Central to these stanzas is an encounter with the "Name Ossip," a reference to Osip Mandel'shtam, whose poetry Celan had been translating in the years preceding *Die Niemandsrose* and to whose memory the book is dedicated. As Leonard Olschner has discovered, Celan's depiction of this encounter as an exchange of arms is taken from a folk rhyme that children recite while clapping their hands in the form of scissors.[48] If we read the exchange of body parts as a concretization of the encounter taking place in translation, translation acquires a new meaning, assuming in fact, the literal meaning of the German word *übersetzen*. This crossing over the Styx, like Orpheus's singing, has the power to recover the dead from Hades, or more precisely, to suspend for a little while their final absorption into it. The theme of revival is also indicated by the birch— a symbol of spring in Russia—that awaits the traveler in the East, and continued in the following stanzas by images of organic growth and reawakening sexuality.

Like Günter Anders, Celan uses the Hades motif to convey the sense of gloom that arises from a destruction so absolute that it annihilates memory itself. The poem invokes the Jewish custom of putting a stone on a grave—"aufs Grab, auf die Gräber, ins Leben" [on the grave, on the graves, into life]. The connection established here between grave and life, which once again harks back to the Hebrew term *beit chayim* for cemetery, suggests that the poem indeed searches for a proper burial rather than a revival of the dead. This possibility of memory and mourning depends on the disruption of linear time, which occurs in the poem as the sounding of a *shofar* (a ram's horn) signals the advent of messianic time: "ein Widderhorn hebt dich /—*Tekiah!*—/ wie ein Posaunenschall über die Nächte hinweg in den Tag, die Auguren / zerfleischen einander, der Mensch / hat seinen Frieden, der Gott / hat den seinen" [a ram's horn lifts you / —*Tekiah!*— / like a trumpet blast out over nights into day, the augurs / tear each other apart, man / has his peace, God / has his]. The *shofar* traditionally announces the beginning of the Jewish New Year (Rosh Ha-Shanah), but the sound also serves as a reminder of the future day of resurrection and return of Israel's scattered remnants to the Holy Land. The fact that the augurs, Roman priests who sought to divine the will of the gods from the flight of birds and other signs of nature, destroy each other indicates that messianic thought, with its idea of unpredictable redemption, replaces the pagan belief in predetermination. The thrust of the poem, however, is to recover the unfulfilled possibilities of the past and to realize in the here and now the change that messianism defers into to an unfathomable future:

> wie heißt es, dein Land
> hinterm Berg, hinterm Jahr?
> Ich weiß, wie es heißt.
> Wie das Wintermärchen, so heißt es,
> es heißt wie das Sommermärchen,
> das Dreijahreland deiner Mutter, das war es,
> das ists,
> es wandert überallhin, wie die Sprache,
> wirf sie weg, wirf sie weg,
> dann hast du sie wieder, wie ihn,
> den Kieselstein aus
> der Mährischen Senke,
> den dein Gedanke nach Prag trug,

aufs Grab, auf die Gräber, ins Leben,

längst
ist er fort, wie die Briefe, wie alle
Laternen, wieder
mußt du ihn suchen, da ist er,
klein ist er, weiß,
um die Ecke, da liegt er,
bei Normandie-Njemen—in Böhmen,
da, da, da,
hinterm Haus, vor dem Haus,
weiß ist er, weiß, er sagt:
Heute—es gilt.
Weiß ist er, weiß, ein Wasser-
strahl findet hindurch, ein Herzstrahl,
ein Fluß,
du kennst seinen Namen, die Ufer
hängen voll Tag, wie der Name,
du tastest ihn ab, mit der Hand:
Alba.
  (*Nr*, 137)

what is it called, your land
behind the mountain, behind the year?
I know what it's called.
Like the winter's tale it's called,
it's called like the summer's tale,
your mother's three-year-land, that was it,
that is it,
it wanders everywhere, like language,
throw it away, throw it away,
then you'll have it again, like
that pebble from
the Moravian Basin
your thought carried to Prague,
on the grave, on the graves, into life,

it's
long gone, like the letters, like all the

> lanterns, you must
> seek it again, there it is,
> it is small, white,
> round the corner, it lies there
> at Normandy-Niemen—in Bohemia,
> there, there, there
> behind the house, in front of the house,
> white it is, white, it says:
> Today's the day.
> White it is, white, a water-
> stream courses on through, a heartstream,
> a river,
> you know its name, the banks
> hang heavy with day, like this name,
> you run your hand over it:
> Alba.
> (*SP*, 207–9)

The mnemonic movement in these concluding stanzas works, in a disjunctive rhythm, to weave a net of connections between places and people of the past. The simile "wie das Wintermärchen" [like the winter's tale] has dual connotations. Shakespeare's *A Winter's Tale* is partially set in Bohemia, the refuge to which Celan's mother fled during World War I. Celan believed the three years she spent there to be crucial for his own existence.[49] The line also calls to mind the Germany satirized in Heine's *Deutschland: Ein Wintermärchen* [*Germany: A Winter's Tale*], thus establishing a connection between Bohemia and Germany. A few lines below, contemplation carries a stone from Moravia to Prague—from the grave of Celan's grandmother to that of Rabbi Löw. Normandy-Niemen, furthermore, is another name for the Normandy Squadron, the only French fighter squadron to serve with the Soviet Army Air Force during World War II, operating in the region around the river Niemen. Celan had seen a documentary on the squadron while vacationing in Normandy in August 1962. The poem's ingathering of names, places, and meanings culminates in the name Alba, which appears in the end like an epiphany in the stone lost and found again. Alba is the Latin name of the river Elbe, which runs through Central Europe. The same Latin word denotes the "morning dawn" associated with the East and the color "white," conflating the stone and the winter's snow and thus the Germany and Bohemia of the winter's tale. Alba is also the short form of the former name of an Italian town today called Celano and is associated with the French revolution.[50] Finally, the Elbe, or more precisely, Turgau on the Elbe, is the site where the Allies met on April 25, 1945, and thus an emblem of the defeat of fascism.

However, like the other elegies, "Es ist alles anders" does not establish Alba as a nostalgic-utopian destination but rather locates a hesitation and self-reflection in the midst of the promise of recuperation. Alba, or Aubade, is also the name of a poetic genre that depicts two lovers at dawn realizing that the night of love is over and their separation impending; the word "Alba" frequently appears in these poems as the call of a night guard who warns the—usually illicit—lovers of the approaching dawn. If we hear this connotation of the word in "Es ist alles anders," the concluding "Alba" functions similarly, a wake-up call that interrupts the dream of nostalgia and reminds the reader that recollection is a transitory, perhaps a futile, undertaking. The daybreak that is associated with the East thus acquires a double meaning, signifying both a hope and a warning, or perhaps, a beginning that remains fraught with the burden of the past. The fact that darkness itself is not unambiguously negative in this poem but initially appears as the means of survival—"die kleinen Geheimnisse sind noch bei sich, / sie werfen noch Schatten, davon / lebst du, leb ich, leben wir" [the little secrets are still intact / they still cast shadows—on this / you live, I live, we live]—also casts doubt on the unambiguously positive meaning of the daylight signified by Alba.

The sense of arrival and closure in the poem is further undermined by the poem's peculiar enactment of a famous mourning ritual, namely that of the little boy whom Freud observed tossing away and retrieving his toys in an effort to master his grief over the absence of his mother. The child accompanied his movements with the sounds of "o" and "a," which Freud identified as the German words *fort* [gone] and *da* [there], articulations of loss and retrieval. Performing similar gestures with Bohemia, the language, and the stone, the speaker in "Es ist alles anders" even approximates the little boy's language as he stammers the particles "fort . . . da, da, da" [gone . . . there, there, there]. The retrieval of Alba is just another instance in this ritual, and there is no indication that this moment moves us out of the transitional space of mourning or ends the poem's hovering between a traumatic past and an indeterminate future.

The emphatic gesture of retrieval does not undo the logic of displacement that shapes the poem as a whole. The recovery of the stone is preceded by a question for the name of a place of origin: "wie heißt es, dein Land / hinterm Berg, hinterm Jahr?" [what is it called, your land / behind the mountain, behind the year?]. This question is never answered but rather displaced in a series of similes first to literary encodings of Bohemia and Germany, then to language, and finally to the memorial stone, all of which are subject to the dynamic of loss and recuperation. In the first lines of the quoted stanzas, the ostentatious, fourfold repetition of "heißt" and its phonetic assonance to "weiß"—"Ich weiß, wie es heißt" [I know what it's called]—exalts the gesture of naming at the expense of the the name itself. The name Alba, which means "weiß" [white] in German and assonates with the exclamation of retrieval—"da" [there]—continues this gesture of retrieval, which constantly fails to recover that which has been lost. Another assonance in the last stanza, which relates the poem's central motif of return and retrieval to the figure of the simile that dominates its structure—"wieder . . . wie der Name" [again . . . like this name]—further enhances the impression of an endless chain of replacements in which whatever is being retrieved is just another substitute, and frequently one of ambiguous character.

This shift from the idea of a telos to a sense of interconnectedness suggests that the poem does not so much recuperate the messianic idea after Auschwitz, as has been claimed; rather it opens up a space for resistance and solidarity in the here and now. One indication of this political thrust is the poem's reference, in the last stanza, to the French fighter squadron that supported the Soviets during the Second World War. Deploying the name of the squadron as if it were a place name— "bei Normandie-Njemen" [at Normandy-Niemen]—the poem turns the flying route of the squadron into a physical connection, like a road between northern France and Russia. Sites of political struggle in Celan, such as Tarussa, St. Petersburg, and Huesca, carry more obvious political meaning, but mythic or literary places names also become historicized and politicized as they enter into the peculiar constellations of public and private meanings in his poems. The interlinking of places in the name Normandy-Niemen, furthermore, epitomizes the deployment of place names in *Die Niemandsrose* to disclose or create a historical affinity between distant places. In the poem "Nachmittag mit

CHAPTER 4

Zirkus und Zitadelle" (*Nr,* 93) ["Afternoon with Circus and Citadel" (*SP,* 183)], the place name "Brest" establishes a connection between France and Russia. A Brest exists in both France and Russia, and both cities have important fortifications, a feature on which the poem expands in its evocation of a visionary encounter between the poem's speaker and Mandel'shtam. Through his peculiar use of place names, Celan allows us to glimpse into this landscape of the past struggles and alliances whose very evocation rescinds the absoluteness of destruction.

Reading Place Names in Celan

In this concluding section, I would like to address the ways in which the connective function of place names extends to Celan's readers, who are being addressed, by means of encrypted historical referentiality, as *Spurensucher* and potential allies in the poet's struggle. Place names, in fact, crystallize a problem of poetic reference in Celan, the question of what role extratextual realia play in a work of poetry that belongs among the most hermetic of the twentieth century. Peter Szondi, Celan's friend and author of several important studies of his poetry, occupies one end of the spectrum of answers. Having witnessed everything Celan experienced in Berlin on the day he composed "Eden," Szondi argues that the poem incorporates the contingent objects and events of empirical reality, yet translates these into phonetic and semantic equivalencies that allow the careful reader to grasp the poem's meaning without knowing its original context.[51] In contrast to Szondi's notion of textual immanence, other critics have emphasized the heuristic nature of Celan's poetry, its dependence upon the reader's willingness and ability to engage in extratextual labor, such as the acquisition of knowledge from remote scientific fields, to ferret out the cryptic meanings of his words. Joel Golb, for instance, reads his poems as allegorical narratives that unfold the diachronic depth dimension of words, a process Golb reconstructs primarily by consulting the Grimm dictionary.[52] However, while Celan himself certainly relied on dictionaries from various disciplines to create his extraordinarily rich semantic universe, readings like that of Golb circumvent a structural problem of his vocabulary: what if a word has a meaning that is nowhere recorded except in the place the word signifies, that is, if the reader is required to be in that very place in order to decipher the word? Such seems to be the case in a striking example of a place name in the poem "Kermorvan":

KERMORVAN
Du Tausendgüldenkraut-Sternchen,
du Erle, du Buche, du Farn:
mit euch Nahen geh ich ins Ferne,—
Wir gehen dir, Heimat, ins Garn.

Schwarz hängt die Kirschlorbeertraube
beim bärtigen Palmenschaft.
Ich liebe, ich hoffe, ich glaube,—
die kleine Steindattel klafft.

Ein Spruch spricht—zu wem? Zu sich selber:
Servir Dieu est régner,—ich kann
ihn lesen, ich kann, es wird heller,
fort aus Kannitverstan.
  (*Nr*, 97, emphasis by Celan)

KERMORVAN
You tiny centaury star,
you alder, beech and fern:
with you near ones I make for afar,—
to our homeland, snared, we return.

By the bearded palm tree's trunk
black hangs the laurel-seed grape.
I love, I hope, I have faith,—
the little date shell's agape.

A sentence speaks—to whom? To itself:
Servir Dieu est régner,—I can
read it, I can, it grows brighter,
away from "kannitverstan."
  (*PPC*, 181, emphasis by Celan, trans. altered)

The title of this poem has created some confusion among scholars. After conducting some research on the possible meaning of Kermorvan, Matthias Loewen went to Brittany in Northern France and found a manor of that name in a region where Celan spent some vacations with his family during the early 1960s.[53] Loewen also discovered that this manor during World War II served as a transitional camp for

CHAPTER 4

presumably Jewish prisoners who were sent from there to Auschwitz and Treblinka and that the manor's wall still features some German-language inscriptions with a distinct Eastern European ring. He argues that the shock Celan must have felt while viewing these inscriptions that were possibly composed by his former countrymen is encoded in the first stanza's "Wir gehen dir, Heimat, ins Garn" [to our homeland, snared, we return]. Since the publication of Loewen's findings, however, his reading has been contested: there is much evidence that "Kermorvan" refers, rather than to the aforementioned manor, to the Château de Kermorvan in Brittany.[54] Celan and his family had rented a vacation apartment in one of the adjoining buildings of the castle in 1961. In that year, a cherry laurel and a palm were growing next to each other in the garden of the castle, and the maxim mentioned in the last stanza—"*Servir Dieu est régner*"—is that of the noble family of Kermorvan, which is inscribed in the coat of arms above the castle's door. The last word of the poem refers to the title of an anecdote from Johann Peter Hebel's *Schatzkästlein* featuring a foreigner in Amsterdam who asks passers-by about a beautiful mansion, a huge ship, and a funeral, apparently ignorant of the fact that they do not understand his language.[55] Each time he receives the answer "Kannitverstan," which means in Dutch "I cannot understand." Mistaking this for an answer to his questions, the traveler draws his own conclusions about the fragility of the human condition.

It is possible to read Celan's poem as a movement from darkness to light, from a sense of betrayal to regained faith. This movement would culminate in the demise of a form of communication in which responses reflect only one's own ignorance, in which everyone speaks, like the foreigner in Hebel's anecdote and the "Spruch" [sentence] in the poem, only to himself. However, this reading misses some important features of the poem and its contexts. Hebel's story is usually read as an illustration of how the ignorance of another language and the ensuing misunderstandings may nevertheless lead to truthful insights. Celan himself famously defended, in his "Meridian" speech, the obscurity of contemporary poetry as the very medium in which an encounter with others may take place. And in the poem itself the supposed passage from darkness to light remains undermined by the word Kermorvan, whose privileged position in the title inevitably makes the reader ponder its meaning. For most readers, the word will sound like a place name but remain enigmatic, and even for those who know the locality, the shift from a sense of betrayal to religiously inspired submissiveness—"*Servir Dieu est régner*"—will seem abrupt. The last stanza's description of an epiphany-like act of reading does not inspire a similar insight in its readers; the maxim inscribed in the castle of Kermorvan remains inaccessible for those who are not in that place. The rhyming and alliterating of Kermorvan—if pronounced in German or Breton rather than French—and "Kannitverstan" emphasize the toponymic character of Kermorvan as well as its incomprehensibility.

Through this persistent invocation of an enigmatic place name, Celan calls for precisely the kind of search undertaken by Loewen, even if that particular search ended up in yet another Kermorvan. If Szondi is right that Celan transforms empirical reality into linguistic structure, part of that structure is an incompleteness that accounts for the peculiar illocutionary force of Celan's poetry. Place names, which signal the impossibility of recovering a word's meaning through either contemplative reading or encyclopedic knowledge, epitomize this illocutionary force, the call upon readers to leave their place and search for meaning in other places. As Celan instructs his readers in his famous poem "Engführung" ["Stretto"], whose beginning deports the reader into an unnameable and unknowable terrain: "VERBRACHT ins / Gelände / mit der untrüglichen Spur: // Gras, auseinandergeschrieben. Die Steine, weiß, / mit den Schatten der Halme: / Lies nicht mehr—schau! / Schau nicht mehr—geh!"[56] [TAKEN OFF into / the terrain / with the unmistakable trace: // Grass, written asunder. The stones, white / with the grassblades' shadows: / Read no more—look! / Look no more—go! (*SP*, 119).]

Writing, then, becomes the accidental and incalculable enterprise captured by Celan in Mandel'shtam's metaphor of "a message in a bottle" (*SP*, 396): the writer of a poem does not know when, where, and by whom its words will be received. Such a mode of writing expresses and contains the experience of randomness and arbitrariness, which is at the core of the survivor guilt from which Celan suffered throughout his postwar life, the tormenting question of why he, among all others, had survived. At the same time it reflects the radical dispersion of memory in a world in which one may unexpectedly stumble over historical sites that, like the Kermorvan discovered by Loewen, are prone to be forgotten by official historiography. The significance Celan accords to the location of memory can be understood as a response to the "missing grave syndrome," that is, the need to first establish special sites in

CHAPTER 4

order to commemorate the dead of the Holocaust. Yet Celan's poems rarely create or refer to full-fleshed sites of memory as Pierre Nora defines them but rather perpetuate a sense of disorientation in their incessant return to places that never fully become available for the imagination. In so doing they mime the structure of traumatic memory. It has been observed that traumatic memories tend to be attached to specific places, a tendency indicated in the very use of the place name "Auschwitz" as a metonym for the mass killings of the Holocaust. In his collection and analysis of testimonies by Holocaust survivors, Lawrence Langer cites Charlotte Delbo as an example of the survivor's inability to transcend the place of her suffering: "The crushing reality of the place, the pain, the exhaustion, the cold, that would later congeal into the hardened skin of memory, prevented her and her companions from fantasizing that they were someone or somewhere else."[57] Langer uses the term "deep memory" to categorize the survivor's way of relating to the camp experience either through noncomprehension or through reenactment, bereft of the ability mentally to transform the past by means of selection, abstraction, or narration.

Jacques Derrida's influential essay "Shibboleth: For Paul Celan" gives hints of how the contingency and dispersion of memory is transmitted to readers. In this essay, Derrida identifies as the structural principle of Celan's poetry the "date," which epitomizes the structure of language itself. Like a date that marks the singularity of an event while mapping it onto the grid of the calendar, each linguistic sign is unique and yet has to efface its own uniqueness in order to become legible. The internal division of language that derives from its communicative function is rendered by the French *partager*, with its double meaning of "to divide" and "to participate." The date is "a cut or incision which the poem bears on its body like a memory, like, at times, several memories in one, the mark of a provenance, of a place and of a time. To speak of an incision or cut is to say that the poem is entered into, that it begins in the wounding of its date."[58] Derrida further draws an analogy between the date and the shibboleth, the password that is invoked several times in Celan's poetry. Referring to the biblical story through which the word "shibboleth" first acquired the meaning of a password, Derrida characterizes the shibboleth as an intrinsically political practice that establishes alliances and enacts exclusions. After their victory over the Ephraimites, the people of Jephthah required everyone at the fords of the Jordan to say "shibboleth," thus forcing the Ephraimites, who were unable to produce the "sh"-sound, to give themselves away. It is decisive here that the outcome of the test does not depend on a person's knowledge of meaning but on his correct pronunciation of a word. A shibboleth is a performative that involves the body, since the speaker has to form his mouth and tongue in a way that will produce the correct pronunciation. The fact that certain people are unable to produce the required sound, regardless of their effort, indicates the analogy between regional dialects and circumcision: in both cases, cultural practices create a physical, permanent mark of difference.

In what looks first like a conceptual slippage, Derrida rethinks the military meaning of the shibboleth. Like the circumcision of words, which affects "first of all the body of the name which finds itself recalled by the wound to its condition as a word, then as carnal mark, written, spaced, and inscribed in a network of other marks, at once both endowed with and deprived of singularity,"[59] a shibboleth is a wound that marks the forced inscription of enunciating subjects—including those belonging to the victorious party—into a social order or cultural community. Celan's deployment of military terminology is marked by a similar doubleness and a similar slippage between self-assertion and vulnerability. The French title of the poem "La Contrescarpe" (*Nr,* 129–31; *GS,* 15–16), for instance, refers to a counter scarp, or fortress wall on a battlefield. The definite article in the title suggests a more specific reference, probably to the Place de la Contrescarpe, a square Celan frequented during his first stay in Paris during the Second World War.[60] The poem includes a reminiscence of Celan's journey from Czernowitz to Paris in November 1938, which led him through Berlin shortly after the so-called *Kristallnacht,* the pogrom during which thousands of synagogues and shops and houses of Jews were destroyed. This reminiscence is preceded by the images of a dove and a ship, the latter of which may refer to Paris, whose coat of arms features a ship, or to Noah's ark, the home of the biblical *Notgemeinschaft* that dispersed after a dove had swerved out and returned with a grass blade, a sign that the deluge had ended. Both images address the communal bonds established in exile:

> Scherte die Brieftaube aus, war ihr Ring
> zu entziffern? (All das
> Gewölk um sie her—es war lesbar.) Litt es
> der Schwarm? Und verstand,
> und flog wie sie fortblieb?

CHAPTER 4

Dachschiefer Helling,—auf Tauben-
kiel gelegt ist, was schwimmt. Durch die Schotten
blutet die Botschaft, Verjährtes
geht jung über Bord:

> Über Krakau
> bist du gekommen, am Anhalter
> Bahnhof
> floß deinen Blicken ein Rauch zu,
> der war schon von morgen. Unter
> Paulownien sahst du die Messer stehn, wieder,
> scharf von Entfernung. Es wurde
> getanzt. (Quatorze
> juillets. Et plus de neuf autres.)
>   (*Nr*, 131)

Did the dove go astray, could her ankle-band
be deciphered? (All the
clouding around her—it was legible.) Did the
flock countenance it? Did they understand,
and fly, when she did not return?

Roof-pitched slipway—that which floats
is laid on dove-keel. The message bleeds
through the bulkheads,
the no longer prosecutable
goes overboard, young again:

> Upon arrival in Berlin,
> via Krakow,
> you were met at the station by a plume of smoke,
> tomorrow's smoke already. Under
> the Paulownia trees
> you saw the knives erect, again,
> sharpened by distance. There was
> dancing. (Quatorze
> juillets. Et plus de neuf autres.)
>   (*GS*, 15–16, trans. altered)

As for the referential matter in the indented stanza, we know that the train that brought Celan from Czernowitz to Paris indeed stopped at the Anhalter Bahnhof in Berlin. The Place de la Contrescarpe is a square with many cafés and bars, and it is quite possible that on the fourteenth of July, the national holiday that commemorates the French Revolution, a public dance, or *bal populaire,* took place there. The fact that the speaker mentions the Paulownia tree, whose name contains Celan's own first name and, in its Slavic ending, the idea of the East, supports this reading. Going to Paris turns out to be a kind of homecoming; the violence witnessed in Berlin is counterbalanced with an image of people gathering to commemorate an act of political resistance. And this resistance is what the poem accomplishes as well. The word "Verjährtes" [the no longer prosecutable] hints at the contemporary debates in West Germany about the juridical limitation of the Nazi crimes, yet the complex temporality of this poetic memory disrupts precisely the logic of these debates. Instead of using temporal distance to mitigate the horrors of the past, poetic retrospection reveals only more horrors as it identifies the smoke arising from the burning synagogues with that from the death camp crematoria. The notion of a gradual overcoming of the past is undermined by the repetitive rhythm of traumatic memory: "Verjährtes / geht jung über Bord" [the no longer prosecutable / goes overboard, young again]. The critique of public memory and jurisdiction in West Germany encoded in these lines suggests that the poem becomes what the title word denotes, a counter scarp on a battlefield. Yet the bleeding and the permeability of boundaries, expressed through the image of leaky bulkheads, indicate that the poem calls for a conscious deployment of vulnerability rather than a quasi-military strategy of self-assertion. If the message that flows from this ship opposes the rituals of *Vergangenheitsbewältigung* in West Germany, the juxtaposition of the message in a bottle with the life-threatening situation of going overboard captures the danger to which such speaking exposes itself.

The cryptic references to personal experience dramatize the disjunction between private reminiscence and public commemoration.[61] This structure of reference accounts at least in part for the powerful demand Celan's poetry places on readers, a demand felt by anyone who reads his poems again and again even though, or rather because, they often elude one's comprehension. Resuming the terminology of Pierre

CHAPTER 4

Nora, we may say that Celan's poems bear witness to the radical destruction of *milieux de mémoire* in the Holocaust without reconstituting *lieux de mémoire*. According to Nora, *lieux de mémoire* are self-enclosed and self-referential, yet at the same time endowed with a symbolic excess that allows for multiple meanings and the momentary experience of what the *milieux de mémoire* did on an everyday basis, the fusion of individual remembrance and collective memory. Celan's poems, however, are deictic rather than self-referential, and they dramatize acts of remembrance that incessantly miss their object. I have argued that part of this deictic structure are place names pointing toward a place that, paradoxically, cannot be named. Such deixis has been explained in terms of a general tendency in modern poetry to address readers who are already partially initiated into the experience to which the poem only alludes.[62] Yet this notion does not quite capture Celan's poetry. Rather than presupposing knowledge, Celan exposes the reader's ignorance and forces her to search for places that cannot be located on cognitive or mnemic maps. His place names are what Jean Laplanche terms "enigmatic signifiers," which propel the subject into an unknown world because they exert a force of address that exceeds, or rather precedes, their referential meaning.[63]

Another word for this structure would be shibboleth, which Derrida uses to describe a non-reciprocal form of communication between a speaker and her addressee, or a poem and its reader. The fact that the poem opens itself up to others by effacing its own singularity means that something is irretrievably lost in the act of communication, and yet, as Derrida emphasizes, this self-effacement takes place only in the encounter with another. Returning once more to "Es ist alles anders," we can see how place names may function as shibboleths that address readers in their particularity. Immediately following the name Normandy-Niemen is a place designation, "in Böhmen" [in Bohemia], which, if pronounced in Yiddish as "in Behmen," rhymes with the name of the fighter squadron. In other words, for readers familiar with the French resistance in northern France and the Yiddish pronunciation of Bohemia, the affinity between the refuge of Celan's mother during the First World War and the military unit of the anti-fascist struggle designated by Normandy-Niemen presents itself more strongly; the compound structure becomes a sign of resistance and survival. But ultimately, the capacity to read and pronounce the shibboleth is a product of chance. The cryptic historical reference of place names in Celan indicates that the contingency of place is never entirely translated into the inner form of poetry but pushes the reader outside of the text, into an unpredictable space in which meaning and intersubjectivity can be found either nowhere or, like the stone in "Es ist alles anders," around the next corner, "hinterm Haus / vor dem Haus" [behind the house, in front of the house].

Conclusion:
Toward the Possibility of a Diasporic Community

In my readings I have shown that postwar German Jewish writers experienced their favorable reception in West Germany after 1960 as a return of the historical events of genocide and mass displacement. Yet however traumatic these crises were, bringing back painful memories of exile and expulsion, they did not silence these authors. Rather, the figures of exile and dispersal that proliferate in their literary texts of the time demonstrate how a sense of irredeemable displacement contains the potential for a productivity marked by critical acuteness. One difficulty in analyzing the nexus between trauma and displacement is the temptation to fall back into a hermeneutic of exile that simply assumes a productive force of exile. Cathy Caruth's classic text on trauma theory, *Unclaimed Experience,* for instance, relies on figures of displacement to propagate a view of trauma as both shattering and liberating. Caruth bases her argument to a great extent on Freud's last book, *Moses and Monotheism.* Briefly summarized, this book advances the thesis that Moses was an Egyptian who imposed the monotheistic doctrine first formulated by Pharaoh Amenhotep IV onto the Hebrews, a group of poor immigrants he led out of Egypt. After some time, the Hebrews reacted to the exacting laws of the new religion and the demands for a constant renunciation of instincts with a rebellion, in which Moses was

CONCLUSION

killed. The murder of Moses was a traumatic event for the perpetrators; it was followed by a period of latency lasting several hundred years, after which monotheism and its strict laws returned and were internalized. Because trauma results from a confrontation with death *and* survival, Caruth concludes, it opens up "the possibility of a future."[1]

This understanding of trauma hinges upon an interpretation of the biblical Exodus as departure rather than return: by transforming the Hebrews into the Jews, God's chosen people, Moses did not so much return them to their former homeland but create a new paradigm of human life, a monotheistic religion with a strong ethical bend. Caruth supports this idea by pointing to the prominence of the word *verlassen* [to leave] in *Moses and Monotheism*, to Freud's interpretation in "Beyond the Pleasure Principle" of the *fort-da* game as a game of departure, and to Freud's own exile as another instance of a departure both forced and liberating. Freud drafted *Moses and Monotheism* during the rise of Nazism and the increasing persecution of Jews and completed the book after leaving Austria for England, where he enjoyed the freedom of expression he had missed in the years before. Though all of this is correct, Caruth's emphasis on these kinds of departures is apt to perpetuate a notion of exile as intrinsically productive because it grants individuals a new perspective on their lives. More precisely, Caruth reformulates this notion into the idea that exile propels traumatized subjects into contact with others and thus ensures the transmission of trauma and the beginning of a history always already shared with others. While this idea resonates, for instance, with Nelly Sachs's understanding of the postwar Jewish diaspora as charged with the task of bearing witness to the Holocaust, Caruth provides few hints as to what such a communication might look like. Rather, she relies, as Ruth Leys puts it, on the idea of a "face-to-face encounter between a victim, who enacts or performs his or her traumatic experience, and a witness who listens and is in turn contaminated by the catastrophe."[2]

In contrast to this idea of a direct contact between survivor and witness, the authors examined in this study write not only from a peculiar distance to their readers but also in a language experienced as a vehicle of violence. Celan's dissemination of language into semantic splinters from disparate vocabularies and epistemes, Weiss's failing attempt to transform the German language into a mere analytical tool, and Sachs's dramatization of conflicting semantics in German and Hebrew instantiate not only a departure to new expressive possibilities but also a return to a scene of split identity. This does not mean that their texts lack the force of address that characterizes testimony but that the passage of their words to their addressees is fraught with additional complications. If the collision of redemptive and catastrophic meanings in Sachs, for instance, transmits the trauma of an irreparably split identity onto readers, this effect differs decisively from the impact of words spoken by a survivor in a more neutral language to a more sympathetic audience. As I have suggested, the texts by postwar German Jewish writers might be strongest where their perpetuation of traumatic ruptures enables them to resist a facile appropriation by the West German public.

One may argue that the reading of these authors in light of their critique of West Germany reiterates the gesture of *Exilliteraturforschung*, that is, that it implicitly defines exile as absence from Germany and focuses on the opposition between those inside and those outside of Germany. This definition would conflict with my claim that the diasporic consciousness after the Holocaust is marked by the absence of a single and clearly defined point of reference. To get beyond the logic of opposition, which always harbors the danger of reducing authors to mere negative reflections of West German culture, it is useful to reconsider the ways that trauma theory and diaspora theory conceptualize community. From the idea that testimony reconstitutes human bonds (Felman and Laub) to the notion of diaspora as a collective identity based on genealogy and contingency (Boyarin and Boyarin), scholars have emphasized communal aspects. In so doing they have drawn on the traditional semantics of the term "diaspora," which signifies the state of dispersal as well as the group of the dispersed, whereas "exile" connotes a more solitary state of separation.[3] Of particular interest is Paul Gilroy's analysis, in *The Black Atlantic*, of the interrelations between black cultures on both sides of the Atlantic. Gilroy is one the few scholars who recognize the indebtedness of postcolonial theory to Jewish thought. He also lays the ground for a reverse borrowing—from postcolonial theory to German Jewish studies—when he points out the analogy between racial slavery and industrial genocide, both of which are distinctively modern phenomena that undermine modernity's promise of emancipation and historical progress. Both testify to the "complicity of rationality and ethnocidal terror"[4] that is equally manifest in racial science and modern eugenics.

Gilroy defines diaspora as a form of transnational connectedness

CONCLUSION

that is devoid of the homogenizing and self-assertive tendencies of nationalism and that incorporates and renders productive a state of vulnerability. He offers a theory of how diasporic discourse helps constitute communities after the radical erosion of communality in a history of dispersal and suffering. Gilroy thus furnishes more relevant concepts of diasporic collective identity than Homi Bhabha, for instance, who is concerned with the generalizable critical potential of diasporic discourse rather than its power to constitute particular groups.[5] Describing diasporas as performative communities emerging from historical trauma, Gilroy emphasizes the phatic aspect of diaspora cultural expressions, or their capacity to initiate and sustain contact between human beings. This capacity is more immediately tangible in the musical performances Gilroy describes, but it is also intrinsic to the literary forms deployed by black modernists. Their experimental, radically unfinished forms of writing have the power to interpellate readers, while the narratives of exile and journeying take on a mnemonic function, "directing the consciousness of the group back to significant, nodal points in its common history and its social memory."[6] Central to Gilroy's concept of diaspora is the redefinition of tradition not as a static archive of past cultural forms but as a process of intragroup communication across temporal and spatial boundaries. Describing the circulation and transmutation of musical forms across the black Atlantic and the elliptic invocations of African origins in this music, he proposes a model of intragroup communication that reflects the heterogeneity and constant remaking of this group and that hinges upon a moment of misrecognition, undiminishable distance, and historical rupture. Such communications produce a "living memory of the changing same."[7] Diaspora cultural expressions constitute hybrid communities, not only because they are inevitably entangled with the surrounding majority cultures, but also because they destabilize the idea of a localizable origin while establishing new—imagined, tenuous—grounds of collective identity. We may recall here Paul Celan's idiosyncratic use of the Jewish mystical tradition and his refusal to cite this tradition as a stable and recognizable entity, which creates new forms of poetic address.

There is, however, a curious loophole in Gilroy's argument. He suggests that the common element between Jewish and black diaspora cultures is their accommodation of traumatic experience—or what he suggestively calls "the condition of being in pain"[8]—and invokes the Holocaust as a major point of reference. His own analysis, however, is

THE POSSIBILITY OF A DIASPORIC COMMUNITY

focused on the late nineteenth and early twentieth century, when black thinkers drew on Jewish concepts of diaspora for a diagnosis of their living situation and formed aspirations toward a national reconstitution after the Zionist model. Gilroy applies the notion of a negative sublime, which he largely derives from the ineffable horror of the Holocaust, retrospectively to black diaspora culture. While this is of course a legitimate theorizing move, his silence about Jewish diaspora cultures after the Holocaust is striking, especially in view of some shared sociocultural characteristics between them and the group he analyzes. Though Gilroy identifies the absence of a shared religion and genealogy among blacks as a distinguishing feature between blacks and Jews, this absence also characterizes the situation of German Jews after the Holocaust. Many of them came from a mixed or assimilated background and felt bound to other Jews at best through the experience of exile and persecution. Do they begin to constitute the kind of community Gilroy describes?

The authors examined in this study certainly do not form a cohesive group. Rather, an absence of communal structures and a pervasive sense of isolation mark their experience more than anything else. In the immediate postwar years, Weiss's sense of nonbelonging and Sachs's apocalyptic images testify to this predicament, as does Celan's melancholic evocation of a Jewish remnant without hope for the future: "Perhaps I am one of the last who must live out to the end the destiny of the Jewish spirit in Europe."[9] This sentiment seems not to have changed much in the course of Celan's life. In 1969, a few months before his suicide, Celan said in an address to the Association of Hebrew Writers in Tel Aviv: "I think I have a notion of what Jewish loneliness can be, and I recognize as well, among so many things, a thankful pride in every green thing planted here that's ready to refresh anyone who comes by" (*SP*, 57). Even in his recognition of the accomplishments of the state of Israel, Celan emphasizes his own position as a traveler who is bound to the group he addresses at best through his knowledge of "Jewish loneliness." As for the poetic dialogue between Sachs and Celan that some critics believe to have been a source of strength for both authors, Jean Bollack has persuasively argued that this communication broke down in the moment of crisis.[10] In a similar vein, Winfried Menninghaus has suggested that this poetic dialogue in effect deracinates the other's poems and thus demarcates the differences between their authors rather than establishing a common ground.[11]

CONCLUSION

Yet despite these rather gloomy views on the possibility of community, each of these literary writers deploys textual strategies that potentially open up subterranean, transitory, fragile spaces of communication between the dispersed. Sachs attempts to create a community of victims by mingling different cultural traditions, notably, German Romantic images with Jewish mystical concepts. This in some ways naive model of cultural synthesis gets a subversive twist through the question marks, hesitations, and self-reflections that Sachs introduces into it. Another example of subterranean communication is the cryptic historic referentiality of Celan's poems, the decoding of which depends on chance. Such references are one element of a partisan poetics that establishes momentary intertextual and intersubjective alliances. The conditions and possibilities of such communication are perhaps best captured in Weiss's *Das Gespäch der drei Gehenden* (1963). As I have shown, this experimental prose text can be read as a conversation between three refugees across broken story lines, or as a faltering dialogue between atomized exiles whose fragmentary speech never reaches an interlocutor without distortion. In this text, the absence of a consistent and stable narrative center entails a creation of transitory centers, purely fictitious grounds of encounter where the threads of different stories converge occasionally. The transitory community that emerges from the accidental encounter, mingling voices, and evasive moments of contact between the three speakers in *Das Gespräch* recalls the diasporic communities described by Gilroy. I have argued that one scene in particular, in which one of the speakers recalls—or imagines—body parts grotesquely piling up in what can only be a mass grave, captures the traumatic core of the exile's experience. The speaker's inability to verbalize what he sees reflects a sense that his own speech—or more precisely, loss of speech—constantly reenacts the death he witnesses. The three speakers, while never explicitly addressing each other, pick up and transform this scenario, fluctuating between reality and fantasy. This exchange, without resolving the trauma, holds it in suspension, thus keeping the speakers from lapsing into silence and constituting a minimal ground of communality.

At the same time, *Das Gespräch* indicates the limited applicability of Gilroy's model to the writing of Peter Weiss. The absence of referential markers and the radical fragmentation of narrative space in *Das Gespräch* suggest that not even the image of a shared geographical origin is available for its speakers. This absence captures the spirit of this generation of German Jewish writers, their sense of an ending that may or may not open up a future. Born before the war and raised with the idea that Jews could be integrated into German culture and society, they witnessed the total collapse of this idea without ever fully embracing another ideal of collective identity. The diasporic poetics of post-Holocaust German Jewish writers articulate not the existence of an alternative form of community but instead its hypothetical conjecture in view of its factual absence.

This tendency toward hypothetical conjecture culminates in Peter Weiss's self-avowed *Wunschautobiographie*,[12] *Die Ästhetik des Widerstands* (1975–81). The book projects data of Weiss's own biography onto the life of a young factory worker whose experience in exile differs decisively from his own, especially in terms of the political solidarity he encounters. The worker—and narrator of the text—engages in the antifascist resistance in Germany, goes on to join the republican forces in the Spanish Civil War, and finally arrives first in Paris and then in Sweden, where he associates with Communists and the circle around Bertolt Brecht. The work, which was written under the influence of the new social movements and the crisis of Western European Marxism, is marked by a fundamental tension. More adamantly than ever before, Weiss posits that the isolation of exile can only be overcome by establishing communal bonds with others; yet at the same time he records the collapse of nearly every community in exile and nearly every effort to build a political alliance. In particular, he describes the failure of the political left to forge a popular front against fascism, a joint force that would be both effective and able to integrate a wide range of psychical temperaments and political practices. In contemplating the reasons for this failure, the narrator is torn between his belief in the necessity of a strong leadership during times of military struggle and his critique of the authoritarian structures of both the Communist Party and the antifascist resistance at large. He recognizes that the coercive character of the popular front reflects not only the exigencies of military battle but also the problematic attempt to construct a collective identity around an abstract political program, for instance in the antifascist resistance in the Spanish Civil War:

> Unsre Zugehörigkeit hatten wir in der politischen Entscheidung gefunden, dieses Handlungsfeld, dieses taktische Bild,

diese Landkarte Spaniens aber war noch nicht verwandelt worden in ein lebendiges Gefüge, in dem es Begegnungen mit Menschen, bestimmte Arten des Sehns, des Ausdrucks gab. (*W,* vol.3, pt. 1, 267)

We had found our sense of belonging in the political decision, but this field of action, this tactical image, this map of Spain had not yet been transformed into a living structure in which encounters with humans, distinct modes of perception and expression had a place.

The narrator's dissatisfaction with the quasi-military idiom of fields, tactics, and maps hints at a critique of what Eric Santner calls a global consciousness. Santner is concerned that the increase of social and cultural interconnections in an age of globalization might amount to little more than an endless expansion of the (capitalist) logic of exchange if it is not accompanied by new modes of relating to others. Most of our social institutions, he argues, integrate individuals by defining their social roles and bestowing upon them a set of predicates needed to fulfill these roles. Santner contrasts this form of social interpellation with divine revelation as conceived by Franz Rosenzweig and seen through the lens of psychoanalytic theory. Revelation signifies here an act of loving attention that singles out a person but that "does not take place on the basis of any distinguishing virtues, any special predicates on the part of the object,"[13] and that disrupts the inherent violence of institutional rituals. Santner suggests that we need to follow this model and recognize the enigmatic singularity of others, or that which is agitating, strange, unresolved in them, rather than reducing them to a set of positive attributes. His term for the ability to form such relations is a "universal" (rather than "global") consciousness:

For global consciousness, conflicts are generated through *external* differences between cultures and societies whereas universality, as I am using the term here, signifies the possibility of a shared opening to the agitation and turbulence *immanent* to any construction of identity, the *Unheimlichkeit* or uncanniness internal to any and every space we call home. In this view, redemption (or, to use the more Freudian term: the cure) signifies not some final overcoming or full integration of this agitation but rather the work of traversing our fantasmatic organizations of it, breaking down our defenses against it. To put it another way, for global consciousness, every stranger is ultimately just like me, ultimately familiar; his or her strangeness is a function of a different vocabulary, a different set of names that can always be translated. For the psychoanalytic conception of universality I will be proposing here, it is just the reverse: the possibility of a "We," of communality, is granted on the basis of the fact that every familiar is ultimately strange and that, indeed, I am even in a crucial sense a stranger to myself.[14]

Conceived in these terms, the antifascist resistance depicted in *Die Ästhetik des Widerstands* must be said to rest on a global consciousness, or a mind-set that reduces the other to a mirror image of the self rather than perceiving her alterity and, in that process, its own alterity. One basis of the resistance movement is an imagined bond with the Soviet Union supported by images from the October Revolution, a bond that inspires a sense of belonging in those who fight fascism on the margins of the political struggle. The power accorded here to images recalls Arjun Appadurai's theory that the global mobility and proliferation of images in the modern age bring about a pervasion of the imagination into every realm of daily life, a pervasion that earlier would only occur at transformative moments such as holidays and revolutions.[15] In this case, the images from the Russian Revolution have the power to efface any doubts of individuals and to forge emotional ties between the exiled antifascists. But they also turn the antifascist community into a unity of monads of identical internal structure: "nichts nahm Gestalt an, wofür nicht schon die Voraussetzungen geschaffen worden waren, wir erkannten, was sich bereits in uns vorgeformt hatte" (*W*, vol. 3, pt. 1, 171) [nothing took form for which the presuppositions had not already been created; we recognized what had been already preformed within us]. The internationalism of the antifascist resistance is figured as an endless expansion of the self.

An alternative mode of being together that is based on a universal consciousness emerges in response to the traumatic experiences of the narrator's mother. The dichotomy between catastrophic and empowering exile we saw in Weiss's earlier work reappears in *Die Ästhetik des Widerstands* in form of a gendered division between exiles

CONCLUSION

who suffer in isolation (mostly women) and exiles who join the international resistance (mostly men). The most striking instance of catastrophic exile occurs when the narrator's mother identifies with the stream of Jewish refugees fleeing East from all over Europe, a process narrated at the beginning of the third book. While the parents are wandering through Czechoslovakia and Poland—even for a while toward Auschwitz, cited in the text in its Polish form "Oswiecim" (*W,* vol. 3. pt. 3, 13)—the mother witnesses a number of horrible events: a tank attack that evidently opens the Second World War, a mass shooting of Jews in Sobibor, and, finally, the bestial murder of a family by the fascists. These experiences push her successively into silence, stupor, and, after the parents' arrival in Sweden have given rise to short-lived hopes for her recuperation, death. As the mother is gradually transformed into a silent allegory of the plight of "racially" persecuted victims, her catastrophic exile becomes marked as both Jewish and female. In a perceptive analysis, Julia Hell has argued that the mother embodies a form of knowledge beyond the dichotomy of mimetic and rational discourse, a "bodily knowledge produced in an act of identification," which in the course of the novel is transmitted onto her son, the narrator.[16] But since this identification is also construed as an act of feminine surrender and scene of abjection, the narrator has to resist his own fall into abjection by transforming helpless passivity into political activity. This mode of defense shapes the novel as a whole, which "develops a specific form of political resistance to images which stage the identification with the victims of the Holocaust."[17]

There are, however, some moments in the novel in which this resistance breaks down and allows us to discern alternative responses to trauma. These moments reverse the hierarchy between words and images characteristic of Weiss's work and more generally question the capacity of language to name, categorize, and explain. *Die Ästhetik des Widerstands* turns the figure of the mother into an image that requires interpretation—which is subsequently offered by male figures such as the narrator, the narrator's father, and the physician Hodann—while casting doubts upon the feasibility of their interpretative project.

Hodann maps the mother's posture after her death onto Albrecht Dürer's famous engraving *Melencolia I,* thus transforming her into a work of art that calls for verbal interpretation. The narrator's comments upon Hodann's comparison indicates one function of the detailed ekphrasis that follows: by transforming the mother into an image and integrating her into a continuum—the artistic tradition of representing limit states—Hodann fixates her experience so that it may be deciphered in the future. Indeed, Hodann believes not only that it will once be possible to verbalize the horrors experienced by the mother but also that this can be done in a language shared and understood by everyone (*W*, vol. 3, pt. 3, 135). The translation of the mother's experience into accessible language occurs already within the text, as can be seen in the different depictions of the massacre in Sobibor. Whereas the first scenes are narrated from the mother's point of view and are barely comprehensible, we gradually and especially after the mother's death get a better sense of the events that happened there. And yet, the specific engraving chosen here is apt to resist Hodann's program of temporalization through interpretation. First, this engraving locates the struggle between silence and communication within the artwork itself. While Hodann initially hails the power of art to communicate experience, he later suggests that the deepest attraction of art might be its ability to lure us into silent melancholy (*W*, vol. 3, pt. 3, 132). Second, the subject matter of Dürer's engraving tends to undermine the dichotomy between silent images and eloquent interpretation. In reading the physical immobility of the female figure as a symptom of increased mental activity, Weiss follows Erwin Panofsky's famous reading of *Melencolia I* as a turning point in the understanding of melancholy.[18] Panofsky and others had argued that Dürer's engraving was the first to depict melancholy as the sign of artistic genius rather than the temper of the misanthropes. Because the female allegory at the center of *Die Ästhetik des Widerstands* is both a work of art and its creator, its detailed description only enhances what James Heffernan has identified as the underlying tension of all ekphrasis: "To represent a painting or sculpture in words is to evoke its power—the power to fix, excite, amaze, entrance, disturb, or intimidate the viewer—even as language strives to keep that power under control."[19]

Rather than provoking a gradual translation of words into images, or of incomprehensible words into comprehensible ones, the mother affects others in ways akin to the tales of the speakers in *Das Gespräch*. As in this earlier text, processes of communication are fundamentally disrupted in *Die Ästhetik des Widerstands*. Though the narrator claims that a special kind of understanding developed between his parents during the mother's crisis, the father and other male characters often do not understand her at all. It is even suggested that their lack

CONCLUSION

of comprehension contributed to her death. And though the father aids the verbalization of the mother's experience, for instance, when he describes their flight through Eastern Europe and fills in the names and topographical markers that are missing from her visions (*W*, vol. 3, pt. 3, 15), his attempts at historical explanation fail conspicuously. In a telling scene the father, who espouses a rational, even economistic interpretation of National Socialism, reacts to the mother's troubling silence by citing a long list of names of German industrial magnates who supported Hitler. He apparently attempts to explain Hitler's rise to power, yet in so doing he only further obscures the matter:

> Während meine Mutter in der Küchennische vom Wandbrett die Teller nahm und sie zum Tisch am Fenster trug, rief er die Namen, die sich in ihm festgefressen hatten, und die so schrill und falsch klangen, wie sie klingen sollten. . . . Krupp, Thyssen, Kirdorf, Stinnes, Vögler, Mannesmann hatten die antibolschewistische Liga gegründet, die Nationalsozialistische Partei finanziert, einige von ihnen auch waren zu deren Mitgliedern geworden. Die Namen hoben sich ab vom sanften Klirren, das aus der Küchennische kam. Einfacher leben und sparen, sagte mein Vater, das hatte uns Mitte der Zwanigerjahre, wie Neunzehnhundert Vierzehn schon, Duisberg zugerufen, der Chef des IG Farben Trusts, des größten Trusts der Welt, und als wir das hörten, da wußten wir, es würde wieder zum Krieg kommen. Meine Mutter ging mit den Bestecken zum Tisch. Mein Vater hatte die Reihe der Namen schon fortgesetzt. Haniel, Wolff, Borsig, Klöckner, Hoesch, Bosch, Blohm, Siemens, einige der Mächtigsten nur nenne er, sagte er. (*W*, vol. 3, pt. 3, 126)

> While my mother in the kitchen nook took down the plates from the shelf and carried them to the table next to the window, he called out the names, which had engrained themselves in him, and which sounded as shrill and wrong as they were supposed to sound. . . . Krupp, Thyssen, Kirdorf, Stinnes, Vögler, Mannesmann had founded the anti-Bolshevik league, they had financed the National Socialist Party, some of them had become members of it. The names stood out against the soft clinking that came from the kitchen

nook. To live more simply and to save, my father said, this is what Duisberg, the boss of the IG Farben Trust, the biggest trust in the world, had shouted to us in the mid-twenties, just as in nineteen hundred fourteen. When we heard this, we knew there would be another war. My mother walked to the table with the cutlery. My father had already continued the series of names. Haniel, Wolff, Borsig, Klöckner, Hoesch, Bosch, Blohm, Siemens, he listed only some of the most powerful, so he said.

These names sound so strange both because their relationship to the mother's experience remains intangible and because their obsessive listing vacates the very gesture of naming.[20] Proper names seldom have a referential meaning, yet they epitomize the power of language to bestow a symbolic identity and position a person within a social structure or symbolic system. Proper names can also be conceived as mimetic ciphers that embody rather than refer to a person; this is what the father has in mind when he attempts to obtain a grasp on people and hold them responsible for their crimes by calling out their names. Yet the father's mind-numbing listing of names undermines both these functions of proper names. In subsuming individual names in an endless chain of similar signs, he perverts the idea of singularity, and in reducing language to asyntactic stammering, he calls into question its ability to assign identities and impose an order on the world. One of the effects of this disarticulation of language is the switch into the subjunctive mood during the father's account of Hitler's rise to power (*W*, vol. 3, pt. 3, 127). This passage anticipates the concluding pages of the book, in which a similar use of the subjunctive makes the future of the past look unreal. Rainer Rother has argued that the use of the subjunctive in these pages allows Weiss to recapitulate postwar developments, including the Cold War and its vacating of utopian politics, without affirming the actual course of history.[21] I would add that in the father's account of the rise of Nazism, temporal disruption is once more both a symptom and a cure of historical trauma. The change into the subjunctive both renders the rise of Nazism more immediate and unsettles its factuality, thus opening up the possibility of imagining alternative courses of history.

Toward the end of her life, the mother increasingly inspires in the father visions whose ultimate origin remains indeterminate:

CONCLUSION

Er sei während der letzten Zeit empfänglich gewesen für Bilder, sagte mein Vater, von denen sich nicht sagen lasse, ob er sie erdacht habe oder ob sie von meiner Mutter ausgesandt worden seien. So habe er sich tanzen sehn mit ihr, mehrmals, in gleicher Weise, auf einer Diele, ohne daß Musik zu hören gewesen sei, mit langsamen Schritten hätten sie sich im Kreis gedreht, sein Arm um ihre Hüfte, ihre Hand auf seiner Schulter, sonderbar hätten sich die Beine angehoben, und lautlos sei das Niedersetzen der Füße gewesen, und wenn er dabei die Liegende angeblickt habe, dann sei ihm gewesen, als lächle ihr Mund. (*W*, vol. 3, pt. 3, 130)

My father said that he had recently been susceptible to images, of which it could not be said whether he had thought them up or whether my mother had sent them out. Thus he had seen himself dancing with her, several times, in the same fashion, in a hallway, no music was audible, with slow steps, they had turned in circles, his arm around her hip, her hand on his shoulder. Their legs lifted themselves strangely, and their feet set themselves down silently, and when he looked at her lying there he had a feeling that her mouth was smiling.

This image of dancing lovers conjures up an affective bond that develops in spite of, or rather because of, the father's utter inability to understand the mother. With an image like this Weiss suggests that the transmission of traumatic knowledge depends not on the availability of exacting words but on the existence of interpersonal relations that can accommodate the other's otherness. Of course, by mapping this experience onto the stereotypical oppositions of active-passive, word-image, and male-female, he might forego the chance to probe more deeply into alternative modes of bonding. But the monumental form of his text and the endless series of words resisting interpretation also signal Weiss's own dissatisfaction with these oppositions. What remains is a vision of how the experience of irredeemable dispersion becomes the very foundation of community in a post-Holocaust world.

Notes

Introduction

1. The attributes "German" and "Jewish" are used here in a wider sense than is customary. "German" refers to writers whose native and main language was German. With "Jewish" I include a writer like Peter Weiss, who neither identified himself as a Jew in any positive way (religious, ethnic, etc.) nor would be regarded as one by Jewish religious laws (his mother was non-Jewish). Nonetheless his sense of self was, at least temporarily, shaped by the knowledge of having been persecuted as a Jew.
2. Dan Diner, ed., *Zivilisationsbruch: Denken nach Auschwitz* (Frankfurt am Main: Fischer, 1988).
3. *Encyclopaedia Judaica* (Jerusalem: Keter, 1972), s.vv. "Diaspora" and "Galut." See also W. D. Davies, who notes that the new terminology expresses the "desire to give expression to the benefits as well as the disadvantages of the Diaspora for the Jewish people." Davies, *The Territorial Dimension of Judaism* (Berkeley: University of California Press, 1982), 116–17.
4. On the shifting conceptions of exile in Jewish thought, see especially Arnold M. Eisen, *Galut: Modern Jewish Reflection on Homelessness and Homecoming* (Bloomington: Indiana University Press, 1986).
5. Barbara Kirshenblatt-Gimblett, "Spaces of Dispersal," *Cultural Anthropology* 9, no. 3 (1994): 343.
6. Khachig Tölölian, "The Nation State and Its Others: In Lieu of a Preface," *Diaspora* 1, no. 1 (1991): 4–5. Quoted in James Clifford, "Diasporas," *Cultural Anthropology* 9, no. 3 (1994): 303.
7. Stuart Hall, "Cultural Identity and Diaspora," in *Identity: Community, Culture, Difference,* ed. Jonathan Rutherford (London: Lawrence and

Wishart, 1990), 235.
8. Although I agree with Daniel Boyarin and Jonathan Boyarin's critique of Hall's essay, especially of its dismissive treatment of Jewish concepts of diaspora (see note 13), I endorse Hall's conceptual expansion of "diaspora" to signify perceptive and discursive modes that are rooted in, but not reducible to, historical experience. On the difference between "exile" and "diaspora," see also Nico Israel, *Outlandish: Writing between Exile and Diaspora* (Palo Alto, Calif.: Stanford University Press, 2000), 3. For further reflections on terminology, see Azade Seyhan, *Writing outside the Nation* (Princeton, N.J.: Princeton University Press, 2001), 9.
9. Homi K. Bhabha, *The Location of Culture* (New York: Routledge, 1994), 139.
10. Daniel Boyarin and Jonathan Boyarin, *Powers of Diaspora: Two Essays on the Relevance of Jewish Culture* (Minneapolis: University of Minnesota Press, 2002), 5.
11. Daniel Boyarin and Jonathan Boyarin, "Diaspora: Generation and the Ground of Jewish Identity," *Critical Inquiry* 19, no. 4 (Spring 1993): 693–725.
12. Ibid, 721.
13. See Hall, "Cultural Identity," 235, and Boyarin and Boyarin, *Powers of Diaspora*, 13.
14. Boyarin and Boyarin, *Powers of Diaspora*, 11.
15. Ibid., 127.
16. See Dan Diner, "Negative Symbiose: Deutsche und Juden nach Auschwitz," *Babylon* 1 (1986): 9–20. For recent reflections on the "German-Jewish symbiosis," see Leslie Morris and Jack Zipes, eds., *Unlikely History: The Changing German-Jewish Symbiosis, 1945–2000* (New York: Palgrave, 2002).
17. This generalization brackets such related issues as the rise of Zionism and the persistence of religious orthodoxy, particularly in some parts of the Habsburg Empire. Furthermore, the project of emancipation clearly remained incomplete, situating Jews rather uneasily within German-speaking cultures. However problematic the integration into new "fatherlands" was, it nonetheless represented a significant shift from the earlier bond to a distant homeland.
18. The existence of multiple points of reference becomes even more important in the second and third generations of German Jewish writers after the Holocaust. See Leslie A. Adelson, "Nichts wie zuhause: Jeannette Lander und Ronnith Neumann auf der utopischen Suche nach jüdischer Identität im westdeutschen Kontext," in *Jüdische Kultur und Weiblichkeit in der Moderne,* ed. Sabine Schilling, Inge Stephan, and Sigrid Weigel (Cologne: Böhlau, 1994), 307–30. See also Sander L. Gilman,

NOTES TO INTRODUCTION

Jews in Today's German Culture (Bloomington: Indiana University Press, 1995); Thomas Nolden, *Junge jüdische Literatur: Konzentrisches Schreiben in der Gegenwart* (Würzberg: Königshausen und Neumann, 1995); Sander L. Gilman and Karen Remmler, eds., *Reemerging Jewish Culture in Germany: Life and Literature since 1989* (New York: New York University Press, 1994).

19. The term diaspora also helps to distinguish my approach from that of German *Exilforschung* (exile research), which has tended to confine exile to the years between 1933–45 and defined it primarily as absence from Germany. See Bernhard Spies, "Exilliteratur—ein abgeschlossenes Kapitel? Überlegungen zu Stand und Perspektiven der literaturwissenschaftlichen Exilforschung," in *Exilforschung: Ein internationales Jahrbuch* 14 (1996): 11–30.

20. See Anson Rabinbach, "The Jewish Question in the German Question," *New German Critique* 44 (Spring–Summer 1988): 159–92. See also Anson Rabinbach, "Introduction: Reflections on Germans and Jews since Auschwitz," in *Germans and Jews since the Holocaust: The Changing Situation in West Germany*, ed. Anson Rabinbach and Jack Zipes (New York: Holmes and Meier, 1986), 3–24.

21. See Jean-Paul Bier, "The Holocaust, West Germany, and Strategies of Oblivion, 1947–1979," in Rabinbach and Zipes, *Germans and Jews since the Holocaust*, 185–207; and Ernestine Schlant, *The Language of Silence: West German Literature and the Holocaust* (New York: Routledge, 1999), 15–16.

22. See Jeffrey Herf, *Divided Memory: The Nazi Past in the Two Germanys* (Cambridge, Mass.: Harvard University Press, 1997), 267–333.

23. Eric L. Santner, *Stranded Objects: Mourning, Memory, and Film in Postwar Germany* (Ithaca, N.Y.: Cornell University Press, 1990), 6.

24. Rabinbach, "The Jewish Question," 167.

25. See Frank Stern, *The Whitewashing of the Yellow Badge: Antisemitism and Philosemitism in Postwar Germany*, trans. William Templer (Oxford: Pergamon, 1992), 265–334.

26. Eleanore Sterling, "Judenfreunde: Fragwürdiger Philosemitismus in der Bundesrepublik," *Die Zeit* (December 10, 1965), quoted in Stern, *The Whitewashing*, 300.

27. Rabinbach, "The Jewish Question," 175.

28. See Shoshana Felman and Dori Laub, *Testimony: Crises of Witnessing in Literature, Psychoanalysis, and History* (New York: Routledge, 1992), 81–82.

29. Ibid., 256.

30. Ibid., 258, emphasis by Felman.

31. Edward Said similarly reinstates a hermeneutic of exile in his influential

article "Reflections on Exile." He describes there the discrepancy between the modernist imagination of exile and its actual experience but in the end shifts back from the harsh reality of exile to the critical consciousness it promotes: "Most people are principally aware of one culture, one setting, one home; exiles are aware of at least two, and this plurality of vision gives rise to an awareness of simultaneous dimensions, an awareness that—to borrow a phrase from music—is *contrapuntal*." Said, *Reflections on Exile and Other Essays* (Cambridge, Mass.: Harvard University Press, 2000), 186.
32. The expression "human being" is, in fact, not quite appropriate because Agamben emphasizes the ways in which testimony articulates the dialectic between the human and the inhuman and between "subjectification" and "desubjectification."
33. Giorgio Agamben, *Remnants of Auschwitz: The Witness and the Archive*, trans. Daniel Heller-Roazen (New York: Zone Books, 1999), 159.
34. Ibid., 161.
35. Ibid., 54.
36. Cathy Caruth similarly claims that exile propels traumatized subjects into contact with others, thereby ensuring the transmission of trauma and the beginning of a history always already shared with others. For a critique of Caruth, see the conclusion of this study.
37. Ruth Klüger, *weiter leben: Eine Jugend* (Munich: Deutscher Taschenbuchverlag, 1997), 270–77. An English version that differs substantially from the German version has appeared under the title *Still Alive: A Holocaust Girlhood Remembered* (New York: Feminist Press at the City University of New York, 2001). My references are to the German version.
38. Klüger, *weiter leben*, 78.
39. Peter Gay, *My German Question: Growing Up in Nazi Berlin* (New Haven, Conn.: Yale University Press, 1998), 1.
40. Ibid., 5.
41. Ibid., 6.
42. Ibid., 191.
43. See Katja Garloff, "The Emigrant as Witness: W. G. Sebald's *Die Ausgewanderten*," *German Quarterly* 77, no. 1 (Winter 2004): 76–93.

Chapter 1

1. See Edward Said, "Intellectual Exile: Expatriates and Marginals," in *Representations of the Intellectual: The 1993 Reith Lectures* (New York: Pantheon Books, 1994), 47–64.
2. See Israel, "Adorno, Los Angeles, and the Dislocation of Culture," in *Outlandish*, 75–122.
3. See Rolf Wiggershaus, *The Frankfurt School: Its History, Theories, and*

Political Significance, trans. Michael Robertson (Cambridge, Mass.: MIT Press, 1994), 404 and 466–68. On the historical circumstances and philosophical consequences of Adorno's exile and return, see also Peter Uwe Hohendahl, *Prismatic Thought: Theodor W. Adorno* (Lincoln: University of Nebraska Press, 1995), 21–44; Martin Jay, *Permanent Exiles: Essays on the Intellectual Migration from Germany to America* (New York: Columbia University Press, 1986), 28–61 and 120–37; and Martin Jay, *Adorno* (Cambridge, Mass.: Harvard University Press, 1984), 31–55.

4. Theodor W. Adorno, "On the Question: 'What is German?'" in *Critical Models: Interventions and Catchworks*, trans. Henry W. Pickford (New York: Columbia University Press, 1998), 212.
5. See Theodor W. Adorno, *The Jargon of Authenticity*, trans. Knut Tarnowski and Frederic Will (Evanston, Ill.: Northwestern University Press, 1973).
6. Ibid., 213.
7. See Anson Rabinbach, *In the Shadow of Catastrophe: German Intellectuals between Apocalypse and Enlightenment* (Berkeley: University of California Press, 1997), 166–98. The connection between Judaism and nomadism is described with particular acuity in a supplement to Adorno's letter to Horkheimer from September 18, 1940, published in Max Horkheimer, *Gesammelte Schriften*, vol. 16, ed. Alfred Schmidt and Gunzelin Schmid Noerr (Frankfurt am Main: Fischer, 1995), 761–64.
8. On Adorno's concept of mimesis, see especially Michael Cahn, "Subversive Mimesis: T. W. Adorno and the Modern Impasse of Critique," in *Mimesis in Contemporary Theory: An Interdisciplinary Approach*, ed. Mihai Spariosu, vol. 1, *The Literary and Philosophical Debate* (Philadelphia, Amsterdam: Jahn Benjamins, 1984), 27–64; Gunter Gebauer and Christoph Wulf, *Mimesis: Culture, Art, Society*, trans. Don Reneau (Berkeley: University of California Press, 1995), 281–93; Miriam Hansen, "Mass Culture as Hieroglyphic Writing: Adorno, Derrida, Kracauer" *New German Critique* 56 (Spring–Summer 1992): 43–73; and Martin Jay, "Mimesis and Mimetology: Adorno and Lacoue-Labarthe," in *The Semblance of Subjectivity: Essays in Adorno's Aesthetic Theory*, ed. Tom Huhn and Lambert Zuidervaart (Cambridge, Mass.: MIT Press, 1997), 29–53.
9. Max Horkheimer and Theodor W. Adorno, *Dialectic of Enlightenment*, trans. John Cumming (New York: Continuum, 1997), 23.
10. Rabinbach, *In the Shadow*, 185.
11. Horkheimer and Adorno, *Dialectic of Enlightenment*, 61.
12. See Theodor W. Adorno, "In Memory of Eichendorff," in *Notes to Literature*, vol. 1, ed. Rolf Tiedemann, trans. Shierry Weber Nicholsen

(New York: Columbia University Press, 1991), 63.
13. Theodor W. Adorno, *Minima Moralia: Reflections from Damaged Life*, trans. E. F. N. Jephcott (London: NLB, 1974), 110, trans. altered.
14. Theodor W. Adorno, "The Essay as Form," in *Notes to Literature*, vol. 1, 4.
15. Ibid., 4.
16. Ibid., 22.
17. Ibid., 12.
18. Ibid., 13.
19. On Adorno's political engagement through essay writing, see Peter Uwe Hohendahl, "The Scholar, the Intellectual, and the Essay: Weber, Lukács, Adorno, and Postwar Germany," *German Quarterly* 70, no. 3 (Summer 1997): 217–32; and Peter J. Burgard, "Adorno, Goethe, and the Politics of the Essay," *Deutsche Vierteljahrsschrift für Literaturwissenschaft und Geistesgeschichte* 1 (1992): 160–91.
20. Adorno, "The Essay as Form," 21.
21. See also Henry Pickford's characterization of Adorno's idea of a "critical model" in "Critical Models: Adorno's Theory and Practice of Cultural Criticism," *Yale Journal of Criticism* 10, no. 2 (1997): 261. On the shift from the writer-reader relation to the text-object relation in Adorno, see Shierry Weber Nicholson, *Exact Imagination, Late Work: On Adorno's Aesthetics* (Cambridge, Mass.: MIT Press, 1997), 105–24.
22. Theodor W. Adorno, "Words from Abroad," in *Notes to Literature*, vol. 1, 185–99.
23. Thomas Y. Levin, "Nationalities of Language: Adorno's *Fremdwörter*. An Introduction to 'On the Question: What is German?'" *New German Critique* 36 (Fall 1985): 117.
24. Hohendahl, *Prismatic Thought*, 115.
25. Ibid.
26. See also Susan Bernstein, "Journalism and German Identity: Communiqués from Heine, Wagner, and Adorno," *New German Critique* 66 (Fall 1995): 65–93.
27. Theodor W. Adorno, "Heine the Wound," in *Notes to Literature*, vol. 1, 83.
28. Ibid.
29. On Adorno's concept of mimetic understanding as an imitation of the process of production, see Christoph Menke, *The Sovereignty of Art: Aesthetic Negativity in Adorno and Derrida*, trans. Neil Solomon (Cambridge, Mass.: MIT Press, 1998), 87–105.
30. Theodor W. Adorno, *Aesthetic Theory*, ed. and trans. Robert Hullot-Kentor (Minneapolis: University of Minnesota Press, 1997), 106.

NOTES TO CHAPTER 1

31. See Bhabha, "Of Mimicry and Man: The Ambivalence of Colonial Discourse," in *The Location of Culture*, 85–92.
32. Adorno, "Heine the Wound," in *Notes to Literature*, vol. 1, 80.
33. Ibid.
34. Ibid., 85.
35. On this projection mechanism, see Diner, "Negative Symbiose," 12–13.
36. Theodor W. Adorno, "The Meaning of Working Through the Past," in *Critical Models*, 83.
37. Ulrich Baer, *Remnants of Song: Trauma and the Experience of Modernity in Charles Baudelaire and Paul Celan* (Palo Alto, Calif.: Stanford University Press, 2000), 295.
38. See Hohendahl, *Prismatic Thought*, 45–72.
39. Adorno, *Minima Moralia*, 66.
40. Adorno, "The Meaning of Working Through the Past," 91.
41. Ibid., 89, my emphasis.
42. Ibid., 91.
43. Ibid., 92, my emphasis.
44. See Sigmund Freud, "Beyond the Pleasure Principle," in *The Standard Edition of the Complete Psychological Works of Sigmund Freud*, ed. and trans. James Strachey (London: Hogarth Press, 1953–75), vol. 18, esp. 24–33; and Walter Benjamin, "On Some Motives in Baudelaire," in Benjamin, *Selected Writings 4: 1938–1940*, ed. Howard Eiland and Michael W. Jennings, trans. Edmund Jephcott et al. (Cambridge, Mass.: Belknap Press of Harvard University Press, 2003), esp. 316–21.
45. See note 23 in the introduction.
46. The title of the essay presents another instance of Adorno's hovering between participation and critique. In omitting the quotation marks around "Working Through the Past," he chooses not to mark this expression as a quotation even though he is fully aware of its slogan character and apologetic tendency.
47. Dominick LaCapra, *History and Memory after Auschwitz* (Ithaca, N.Y.: Cornell University Press, 1998), 69. For LaCapra's references to Adorno's essay, see ibid., 51, and his *Representing the Holocaust: History, Theory, Trauma* (Ithaca, N.Y.: Cornell University Press, 1994), 46n, 58n.
48. See Werner Hamacher, "Working Through Working," trans. Matthew T. Hartman, *Modernism / modernity* 3, no. 1 (January 1996): 46.
49. One would have to add that Adorno thus reworks the term *Aufarbeitung* quite thoroughly. See Pickford's remarks on the original meaning of term as an "unpleasant obligation" in Adorno, *Critical Models*, 337–38.

NOTES TO CHAPTER 1

50. Adorno, "The Meaning of Working Through the Past," in *Critical Models*, 89.
51. Ibid., 103, trans. altered.
52. See Hannah Arendt, "The Jew as Pariah: A Hidden Tradition" (April 1944), in *The Jew as Pariah: Jewish Identity and Politics in the Modern Age*, ed. Ron H. Feldman (New York: Grove Press, 1978), 67–90. Arendt had already used the pariah/parvenu distinction in her biography of Rahel Varnhagen, the first draft of which she completed in 1933. See Hannah Arendt, *Rahel Varnhagen: The Life of a Jewess*, ed. Liliane Weissberg, trans. Richard and Clara Winston, first complete edition (Baltimore: Johns Hopkins University Press, 1997), esp. 4 and 237–49.
53. Arendt, "The Jew as Pariah," 79.
54. Walter Benjamin, "On the Concept of History," in *Selected Writings 4*, 396.
55. See Michael André Bernstein, *Foregone Conclusions: Against Apocalyptic History* (Berkeley: University of California Press, 1994).
56. On Anders's biography and philosophy, see Micha Brumlik, "Günther Anders: Zur Existenzialontologie der Emigration," in *Zivilisationsbruch: Denken nach Auschwitz*, ed. Dan Diner (Frankfurt am Main: Fischer, 1988), 110–49; Elke Schubert, *Günther Anders* (Reinbek bei Hamburg: Rowohlt, 1992); Evelyn Adunka, "Günther Anders und das jüdische Erbe," in *Günther Anders kontrovers*, ed. Konrad Paul Liessmann (Munich: Beck, 1992), 72–80.
57. Günther Anders, *Die Schrift an der Wand: Tagebücher 1941 bis 1966* (Munich: Beck, 1967), 67–68. Emphasis by Anders.
58. Ibid., 100.
59. See Susan Stewart, *On Longing: Narratives of the Miniature, the Gigantic, the Souvenir, the Collection* (Baltimore: Johns Hopkins University Press, 1984).
60. Anders, *Die Schrift an der Wand*, 261–68.
61. This incompleteness of death is already implied in the metaphor of Hades, which in Greek mythology is imagined as a place in which the dead live a tasteless and colorless life as bodiless phantoms, often with a shadowy continuance of their former occupations. I will return to the Hades metaphor in my analysis of Paul Celan's revisiting of Eastern Europe (see chapter 4).
62. Anders, *Die Schrift an der Wand*, 352.
63. Ibid.
64. Ibid., 337. The restoration of a proper diachronic order is a concern throughout the book. See, for instance, Anders's discussion of the book by two former German generals, titled *So kämpfte ich in Breslau [Thus I Fought in Breslau]*. His indignation about the book derives not only

NOTES TO CHAPTER 1

from its revisionist views of World War II and idealizing depiction of the German soldiers but also from the way in which its maps pervert the course of history by synchronizing different diachronic layers of the city. A military map from 1945, for instance, indicates a synagogue that had been destroyed by then (330), and another map shows both a runway built during the final days of World War II and street names from the Weimar Republic (407). Hints of Anders's own struggle to maintain or recuperate some distance from the past can also be found in the way he repeatedly reminds himself and his readers of the rights of the Poles to be here, as if to contain his own tendency to conjure up the past. The fact that he pays only secret visits to the street where his family used to live further indicates uneasiness regarding his own implication in the world of his parents.

65. Anders, *Die Schrift an der Wand*, 340.
66. Ibid.
67. Ibid., 345.
68. See Paula E. Hyman, *Gender and Assimilation in Modern Jewish History: The Roles and Representation of Women* (Seattle: University of Washington Press, 1995), esp. 10–49.
69. Günther Anders, *Wir Eichmannsöhne: Offener Brief an Klaus Eichmann* (Munich: Beck, 1964).
70. For Améry's deliberate address of a German audience, see his *At the Mind's Limits: Contemplations by a Survivor on Auschwitz and Its Realities*, trans. Sidney Rosenfeld and Stella P. Rosenfeld (Bloomington: Indiana University Press, 1980), xiv.
71. Améry, *At the Mind's Limits*, 53. On Améry's relationship to the German language, see his "Die deutsche Sprachwelt," in *Der Grenzgänger: Gespräch mit Ingo Hermann in der Reihe 'Zeugen des Jahrhunderts'* (Göttingen: Lamuv, 1992), 83–86. See also Petra S. Fiero, *Schreiben gegen Schweigen: Grenzerfahrungen in Jean Amérys autobiographischem Werk* (Hildesheim: Olms, 1997), 71–130.
72. Améry, *At the Mind's Limits*, 84. For Améry's self-understanding as a "catastrophe Jew," see especially the last essay from *At the Mind's Limits*. See also Irene Heidelberger-Leonard, "Jean Améry's Selbstverständnis als Jude," in *Über Jean Améry*, ed. Irene Heidelberger-Leonard (Heidelberg: Winter, 1990), 17–27.
73. See Jean Améry "Jargon der Dialektik" (1967), in *Widersprüche* (Stuttgart: Ullstein, 1970), esp. 72–73. For Améry's critique of the Frankfurt School, see also Detlev Claussen, "Eine kritische Differenz: Zum Konflikt Jean Améry's mit Theodor W. Adorno und Max Horkheimer," in *Jean Améry (Hans Maier)*, ed. Stephan Steiner (Basel: Stroemfeld, 1996), 197–207.

74. Améry, *At the Mind's Limits*, xiii.
75. For an analysis of Améry's exile and his ambivalent relationship to Austria and the Austrian discourse on *Heimat*, see also W. G. Sebald, "Verlorenes Land: Jean Améry und Österreich," *Text und Kritik* 99 (1988): 20–29.
76. Peitsch cites, for example, Alfred Andersch's request that the exiles should switch from "resentment" to "objectification" [Objektivierung]. See Helmut Peitsch, "Die Gruppe 47 und die Exilliteratur—ein Mißverständnis?" in *Die Gruppe 47 in der Geschichte der Bundesrepublik*, ed. Justus Fetscher, Eberhard Lämmert, and Jürgen Schutte (Würzburg: Könighausen and Neumann, 1991), 109. Objectification soon came to denote a rejection of the idea of collective guilt and to imply an exculpation of large parts of the German population, especially of its army.
77. Améry, *At the Mind's Limits*, 68.
78. This is not to deny positive effects on an individual level. According to Hans Keilson, the fact that *Wiedergutmachung* allowed victims to recognize themselves as victims potentially helped them to overcome traumatization and to regain a sense of self and agency. See Keilson, "Die Reparationsverträge und die Folgen der 'Wiedergutmachung,'" in *Jüdisches Leben in Deutschland seit 1945*, ed. Micha Brumlik et al. (Frankfurt am Main: Jüdischer Verlag bei Athenäum, 1986), 121–39.
79. Améry, *At the Mind's Limits*, 63. In the foreword to the second German edition, Améry further elaborates the meaning of this address: "But new generations, molded by origin and environment, are constantly rising in both camps, and between them the old unbridgeable chasm is opening again. Someday *time* will close it, that is certain. But it must not be done by hollow, thoughtless, utterly false conciliatoriness, which already now is accelerating the time process. On the contrary: since it is a *moral* chasm, let it for now remain wide open; this, too, is the reason for the new edition of my book" (ibid., ix, emphasis by Améry).
80. Ibid., 62.
81. Ibid., 63.
82. Ibid., 81.
83. See Jürgen Habermas, *The Structural Transformation of the Public Sphere: An Inquiry into a Category of Bourgeois Society*, trans. Thomas Burger with the assistance of Frederic Lawrence (Cambridge, Mass.: MIT Press, 1989), 49–50.
84. Améry, *At the Mind's Limits*, 66.
85. Ibid., 81.
86. Moishe Postone, "Anti-Semitism and National Socialism," *New German Critique* 19 (Winter 1980): 101–2.
87. Améry, *At the Mind's Limits*, 70, emphasis by Améry. For a philosophi-

cally oriented analysis of this concept of historical intervention and its roots in Hegel, see Jean-Michel Chaumont, "Geschichtliche Verantwortung und menschliche Würde bei Jean Améry," in *Über Jean Améry,* 29–47.
88. Améry, *At the Mind's Limits,* 78.

Chapter 2

1. Peter Weiss, *Notizbücher, 1960–1971* (Frankfurt am Main: Suhrkamp, 1982), 54. The notebooks were published only after the great success of the *Notizbücher, 1971–1980,* which appeared at the request of Suhrkamp as a commentary to *Die Ästhetik des Widerstands* [The Aesthetics of Resistance]. Although they came out only after his death, the *Notizbücher, 1960–1971* were prepared for publication by Weiss himself. Unfortunately, the Suhrkamp edition fails to make the readers aware of the fact that Weiss edited his original notes quite extensively: not only did he omit some notes, but he inserted whole passages, that is, part of the text was actually written around 1980, not during the 1960s. This is important because the alterations affect some of the most explicit passages on Peter Weiss's relationship to the West German literary scene. The published version tends to present Weiss's position as an outsider of the German cultural scene in a rather abstract and rationalizing manner at the expense of more impulsive, emotional impressions. The quotes of this chapter are drawn from the published *Notizbücher, 1960–1971,* hereafter referred to in text as *Nb.* Unless otherwise noted, all quotations are also in the unpublished version, although sometimes with slightly different wording.
2. The book was originally written in 1952, but first published in 1960. Excerpts of it appeared in the journal *Akzente,* no. 3 (June 1959): 228–38.
3. See for example Rainer Gerlach, "Isolation und Befreiung: Zum literarischen Frühwerk von Peter Weiss," in *Peter Weiss,* ed. Rainer Gerlach (Frankfurt am Main: Suhrkamp, 1984), 177.
4. See Arlene A. Teraoka, *East, West, and Others: The Third World in Postwar German Literature* (Lincoln: University of Nebraska Press, 1996), 27–47, 74–78.
5. See Alfons Söllner, *Peter Weiss und die Deutschen: Die Entstehung einer politischen Ästhetik wider die Verdrängung* (Opladen: Westdeutscher Verlag, 1988). Among the critics who have established Weiss's *Unzugehörigkeit* [nonbelonging] as a constant throughout his work are Jochen Vogt, *Peter Weiss* (Reinbek bei Hamburg: Rowohlt, 1987); and Juliane Kuhn, *"Wir setzten unser Exil fort": Facetten des Exils im literarischen Werk von Peter Weiss* (St. Ingbert: Röhrig, 1995).

NOTES TO CHAPTER 2

6. The focus on the confrontation between the emigrant and his former home, which comes to a provisional close with *Die Ermittlung*, determined my choice of texts and time frame in this chapter. I thus decided to analyze only in passing the play that made Peter Weiss famous to an international audience, *Marat/Sade*, which premiered in 1964. However, my analysis of the underpinnings of Peter Weiss's politicization also sheds new light on his representation of the French revolutionary and hypersensitive outsider, Marat.
7. See also the story by Tadeusz Borowski, "This Way for the Gas, Ladies and Gentlemen," in *This Way for the Gas, Ladies and Gentlemen*, trans. Barbara Vedder (New York: Penguin Books, 1976), 29–49.
8. See Klaus Briegleb, "'Neuanfang' in der westdeutschen Nachkriegsliteratur—Die Gruppe 47 in den Jahren 1947–1951," in *Bestandsaufnahme: Studien zur Gruppe 47*, ed. Stephan Braese (Berlin: Schmidt, 1999), 35–64.
9. See Peitsch, "Die Gruppe 47 und die Exilliteratur," 120.
10. Richter to Dr. Leonhardt, March 3, 1962. Hans Werner Richter-Archiv, Stiftung Archiv der Akademie der Künste, Berlin (hereafter referred to in text as SAdK), 72/86/520-2.
11. Peter Weiss-Archiv, SAdK, 76/86/7-47.
12. See also Peter Weiss, *Notizbücher, 1971–1980* (Frankfurt am Main: Suhrkamp, 1981), 731, 734; and Sven Kramer, "Zusammenstoß in Princeton—Peter Weiss und die Gruppe 47," in *Bestandsaufnahme*, 155–74. Helmut Müssener draws attention to the fact that Richter's and Grass's rhetoric closely resembled the attacks Christian Democrats were simultaneously launching against Social Democrats who emigrated during the war, which shows that that anti-emigrant sentiments were not confined to the politically conservative. See Müssener, "'Du bist draußen gewesen.' Die unmögliche Heimkehr des exilierten Schriftstellers Peter Weiss," in *Die Gruppe 47 in der Geschichte der Bundesrepublik*, 136. In this context, it is also important to remember that "cosmopolitanism" has often served as a euphemism insinuating that Jews have no bonds to the nation they live in, fostering a notion that they are second-class citizens. As Frank Stern has shown, postwar Germany's philosemitism has created an inverted variant of this political stereotype. See Stern, "Philosemitismus: Stereotype über den Feind, den man zu lieben hat," *Babylon* 8 (1991): 21.
13. Peter Weiss-Archiv, SAdK, 76/86/2190. Letter from January 28, 1965.
14. Peter Weiss, "Unter dem Hirseberg," in *Rapporte 2* (Frankfurt am Main: Suhrkamp, 1971), 12.
15. See Ingo Breuer, "Der Jude Marat: Identifikationsprobleme bei Peter Weiss," in *Peter Weiss: Neue Fragen an alte Texte*, ed. Irene Heidelberger-

Leonard (Opladen: WestdeutscherVerlag, 1994), 70–71.
16. Urs Jenny,"'Abschied von den Eltern'" (1963), in *Über Peter Weiss*, ed. Volker Canaris (Frankfurt am Main: Suhrkamp, 1970), 47.
17. The word "exile" appears already in a pre-1952 Swedish text variant related to *Abschied von den Eltern*, although not in very prominent places. The unpublished manuscript *Abwechselnd lag der Garten*, which was probably written in 1958 or at the beginning of 1959 and is already quite similar to *Abschied von den Eltern*, returns to the notion of exile in the narrator's childhood alienation. I am grateful to Jürgen Schutte for the details about these earlier sketches. During my own research in the Peter Weiss-Archiv, I noticed that *Abschied von den Eltern* (written between 1959 and 1960) foregrounds the theme of exile more strongly than *Abwechselnd lag der Garten*. Some of the most explicit phrases first appear in *Abschied von den Eltern*, for example: "Diese Spiele waren wie Psychodramen, in denen wir uns mit der Emigration auseinandersetzten, in meiner Arbeit war alles nur ein Abgewandtsein und ein Verbergen." Peter Weiss, *Werke in sechs Bänden* (Frankfurt am Main: Suhrkamp 1991), vol. 2, 123. This edition will hereafter be referred to in text as *W*. "These games were like psychodramas in which we confronted emigration, and in my work everything was only turning aside and concealment." Peter Weiss, *Exile*, trans. E. B. Garside, Alastair Hamilton, and Christopher Levenson (New York: Delacorte Press, 1968), 70, trans. altered. This edition contains the translations of both *Abschied von den Eltern* and *Fluchtpunkt*. *Exile* will hereafter be referred to in the text as *Ex*.
18. In *Abschied von den Eltern*, secrecy and uncanniness characterize both the childhood—witness the narrator's reading of forbidden books, his nightly and incestuous encounters with his sister, and his secret spying in the loft for evidence of his parents' identity—and the process of its recollection. The novel starts out with an account of his father's last trip to Belgium, where he went, as the narrator surmises, "um wie ein verwundetes Tier im Versteck zu sterben" (*W*, 2:59) ["to die like a wounded animal in its lair" (*Ex*, 3)]. Later the narrator hides his father's ashes in a cupboard in the hotel and secretly takes away some of his parents' diaries.
19. Weiss himself invokes this tradition in interviews and letters from the 1960s in which he refers to himself as a *Weltbürger*. In his letter to Marcel Reich-Ranicki from October 3, 1965, he claims that his identity as a *Weltbürger* allows him to regard German problems within a universalizing framework: "Because I am not tied to Germany, I see it simply as one small part of the earth's continents; and the conflict there, which constantly erupts anew and compounds itself, revolves around other issues than the complacency that characterizes the official politics of West Germany." Peter Weiss-Archiv, SAdK, Berlin, 76/86/2172-1. For Weiss's

self-labeling as a *Weltbürger*, see further below in this letter (76/86/2172-2).
20. On the Greek origins of the concept, see Joachim Ritter and Karlfried Gründer, eds., *Historisches Wörterbuch der Philosophie*, vol. 4 (Basel and Stuttgart: Schwabe, 1976), s.v. "Kosmopolit, Kosmopolitanismus." Although cosmopolitanism thrived in times when the significance of the individual *polis* was diminishing, it also proved a doctrine well-suited for a politics of ethnocentric expansionism.
21. Johann Wolfgang von Goethe, *Collected Works*, vol. 3: *Essays on Art and Literature*, ed. John Gearey, trans. Ellen von Nardroff and Ernest H. von Nardroff (New York: Suhrkamp, 1986), 225.
22. See Immanuel Kant, *The Cambridge Edition of the Works of Immanuel Kant: Practical Philosophy*, ed. and trans. Mary J. Gregor. (Cambridge: Cambridge University Press, 1996), 328-31.
23. Such an interpretation is not uncommon in modern (Jewish) writing. Stefan Heym's *Ahasver* (Munich: Bertelsmann, 1981) is another example.
24. It is never entirely clear if Anatol is indeed Jewish. The fact that he has his wife buried in Greek-Orthodox fashion and that he has made icons of her does suggest that he might not be Jewish. Yet this takes nothing away from my interpretation that Anatol symbolizes Jewish exile.
25. See Gilroy's analysis of Du Bois's modernist writing in his *The Black Atlantic: Modernity and Double Consciousness* (Cambridge, Mass.: Harvard University Press, 1993), 115.
26. *W*, 2:297. Weiss, *The Conversation of the Three Walkers and The Shadow of the Coachman's Body*, trans. S. M. Cupitt (London: Calder and Boyars, 1972), 7. Hereafter referred to in text as *C*. If I refer below to "speakers," it has to be kept in mind that they are never identifiable as persons and that their voices sometimes merge and affect each other's. There is, nonetheless, enough continuity between the different segments that we can attribute most of them to one of three speakers whom I will simply call A, B, and C. Helmut Lüttmann suggests a plausible sequence of the speakers in his *Die Prosawerke von Peter Weiss* (Hamburg: Lüdke, 1972), 133.
27. Mikhail M. Bakhtin, "Forms of Time and of the Chronotope in the Novel," in *The Dialogic Imagination: Four Essays*, ed. Michael Holquist, trans. Caryl Emerson and Michael Holquist (Austin: University of Texas Press, 1981), 84-258.
28. Michel de Certeau, *The Practice of Everyday Life*, trans. Steven Rendall (Berkeley: University of California Press, 1984), 93. Emphasis by de Certeau.
29. The exile's language dilemma is also pointedly captured in Weiss's

address "Laokoon oder Über die Grenzen der Sprache" [Laocoon, or On the Limits of Language], in *Rapporte*, (Frankfurt am Main: Suhrkamp, 1968), 170–87. In this speech Weiss describes language as the very agent of persecution and expulsion.

30. See the wording Weiss uses to describe his early writing attempts in exile: "doch auch in diesem Fragmentarischen, in diesen zerknitterten Zeugnisses einer krankhaften Einsamkeit, kann ich nicht unbrauchbaren Abfall sehn, nur wert, in den Verbrennungsofen zu fallen" (*W*, 2:461). [Yet in these fragments, in these crumpled documents of a miserable isolation, I cannot see useless refuse, worthy only of the incinerator.]

31. The discrepancy between meaningful language and traumatic experience becomes even more tangible when the narrator, shortly thereafter, uses narrative structures to render his experiences. Interspersed with qualifications and hesitations, these structures are indicative of his failing attempt to verbalize unspeakable horror. While developing increasingly complex semantic units, the narrator exposes their stereotypical character and ultimate inadequacy: "und *ich wollte mir meine Lage vereinfachen*, nun ja, dachte ich, ich bin von meiner Frau weggerissen worden, und meine Kinder hat man an der Wand zerschlagen, *wahrscheinlich* hat man mich in ein Gefängnis geschmissen und dann, *wie üblich*, in ein Massengrab" (*W*, 2:338, my emphasis). [*I wanted to simplify my position*, well then, I thought, I have been torn from my wife, my children have been dashed against a wall, they *probably* threw me into a prison and then, *as they usually do*, into a mass grave" (*C*, 76, my emphasis).]

32. See for example the three descriptions of the hideout. Speaker A conflates the words of the ferryman he remembers—perhaps misremembers—with those of C, which he has just heard, and then C uses the words he heard from A to recast the original scene. For instance, first speaker C describes his hideout as located "unter einem Bretterhaufen" (*W*, 2:318) [under a pile of planks (*C*, 42)] nearby a railway bridge; then speaker A describes a similar site that includes "Packpapier und Wellpappe" (*W*, 2:324) [wrapping paper and corrugated cardboard (*C*, 53, trans. altered)]; and then speaker C changes his own depiction of his hideout to "unter Brettern and aufgeweichter Pappe" (*W*, 2:337) [under planks and sodden cardboard (*C*, 74)].

33. The text remained a fragment and was first published in 1968.

34. For some documentation on the application process, see the letters by Weiss's lawyers Kroll and Gregor. "Entschädigungssache Eugen Weiss," Peter Weiss-Archiv, SAdK, 76/86/1272-1 to 76/86/1272-5.

35. Peter Weiss-Archiv, SAdK, Notizbuch 2, 76/86/2-53. Emphasis by Weiss. In the published *Notizbücher*, this note would have appeared on 110. Weiss's notebooks also contain a reminiscence of what seems to

have been Weiss's own circumcision during his first years of exile in Sweden. Unfortunately, we have little documentation of those years and of the circumstances that may have convinced Weiss to undergo circumcision. The description is nonetheless highly interesting. It is not the act of circumcision itself that is depicted but the negative reaction to it on the face of the female assistant; the circumcised penis, then, is not a positive sign of Jewish identity but a sign of the disgust felt by others: "I was circumcised when already an adult by the doctor in Alingsås. His nurse was visibly disgusted. Myself—I felt nothing. I only saw her contorted face" (*Nb*, 105). For the significance of circumcision as a mark of male Jewish difference, see Sander L. Gilman, "Male Sexuality and Contemporary Jewish Literature in German: The Damaged Body as the Image of the Damaged Soul," in *Reemerging Jewish Culture in Germany*, 210–49.

36. Weiss, "Bericht," 130.
37. For examples of this tradition see Oliver Goldsmith, *The Citizen of the World* (London: Folio Society, n.d.); and Charles-Louis de Secondat, baron de Montesquieu, *Persian Letters*, trans. John Ozell (New York: Garland, 1972).
38. Weiss, "Bericht," 121.
39. Weiss, "Bericht," 126.
40. Weiss, "Bericht," 129.
41. English translations of *Die Ermittlung* are from Peter Weiss, *The Investigation*, trans. Jon Swan and Ulu Grosbard, rev. Robert Cohen, in *Marat/Sade, The Investigation, The Shadow of the Body of the Coachman*, ed. Robert Cohen (New York: Continuum, 1998), which is hereafter referred to in text as *I*.
42. Felman and Laub, *Testimony*, 62.
43. For a comprehensive reconstruction of the relationship between Weiss's *Divine Comedy* project and *Die Ermittlung*, see Christoph Weiß, *Auschwitz in der geteilten Welt: Peter Weiss und die 'Ermittlung' im Kalten Krieg* (St. Ingbert: Röhrig, 2000), 55–148.
44. Martin Walser, "Unser Auschwitz," *Kursbuch* 1 (1965): 190–91.
45. See: "Inferno / accommodates all those who in the opinion of the earlier Dante / were condemned to eternal damnation, but who today / tarry here, with us, the living, / and they continue their deeds unpenalized, and live content, / with their deeds, respected and admired by many. Everything / is firm here, well-oiled, certain, never doubted; any suffering / is pushed far away." Weiss, *Rapporte*, 137. *Inferno* and *Paradiso* refer to the parts of Dante's *Commedia*.
46. "Lynx: We will do anything to be helpful to Dante Alighieri / in his difficult undertaking / Lion: Whoever comes as a friend / we smooth his

path in our land of peace and justice / Lynx: Just as we are on our guard against those forces / that intend to disturb and endanger the harmony we've achieved." Peter Weiss-Archiv, SAdK, 76/86/6095-2, folder 17— *Inferno* 1-1.
47. "She-wolf: It remains to say that, as Virgil's notebooks indicate, certain groups here / have long been in contact with Aligheri. / Lion: Of course, those leftist literary types. Completely non-threatening, basically. / Wolf: And groups of the intellectual youth. They say that his works are highly esteemed there. / Lion: All the better. Our invitation will show even more (he cites ironically) / how free and progressive we are." Peter Weiss-Archiv, SAdK, 76/86/60951-2, folder 17, *Inferno* 1-2.
48. "You built gigantic structures / in commemoration of the ideals of your mind. / You developed indignation at the injustices / which you believed to perceive from your tower, / . . . / And whom did you glorify / but yourself." Peter Weiss-Archiv, SAdK, 76/86/6095-2, folder 18—26/3.
49. See James E. Young, *Writing and Rewriting the Holocaust: Narrative and the Consequences of Interpretation* (Bloomington: Indiana University Press, 1988), 64–80. See also Andreas Huyssen, *After the Great Divide: Modernism, Mass Culture, Postmodernism* (Bloomington: Indiana University Press, 1986), 111. Young goes further than Huyssen, contending that Weiss consciously uses the documentary form in order to make his ideological point of view more credible. For an insightful critique of Young and other critics of *Die Ermittlung*, see Robert Cohen, "The Political Aesthetics of Holocaust Literature: Peter Weiss's *The Investigation* and Its Critics," *History and Memory* 10, no. 2 (Fall 1998): 43–67.
50. This representation of the witnesses is one of the few and striking instances where Weiss departs from the documents, which frequently depict witnesses as being horrified, angry, or crying. See Bernd Naumann, *Auschwitz: A Report on the Proceedings against Robert Karl Ludwig Mulka and Others before the Court at Frankfurt*, trans. Jean Steinberg (New York: Praeger, 1966), 89, 108, 115, 123.
51. Only in one case does a stage direction refer to a witness, that is, when a woman falls into silence after having been asked to testify to the medical experiments to which she was subjected. However, this silence is not an expressive silence; it evokes an extreme absence of affect, a numbness that is also palpable in the witness's depersonalized language as she resumes her speech: "Die übrigen Ärzte des Lagers / erstellten das Menschenmaterial" (*W*, 5:88). [The rest of the camp doctors supplied him / with the subjects he worked on (*I*, 194).]
52. On the form of the oratorio, see also Erika Salloch, *Peter Weiss's* Die Ermittlung: Zur Struktur des Dokumentartheaters (Frankfurt am Main:

Athenäum, 1972), 137.
53. On the function of the chorus as public in Greek drama, see Hans-Thies Lehmann, *Theater und Mythos: Die Konstitution des Subjekts im Diskurs der antiken Tragödie* (Stuttgart: Metzler, 1991), 48.
54. The play also attempts to establish a truth by means other than description. Witness 3, who explains fascism in terms of its links to capitalism, stands for the possibility of political resistance. He speaks with more emphasis and persuasiveness than most of the others. I argue, however, that even his position is undermined by the aporetic constellation created when a witness stands in front of a German audience and uses the German language.
55. Huyssen, *After the Great Divide*, 110.
56. Söllner, *Peter Weiss und die Deutschen*, 181–85.
57. See Pierre Nora, "Between Memory and History: Les Lieux de Mémoire," *Representations* 26 (Spring 1989): 7–24.
58. Peter Weiss, "Meine Ortschaft," in *Rapporte*, 115.

Chapter 3

1. Nelly Sachs, *Briefe der Nelly Sachs*, ed. Ruth Dinesen and Helmut Müssener (Frankfurt am Main: Suhrkamp, 1984), 281, 282. The letter was written to Margaretha and Bengt Holmqvist on June 23, 1962, less than a month after Adolf Eichmann's execution in Jerusalem.
2. Nelly Sachs, *Fahrt ins Staublose* (Frankfurt am Main: Suhrkamp, 1961), 262. This edition is a compilation of poetry from Sachs's early and middle period. It contains several poem collections, some of which had been published before. The following poems from this edition will be quoted with page numbers in brackets and an abbreviation indicating the collection of which they were originally part. The following abbreviations will be used: S (*Sternverdunklung*, 1949 [*Eclipse of the Stars*]); N (*Und niemand weiß weiter*, 1957 [*And No One Knows How to Go On*]); F (*Flucht und Verwandlung*, 1959 [*Flight and Metamorphosis*]); T (*Noch feiert Tod das Leben*, ca. 1961 [*Death Still Celebrates Life*]). The English translations are taken either from Nelly Sachs, *O the Chimneys: Selected Poems*, trans. Michael Hamburger et al. (New York: Farrar, Straus and Giroux, 1967), which will hereafter be referred to in text as *OTC*, or from Nelly Sachs, *The Seeker and Other Poems*, trans. Ruth and Matthew Mead and Michael Hamburger (New York: Farrar, Straus and Giroux, 1970), which will hereafter be referred to in text as abbreviated *TS*. Unless otherwise noted, all emphases in Sachs's poems are mine.
3. Hans Magnus Enzensberger, "Die Steine der Freiheit," *Merkur* 13, no. 8 (August 1959): 772. For the redeemer topos, see also the prize diploma of the *Annette von Droste-Hülshoff-Preis für Dichterinnen 1960*: "We thank

[Nelly Sachs], the Jewish woman of German extraction, for preserving in her poetry the quality of the German language and the possibility for this language to become a vessel of mercy, in spite of its merciless abuse in the mouth of the hangmen." Nelly Sachs-Archiv, Stadt- und Landesbibliothek Dortmund, Presse 151. On Nelly Sachs's reception in West Germany, see Erhard Bahr, *Nelly Sachs* (Munich: Beck, 1980), 9–28; Ruth Dinesen, "Verehrung und Verwerfung: Nelly Sachs—Kontroverse um eine Dichterin," in *Kontroversen, alte und neue: Akten des VII. Internationalen Germanisten-Kongresses Göttingen 1985*, ed. Karl Pestalozzi, Alexander von Bormann, and Thomas Koebner (Tübingen: Niemeyer, 1986), 130–37; Leonard Olschner, "Der mühsame Weg von Nelly Sachs' Poesie ins literarische Bewußtsein," in *Die Resonanz des Exils: Gelungene und mißlungene Rezeption deutschsprachiger Exilautoren*, ed. Dieter Sevin (Amsterdam: Rodopi, 1992), 267–81; and Michael Braun, "Phasen, Probleme und Perspektiven der Nelly-Sachs-Rezeption: Forschungsbericht und Bibliographie," in *Nelly Sachs: Neue Interpretationen*, ed. Michael Kessler and Jürgen Wertheimer (Tübingen: Stauffenburg, 1994), 375–93.

4. There are some hints that these institutions sought contact with Sachs even before she was noticed by the German reading public. *Friede mit Israel: Mitteilungsblatt der Gesellschaft für Christlich-Jüdische Zusammenarbeit* (Hamburg) published some of her poems and a review article about her around 1956. See Sachs's letter to Johannes Edfelt, December 9, 1956, in *Briefe*, 155.

5. See Uwe Naumann's survey over the reception of the play, "Ein Stück der Versöhnung: Zur Uraufführung des Mysterienspiels *Eli* von Nelly Sachs (1962)," *Exilforschung: Ein Internationales Jahrbuch* 4 (1986): 98–114.

6. See Y. Michal Bodemann, "Staat und Ethnizität: Der Aufbau der jüdischen Gemeinden im Kalten Krieg," in *Jüdisches Leben in Deutschland seit 1945*, ed. Micha Brumlik et al. (Frankfurt am Main: Jüdischer Verlag bei Athenäum, 1986), 49–69.

7. See Martin Stöhr, "Gespräche nach Abels Ermordung: Die Anfänge des jüdisch-christlichen Dialogs," in *Jüdisches Leben in Deutschland seit 1945*, esp. 221–22. On the constitutive phase of the *Gesellschaften für Christlich-Jüdische Zusammenarbeit*, their apologetic tendency, and their function in restoring the German reputation abroad, see Josef Foschepoth, *Im Schatten der Vergangenheit: Die Anfänge der Gesellschaften für Christlich-Jüdische Zusammenarbeit* (Göttingen: Vandenhoeck and Ruprecht, 1993).

8. "Grußworte des Präsidenten der Bundesrepublik Deutschland," in *Nelly Sachs: Ansprachen anläßlich der Verleihung des Friedenspreises des Deutschen Buchhandels* (Frankfurt am Main: Börsenverein des Deutschen

NOTES TO CHAPTER 3

Buchhandels, 1965), 9–10.
9. *Nelly Sachs: Ansprachen,* 14.
10. See Diner, "Negative Symbiose," 12–13.
11. For the construction of antithetical images of male and the female Jews, see Sander L. Gilman, "Salome, Syphilis, Sarah Bernhardt and the 'Modern Jewess,'" *German Quarterly* 66, no. 2 (Spring 1993): 195–211. For the gender ideology at work in Nelly Sachs's reception, see Willy Brundert's speech during the *Friedenspreis* ceremony: "Who else but woman would naturally be called upon to proclaim to the world, sensitively and thus all the more efficiently, the high ethical goals of love of peace, humanity, and international understanding?" *Nelly Sachs: Ansprachen,* 21.
12. See Huyssen, *After the Great Divide,* 100–101.
13. See Bruno Bettelheim, *The Informed Heart: Autonomy in a Mass Age* (New York: Avon, 1971), 252–54.
14. Frances Goodrich and Albert Hackett, *The Diary of Anne Frank* (New York: Random House, 1956), 174. In the book, this sentence is the second to last line; in the film it is the very last line.
15. See for example an essay by Hellmut Geißner, broadcasted December 9, 1961, by the Saarländischer Rundfunk: "Only her long-standing friendship with Selma Lagerlöf, to whom Nelly Sachs in 1921 dedicated her first book *Legenden und Erzählungen,* and the intervention of the Swedish royal house made it possible for her and her aged mother to fly to Stockholm." Nelly Sachs-Archiv, Presse 158, 1. See also Ruth Dinesen, *Nelly Sachs: Eine Biographie,* trans. Gabriele Gerecke (Frankfurt am Main: Suhrkamp, 1992), 108.
16. Quoted in Jakob Hessing, *Die Heimkehr einer jüdischen Emigrantin: Else Lasker-Schülers mythisierende Rezeption 1945 bis 1971* (Tübingen: Niemeyer, 1993), 30.
17. See Gershom Scholem, "Against the Myth of the German-Jewish Dialogue" (1962); "Once More: The German-Jewish Dialogue" (1965); "Jews and Germans" (1966), trans. Werner J. Dannhauser, in *On Jews and Judaism in Crisis,* ed. Werner J. Dannhauser (New York: Schocken Books, 1978), 61–92.
18. Scholem, "Against the Myth of the German-Jewish Dialogue," 61.
19. For the public's attention to dead Jews and the lack of interest in living Jews, see Sander L. Gilman, "Jewish Writers in Contemporary Germany: The Dead Author Speaks," in *Inscribing the Other* (Lincoln: University of Nebraska Press, 1991), 249–78.
20. Sachs's tendency to veil her private self with an aura of secrecy reinforces this separation between public and private: "I think you do not yet know how much I fear the public. I publish things—now at the end of my

NOTES TO CHAPTER 3

life—since new young people want to have them—, but I myself want to disappear into the dark. Of course my outward and inward life is based on a fate, whose secret only my mother knew—and which no one else will know." Letter to Walter A. Berendsohn, December 15, 1959. Sachs, *Briefe*, 238.

21. See Sachs's letter to Alfred Andersch, October 30, 1957: "But this [*Eli*] is nothing for Germany, I know and I feel it. It is my first work, written in the fire of terrible suffering, around the same time as *Die Wohnungen des Todes*." Sachs, *Briefe*, 170.
22. Letter to Alfred Andersch, October 1, 1957. Sachs, *Briefe*, 168.
23. Letter to Walter A. Berendsohn, November 28, 1957. Sachs, *Briefe*, 178. For other examples of such quotes, see ibid., 160, 166.
24. See her letter to Peter Hamm, May 10, 1958, in Sachs, *Briefe*, 190. For the symbolic effect of cultural relationships, see also the letter to the Catholic priest and writer Albrecht Goes, July 16, 1951: "I cannot express in words what a gift you sent me with this holy book *Unsere letzte Stunde*. But now it is with me all the time. It came in the same mail as a book of stories [Legendenbuch] by the Hebrew writer Agnon, who is currently in Stockholm, and the holy Hasidim always lie like a profound symbol next to your blessed "poetry of departure" [Ausgangsdichtung]." Sachs, *Briefe*, 130.
25. Letter to Johannes Edfelt, September 12, 1956. Sachs, *Briefe*, 155.
26. Letter to Brita and Johannes Edfelt, March 21, 1956. Sachs, *Briefe*, 160.
27. Letter to Johannes Edfelt, August 25, 1959. Sachs, *Briefe*, 228.
28. Letter to Walter A. Berendsohn, March 24, 1948. Sachs, *Briefe*, 92. Berendsohn, originally a professor of German literature in Hamburg, like Sachs had found refuge in Stockholm and later came to play a crucial role in disseminating her work in both Sweden and Germany. Although he never immigrated to Israel, Berendsohn ardently supported Zionism. In 1951, he traveled through Israel and wrote an enthusiastic report on the building of the new state. See Walter A. Berendsohn, *Aufbauarbeit in Israel* (Berlin: Bernhard and Graefe, 1953). In one of her earliest letters to Berendsohn, Sachs defines her position as follows: "I am not a Zionist in the contemporary sense of the word; I believe that our homeland is wherever the springs of eternity flow." Letter to Walter A. Berendsohn, September 12, 1944. Sachs, *Briefe*, 41.
29. Ytzak Baer, *Galut*, trans. Robert Warshow (New York: Schocken Books, 1947), 9.
30. Arnold Eisen has further shown that in modern times the concept of the land of Israel underwent a demystification, resymbolization, and politicization. See Eisen, "Off Center: The Concept of the Land of Israel in Modern Jewish Thought," in *The Land of Israel: Jewish Perspectives*, ed.

Lawrence A. Hoffman (Notre Dame, Ind.: University of Notre Dame Press, 1986), 263–96. For concepts of Jewish diaspora and the land of Israel, see also: Jacob Neusner, *Self-Fulfilling Prophecy: Exile and Return in the History of Judaism* (Boston: Beacon, 1987); Eliezer Schweid, "Land of Israel," in *Contemporary Jewish Religious Thought: Original Essays on Critical Concepts, Movements, and Beliefs*, ed. Arthur A. Cohen and Paul Mendes-Flohr (New York: Free Press, 1987), 535–41; Ben Halpern, *The Idea of the Jewish State*, 2nd ed. (Cambridge, Mass.: Harvard University Press, 1969).

31. Halpern, *The Jewish State*, 73.
32. That the implied addressee of Sachs's poetry was humanity in general is documented, for instance, in her comments on the political conflicts that accompanied the establishment of the state of Israel, which she links to the Nazi persecution of Jews as well as well as to her own task as a writer: "If only there would be peace again in Erez Israel. It is strange how quickly the Jewish fate gets buried under current events, as if humanity were glad to be free of a responsibility to which it once did not measure up. If I could only contribute something to keep the memory alive, that would have been worth giving my life." Letter to Walter A. Berendsohn, May 21, 1948. Berendsohn, *Nelly Sachs: Einführung in das Werk der Dichterin jüdischen Schicksals* (Darmstadt: Agora, 1974), 145.
33. The word is from the introduction to the Sabbath Eve Kiddush (originally from Gen. 2:1) and refers to the completion of creation.
34. On the figure of Ruth as an exhortation to tolerance, see Russell A. Berman, "'Der begrabenen Blitze Wohnstatt': Trennung, Heimkehr und Sehnsucht in der Lyrik von Nelly Sachs," in *Im Zeichen Hiobs: Jüdische Schriftsteller und deutsche Literatur im 20. Jahrhundert*, ed. Gunter E. Grimm and Hans-Peter Bayerdörfer (Königstein/Ts.: Athenäum, 1985), 287.
35. See also Mark H. Gelber, "Nelly Sachs und das Land Israel: Die mystisch-poetischen Funktionen der geographisch-räumlich Assoziationen," in *Nelly Sachs: Neue Interpretationen*, 169–78.
36. Alain Finkielkraut, *The Imaginary Jew*, trans. Kevin O'Neill and David Suchoff (Lincoln: University of Nebraska Press, 1994), 124–25. Emphasis by Finkielkraut.
37. Nelly Sachs was not able to attend the lectures but received copies from Bergmann. See her letters to Bergmann 1947–48 in *Briefe*, 85–90.
38. See Paul Mendes-Flohr, "Franz Rosenzweig and the Crisis of Historicism," in *The Philosophy of Franz Rosenzweig*, ed. Paul Mendes-Flohr (Hanover, N.H.: University Press of New England, 1988), 138–61.
39. Diner, "Negative Symbiose," 20.

40. See Dominick LaCapra, *Writing History, Writing Trauma* (Baltimore: Johns Hopkins University Press, 2001), 79.
41. See Steven M. Wasserstrom, *Between Muslim and Jew: The Problem of Symbiosis under Early Islam* (Princeton, N.J.: Princeton University Press, 1995), esp. the introductory discussion of the term "symbiosis."
42. See Franz Rosenzweig, *The Star of Redemption*, trans. William H. Hallo (New York: Holt, Rinehart, and Winston, 1971), 300.
43. Nelly Sachs, *Abram im Salz*, in *Zeichen im Sand: Die szenischen Dichtungen der Nelly Sachs* (Frankfurt am Main: Suhrkamp, 1962), 119. Emphasis by Sachs. For a more comprehensive interpretation of the play, see Dorothee Ostmeier, *Sprache des Dramas, Drama der Sprache: Zur Poetik der Nelly Sachs* (Tübingen: Niemeyer, 1997), 40–74.
44. In a letter, Sachs describes Abraham's father in words that evoke the image of a religiously and politically indifferent German Jew of the 1930s: "Abraham's weak and doubting father, who gladly worships everything as long as the peace of his everyday life in ensured, and who decides to flee only when his son is about to be thrown in the oven." Letter to Walter Berendsohn, September 1, 1946. Berendsohn, *Nelly Sachs*, 135.
45. Sachs, *Abram im Salz*, in *Zeichen im Sand*, 120.
46. Ibid., 95.
47. Ibid., 122.
48. See Jakob Grimm and Wilhelm Grimm, eds., *Deutsches Wörterbuch*, rev. Karl Euling (Leipzig: Hirzel, 1936), s.vv. "Ur," "Urbild," "Urmensch."
49. The commentary of Rashi on Gen. 11:28 mentions this midrashic exegesis. See *Chumash with Rashi's Commentary*, ed. and trans. Rabbi A. M. Silbermann (Jerusalem: Silbermann Family, 1934), 47.
50. See for instance Sachs, *Eli*, in *Zeichen im Sand*, 34, 90 (hereafter referred to in the text as *E*), and *Abram im Salz*, in *Zeichen im Sand*, 112.
51. Sander Gilman, *Jewish Self-Hatred: Anti-Semitism and the Hidden Language of the Jews* (Baltimore: Johns Hopkins University Press, 1986), 270.
52. See Dietz Bering, *Der Name als Stigma: Antisemitismus im deutschen Alltag, 1812–1933* (Stuttgart: Klett-Cotta, 1987), 15–25 and 232–37. According to Bering, names functioned since the nineteenth century as means to stigmatize Jews. Originally not a Hebrew but a Greek name, "Isidor" became a favorite name among assimilating Jews because of its phonetic assonance to popular Jewish names such as "Isaak" "and "Israel." Since it was rarely chosen by Christians, it developed into a distinctively Jewish name. According to Bering, it carried the strongest antisemitic stigma of all Jewish names.
53. For a survey of the different adaptations of the Melusine theme, see Irm-

gard Roebling, ed., *Sehnsucht und Sirene: Vierzehn Abhandlungen zu Wasserphantasien* (Pfaffenweiler: Centaurus, 1992). For insightful remarks on Sachs's Melusine cycle, see Anke Bennholdt-Thomsen and Alfredo Guzzoni, "Melusine: Herkunft und Bedeutung bei Nelly Sachs," *Euphorion* 81, no. 2 (1987): 156–70.

54. Ludwig Tieck's Romantic adaptation of the Genoveva legend depicts Genoveva with notable German nationalist undertones. See Ludwig Tieck, "Leben und Tod der heiligen Genoveva: Ein Trauerspiel," in *Schriften*, vol. 2 (Berlin: Reimer, 1828), 1–272. For the figure of the *shekhinah*, see Gershom G. Scholem, *Von der mystischen Gestalt der Gottheit* (Frankfurt am Main: Suhrkamp, 1973), 135–92. Kathrin M. Bower points out further parallels between Sachs's and Martin Buber's representation of the shekhinah in *Ethics and Remembrance in the Poetry of Nelly Sachs and Rose Ausländer* (Rochester, N.Y.: Camden House, 2000), 68.

55. See Bennholdt-Thomsen and Guzzoni, "Melusine," 160.

56. Bakhtin contrasts unconscious hybridity, which occurs almost automatically in most linguistic utterances and constitutes the main vehicle of linguistic development, with intentional hybridity, a critical strategy that undoes the monological voice of authority by setting two voices against each other, such that a dialectical tension emerges between them, and one voice unmasks the other. See Bakhtin, *The Dialogic Imagination: Four Essays*, 358–61.

57. See Roman Jakobson, "Linguistics and Poetics," in *Language in Literature*, ed. Krystyna Pomorska and Stephen Rudy (Cambridge, Mass.: Belknap Press of Harvard University Press, 1987), 71.

58. See Gabriele Fritsch-Vivié, *Nelly Sachs* (Reinbek bei Hamburg: Rowohlt, 1993), 118.

59. See Wolfgang Benz, ed., *Die Juden in Deutschland, 1933–1945* (Munich: Beck, 1988), esp. 596–613. Sachs herself compared the persecution to which she felt subject to the Gestapo terror against intellectuals (Sachs, *Briefe*, 280). She further captured the claustrophobia that shaped every aspect of her life in Germany during the late 1930s in a dense prose text titled "Leben unter Bedrohung," in Berendsohn, *Nelly Sachs*, 9–12.

60. See Dinesen, *Nelly Sachs*, 238.

61. See Eric L. Santner, *My Own Private Germany: Daniel Paul Schreber's Secret History of Modernity* (Princeton, N.J.: Princeton University Press, 1996).

62. For the centrality of the Eichmann trial for Sachs's persecution fears, see also a letter she wrote to Gunnar Ekelöf while in the hospital, June 6, 1961: "But I will have to stay here in my refuge until the trial in

Jerusalem is over, and after that—I don't know whether they will leave me in peace." Quoted in Dinesen, *Nelly Sachs*, 337.

63. For the political dimension of the trial, see Hannah Arendt, *Eichmann in Jerusalem: A Report on the Banality of Evil*, revised and enlarged edition (New York: Viking Press, 1964), esp. 253–79. See also Manès Sperber, "Churban oder die unfaßbare Gewißheit," in *Die Kontroverse: Hannah Arendt, Eichmann und die Juden*, ed. F. A. Krummacher (Munich: Nymphenburger Verlagshandlung, 1964), esp. 28–29. In recent years, the political dimension of the Eichmann trial has once again become the subject of intense debate. Continuing her earlier work on survivor testimony, Shoshana Felman has argued that the trial added "*a new idiom* to the discourse on the Holocaust." Felman, "Theaters of Justice: Arendt in Jerusalem, the Eichmann Trial, and the Redefinition of Legal Meaning in the Wake of the Holocaust," *Critical Inquiry* 27, no. 2 (Winter 2001): 201. Emphasis by Felman. In contrast, Benjamin Robinson has criticized the conflation of justice and national sovereignty in the trial, and its political instrumentalization for cold-war political agendas. See Robinson, "*The Specialist* on the Eichmann Precedent: Morality, Law, and Military Sovereignty," *Critical Inquiry* 30, no. 1 (Autumn 2003): 63–97.

64. "Dear Mr. President, I wish to tell you, in words that took shape in deepest suffering, what moves me most deeply . . . . Do not pronounce a judgment against Eichmann. Even in Germany, there were the righteous; for their sakes let there be an era of mercy." Letter to David Ben-Gurion, March 27, 1962. Quoted in Dinesen, *Nelly Sachs*, 338. For the legend of the thirty-six hidden righteous, see Gershom Scholem, "Die 36 verborgenen Gerechten in der jüdischen Tradition," in *Judaica 1* (Frankfurt am Main: Suhrkamp, 1963), 216–25.

65. See also Michael Kessler, "Dichte der Abwesenheit: Transzendenz und Transzendieren im Werk der Nelly Sachs," in *Nelly Sachs: Neue Interpretationen*, 253.

66. Although madness traditionally counts as an attribute of the prophet, it derives here not from divine inspiration but from illness, and it is difficult not to hear some desperation in the final line.

67. See also other examples of deictic poems in *Noch feiert Tod das Leben:* "Vor meinem Fenster" (*T*, 346) [In Front of My Window"], "Hinter der Tür" (*T*, 348) ["Behind the door," *OTC*, 211], and "Da" (*T*, 374) ["There," *OTC*, 363]. These poems describe everyday spaces as infused with the threat of the past and fail to construct symbolic places that would elude this threat.

68. Nelly Sachs, *Suche nach Lebenden* (Frankfurt am Main: Suhrkamp, 1971), 120, hereafter referred to in text as *SNL*.

NOTES TO CHAPTER 4

69. Bahr, *Nelly Sachs*, 152.
70. See Paul Kersten, *Die Metaphorik in der Lyrik von Nelly Sachs: Mit einer Wortkonkordanz und einer Nelly Sachs-Bibliographie* (Hamburg: Lüdke, 1970).
71. Paul Celan, *Collected Prose*, trans. Rosmarie Waldrop (Manchester: Carcanet, 1986), 15–16, trans. altered.

Chapter 4

1. Claire Goll had accused Celan of plagiarizing her husband's poetry as early as 1953 but managed to attract wider public attention only after the appearance of her article in the Munich literary magazine *Baubudenpoet*. For a comprehensive documentation of the affair, see Barbara Wiedemann, ed. and comp., *Paul Celan—Die Goll-Affäre: Dokumente zu einer "Infamie"* (Frankfurt am Main: Suhrkamp, 2000). For Celan's tense relationship with the Gruppe 47 around the same time, see Klaus Briegleb, "Ingeborg Bachmann, Paul Celan: Ihr (Nicht-)Ort in der Gruppe 47 (1952–1964/65)," in *Ingeborg Bachmann und Paul Celan: Poetische Korrespondenzen*, ed. Bernhard Böschenstein and Sigrid Weigel (Frankfurt am Main: Suhrkamp, 1997), 59–68.
2. Françoise Meltzer, *Hot Property: The Stakes and Claims of Literary Originality* (Chicago: University of Chicago Press, 1994), 46.
3. Letter to Petre Solomon, September 5, 1962. Solomon, "Briefwechsel mit Paul Celan, 1957–1962," *Neue Literatur* 32, no. 11 (November 1981): 78. Emphasis by Celan. The letter was originally written in French.
4. Israel Chalfen, *Paul Celan: A Biography of His Youth*, trans. Maximilian Bleyleben (New York: Persea Books, 1991), 184.
5. János Szász, "'Es ist nicht so einfach . . .': Erinnerungen an Paul Celan: Seiten aus einem amerikanischen Tagebuch," *Neue Literatur* 26, no. 11 (November 1975): 27.
6. Letter to Petre Solomon from the summer of 1957. Solomon, "Briefwechsel," 73. The letter was originally written in Rumanian.
7. Letter to Walter Jens from 1961. Quoted in John Felstiner, *Paul Celan: Poet, Survivor, Jew* (New Haven, Conn.: Yale University Press, 1995), 177.
8. See Reinhard Döhl, "Geschichte und Kritik eines Angriffs: Zu den Behauptungen gegen Paul Celan," *Deutsche Akademie für Sprache und Dichtung: Jahrbuch 1960*: 101–32.
9. Letter to Alfred Margul-Sperber, June 30, 1960. Celan, "Briefe an Alfred Margul-Sperber," *Neue Literatur* 26, no. 7 (July 1975): 56. Emphasis by Celan.
10. For an account of the meeting between Sachs and Celan in Zurich, see

Dinesen, *Nelly Sachs,* 299–300.
11. Letter to Alfred Margul-Sperber, February 8, 1962. Celan, "Briefe," 57.
12. See Jean Bollack, "Paul Celan und Nelly Sachs: Geschichte eines Kampfes," *Neue Rundschau* 105, no. 4 (1994): 127–28.
13. Uta Werner, *Textgräber: Paul Celans geologische Lyrik* (Munich: Fink, 1998).
14. Ulrich Baer, *Remnants of Song,* 241. See also Peter Szondi, "Reading 'Engführung,'" in *Celan Studies,* ed. Jean Bollack et al., trans. Susan Bernofsky with Harvey Mendelsohn (Palo Alto, Calif.: Stanford University Press, 2003), 27–82.
15. Letter to Petre Solomon, March 26, 1962. Solomon, "Briefwechsel," 76. Emphasis by Celan. The letter was originally written in French. On Celan's renewed interest in Eastern Europe, see especially Felstiner, *Paul Celan,* 185–99.
16. Bollack, "Paul Celan und Nelly Sachs," 128. Emphasis by Bollack.
17. *Selected Poems and Prose of Paul Celan,* trans. John Felstiner (New York: Norton, 2001), 413. Emphasis by Celan. This edition will hereafter be referred to in text as *PPC*. The edition contains fine translations of most of the poems discussed in this chapter and will be referenced throughout. However, I have altered all translations of poems to some degree, often inspired by the equally fine translations in *Poems of Paul Celan,* trans. Michael Hamburger, rev. and exp. ed. (New York: Persea Books, 2002).
18. Paul Celan, *Die Niemandsrose, Tübinger Ausgabe,* ed. Jürgen Wertheimer (Frankfurt am Main: Suhrkamp, 1996), 41. This edition, which includes earlier versions of the poems and annotations, will hereafter be referred to in text as *Nr.* Unless otherwise noted, the quotes in this chapter are drawn from the final version of the poems. I have made extensive use of the annotations in this volume and, especially, in Jürgen Lehmann, ed., *Kommentar zu Paul Celans "Die Niemandsrose,"* with the assistance of Christine Ivanović, 2nd ed. (Heidelberg: Winter, 1998). This commentary also contains a comprehensive bibliography of scholarly articles on the individual poems. To keep the chapter readable, I do not note each instance in which I cull factual knowledge from these important sources. One particularly helpful article on "Eine Gauner- und Ganovenweise" is Manfred Geier, "Poetisierung der Bedeutung: Zu Struktur und Funktion des sprachlichen Zeichens in einem Gedicht von Celan," in *Paul Celan,* ed. Werner Hamacher and Winfried Menninghaus (Frankfurt am Main: Suhrkamp, 1988), 239–71. Another important article that addresses questions of place and origin in this poem is Amir Eshel and Thomas Sparr, "Zur Topographie der Herkunft in der Lyrik von Dan Pagis und Paul Celan," in *Von Franzos zu Canetti: Jüdische Autoren aus Österreich,* ed. Mark Gelber, Hans Otto Horch, and Sigurd Paul Scheichl

(Tübingen: Niemeyer, 1996), 115–28.
19. Winfried Menninghaus, "'Czernowitz / Bukowina' als Topos deutsch-jüdischer Geschichte und Literatur," *Merkur* 53, no. 3–4 (March–April 1999): 349. For a cultural history of the Bukovina, see Andrei Corbea-Hoisie, *Czernowitzer Geschichten: Über eine städtische Kultur in Mittelosteuropa* (Vienna: Böhlau, 2003).
20. The poem's initial title was "Eine deutsche Weise, gesungen von Paul Celan / im Februar 1961" (*Nr,* 40), and an intermediate title read "Eine Gauner- und Ganovenweise, im Jahre 1961 gesungen von Pawel Lwowitsch Tselan, Russkij poët in partibus nemetskich infidelium." This title presents Celan as a Russian poet residing in the midst of German infidels or disbelievers; "in partibus infidelium" is the Latin designation for bishops whose dioceses were under heathen rule, and "nemetsky" is the Russian word for "German."
21. François Villon, *Complete Poems,* ed. and trans. Barbara N. Sargent-Baur (Toronto: University of Toronto Press, 1994), 272–73. This reversal is even more conspicuous in the French original: "Je suis François, dont il me poise, / Né de Paris emprès Pontoise. / Et de la corde d'une toise / Saura mon col que mon cul poise."
22. For Sadagora's reputation, see Chalfen, *Paul Celan,* 29. The Jewish alignment with German culture in the Bukovina acquired, of course, another meaning after the Romanian government took over beginning in 1918. With Romanian nationalism and antisemitism rising in the following years, German culture became itself a minority culture and for many Jews an expression of resistance to Romanian hegemony. From the vantage point of the Holocaust, however, the Jewish commitment to German culture—which led the young Celan, for example, to disregard Yiddish as a corrupt language—appears nonetheless as problematic.
23. See Heinrich Heine, *Sämtliche Schriften,* vol. 1, *Schriften 1817–1840,* ed. Klaus Briegleb (Frankfurt am Main: Ullstein, 1981), 271.
24. Heinrich Heine, *The Rabbi of Bacharach,* trans. Charles Godfrey Leland, in *Jewish Stories and Hebrew Melodies* (New York: Markus Wiener, 1987), 80.
25. On this concept, see p. 40 of this book.
26. See Eccles. 12:5 and Jer. 1:11–12. The image in Jeremiah is based on the wordplay of the Hebrew *shaked* [almond] and *shakad* [to keep watch]. For the almond rod as a symbol of divinely ordained authority, see Num. 17:23. The almond tree also recalls the name of Osip Mandel'shtam. Because of its bitter and sweet fruits, it in baroque emblems further came to signify Jesus's suffering and its redemptive effect.
27. The song from which Celan quotes reads: "Wir kamen nach *Friaul / Da hättn wir* allesamt groß Maul / Strampedemi / Ala mi presente al vos-

tra signori"; an earlier version had "die Pest" instead of "groß Maul." Ludwig Erk, comp., *Deutscher Liederhort: Auswahl der vorzüglichen Volkslieder,* rev. Franz M. Böhme, vol. 3 (Leipzig: Breitkopf and Härtel, 1894), no. 1286.

28. Gershom Scholem, *Major Trends in Jewish Mysticism* (1946; reprint, New York: Schocken Books, 1988), 248. In his French copy of the book, Celan not only marked the whole passage on the psalms, but also penciled on the bottom on the page a reference to his own poem "Engführung" ["Stretto"]—"18.7.1960: 'die Rillen, die Psalmen'!!!" [7/18/1960: 'the grooves, the psalms'!!!]. See G. G. Scholem, *Les Grands Courants de la mystique juive,* trans. M. M. Davy (Paris: Payot, 1950), 265. The book is located in the Deutsches Literaturarchiv, Marbach. See Deutsches Literaturarchiv in Marbach, *Katalog der Bibliothek Paul Celans (Paris und Moisville) in vier Bänden,* comp. Dietlind Meinecke and Stefan Reichert, vol. 3, part 1, p. 80.

29. See Joachim Schulze, "Rauchspur und Sefira: Über die Grundlagen von Paul Celans Kabbala-Rezeption," *Celan-Jahrbuch* 4 (1991): 211. For the phallic symbolism, see Scholem's *Von der mystischen Gestalt der Gottheit,* 101 and 103. Celan was given a copy of the original edition (Zürich: Rhein-Verlag, 1962) in 1967, which does not preclude the possibility that he read the book before that. See also Celan's more explicit allusion to this motif in the poem "Aus Engelsmaterie" ["Out of Angel Flesh"] in *Fadensonnen,* Tübinger Ausgabe, ed. Jürgen Wertheimer (Frankfurt am Main: Suhrkamp, 1996), 161: "phallisch / vereint im Einen . . . vom Osten gestreut, einzubringen im Westen" [phallically united in the One . . . seed scattered in the East to be gathered in the West (*Glottal Stop: 101 Poems by Paul Celan,* trans. Nikolai Popov and Heather McHugh [Hanover, N.H.: Wesleyan University Press/University Press of New England, 2000], 70, hereafter referred to in text as *GS*.)].

30. See Hendrik Birus, "Hommage à quelqu'un: Paul Celans *Hüttenfenster*—ein 'Wink' für Johannes Bobrowski?," in *Hermenautik—Hermeneutik: Literarische und geisteswissenschaftliche Beiträge zu Ehren von Peter Horst Neumann,* ed. Holger Helbig, Bettina Knauer, and Gunnar Och (Würzburg: Königshausen & Neumann, 1996), 269–77.

31. Letter by Bobrowski from October 9, 1956. Quoted in Birus, "Hommage," 275.

32. For Celan's critique of the poem, see his letter to Alfred Margul-Sperber from September 12, 1962. Celan, "Briefe," 59.

33. Letter to Gottfried Bermann Fischer, December 14, 1963, in *Paul Celan,* ed. Werner Hamacher and Winfried Menninghaus (Frankfurt am Main: Suhrkamp, 1988), 22. Emphasis by Celan.

34. See Rilke's letter to Witold Hulewitz, quoted in Wolfram Groddeck,

"Nachwort," in Rainer Maria Rilke, *Duineser Elegien, Die Sonette an Orpheus* (Stuttgart: Reclam, 1997), 141–42. The figure of death in Celan's poem further evokes the angel of death described in Baudelaire's "La Mort des pauvres," an intertextual allusion that is supported by the word "magnetisch" [magnetically], which in Baudelaire's poem describes the lure of death for the poor. See Celan's translation in *Gesammelte Werke*, ed. Beda Allemann and Stefan Reichert, vol. 4 (Frankfurt am Main: Suhrkamp, 1983), 821.

35. Johannes Bobrowski, *Gesammelte Werke*, vol. 1, ed. Eberhard Haufe (Stuttgart: Deutsche Verlags-Anstalt, 1987), 34.
36. Ibid.
37. The reading of the last line as a reference to two different forms or qualities of light can be supported by the fact that Celan temporarily considered the formulation "mit // dem Licht und der Leuchte" (*Nr*, 122). For a reconstruction of the poem's possible references to the Kabbalah, see Jean Firges, *Vom Osten gestreut, einzubringen im Westen: Jüdische Mystik in der Dichtung Paul Celans* (Annweiler am Trifels: Sonnenberg, 1999), 122; and Schulze, "Rauchspur," 231–34. For a rich and complex reading of the poem that takes its lead from such allusions to the Kabbalah, see Rochelle Tobias's forthcoming book *The Unnatural World: Stones, Stars and Bodies in Paul Celan's Work*. According to Tobias, the poem makes minor messianic claims, attempting to redeem individual things without purporting to redeem history.
38. See Scholem, *Jewish Mysticism*, 222.
39. These lines hark back to a sentence in the *Sohar*, according to which consonants are bodies and vowels are souls. See Gershom Scholem, *Die Geheimnisse der Schöpfung: Ein Kapitel aus dem Sohar* (Berlin: Bücherei des Schocken Verlags, 1935), 49. In Celan's copy of this book this sentence is underlined. The book is located in the Deutsches Literaturarchiv in Marbach. See *Katalog der Bibliothek Paul Celans*, vol. 4, part 1, no. 295.
40. The German word used by Celan, "Davidsschild" [shield of David], is the literal translation of the Hebrew *magen david*, which is usually translated as "Star of David."
41. For the more narrow definition of intertextuality, see Renate Lachmann, *Memory and Literature: Intertextuality in Russian Modernism*, trans. Roy Sellars and Anthony Wall (Minneapolis: University of Minnesota Press, 1997). On intertextuality in Celan, especially in its personal and intersubjective dimensions, see Sigrid Weigel, "Die Erinnerungs- und Erregungsspuren von Zitat und Lektüre: Die Intertextualität Bachmann-Celan, gelesen mit Benjamin," in *Ingeborg Bachmann und Paul Celan*, 231–49; and Michael Eskin, *Ethics and Dialogue in the Works of Levinas*,

Bakhtin, Mandel'shtam, and Celan (Oxford: Oxford University Press, 2000), esp. 226–67.

42. Paul Celan, *Speech-Grille and Selected Poems*, trans. Joachim Neugroschel (New York: Dutton, 1971), 207–11, hereafter referred to in text as *SG*. In what follows, I use a slightly altered translation.

43. The quote is commonly translated as "All poets are Jews," but the Russian word Tsvetaeva uses is actually a derogatory one. See Felstiner, *Paul Celan*, 197.

44. "Colchicum autumnale" is the Latin name of the meadow saffron. Christopher Perels has argued that the meadow saffron, in Hölderlin a symbol of hope and in the Jewish tradition an emblem of the chosen people and its life in eschatological dimensions, comes in Celan to crystallize a paradoxical temporality, the tension between eschatological hope and the experience of radical finitude. See Perels, "Zeitlose und Kolchis: Zur Entwicklung eines Motivkomplexes bei Paul Celan," *Germanisch-Romanische Monatsschrift* 29 (1979): 70.

45. See the similarly ambiguous endings of "In der Luft," which perverts the very idea of redemption and issues in a similar sense of belatedness—"um / wessen / Sternzeit zu spät?" (*Nr*, 147) [by / whose / star time too late? (*SP*, 213)]—and of "Hinausgekrönt," which ends with a resolution to leave behind the most salient symbol of dispersion: "Und wir schicken / keinen der Unsern hinunter / zu dir, / Babel." (*Nr*, 111) [And we send / none of ours downward / to you, / Babel. (*SP*, 193)]. This concluding address curiously focuses the reader's attention on the word "Babel," which is cast as the destination of the poem. The weight which the word "Babel" attains in its very rejection indicates just how fragile the possibility of an end of exile is.

46. Peter M. Sacks, *The English Elegy: Studies in the Genre from Spenser to Yeats* (Baltimore: Johns Hopkins University Press, 1985), 5. In this study, Sacks shows the affinities between the formal principles of elegy and the psychical mechanisms of mourning.

47. See Celan's translation of the poem in *Gesammelte Werke*, vol. 5, 194–213. The title derives from the Russian *inoi* [other] and means "otherland" or utopia.

48. See Leonard Olschner, *Der feste Buchstab: Erläuterungen zu Paul Celans Gedichtübertragungen* (Göttingen: Vandenhoeck and Ruprecht, 1985), 249.

49. See his letter to Reinhard Federmann from March 3, 1962, in Celan, "Briefe" [to Reinhard Federmann], *Die Pestsäule* 1, no. 1 (1972): 19.

50. See Olschner, *Der feste Buchstab*, 247, and Bernhard Böschenstein, "Celan und Mandel'shtam: Beobachtungen zu ihrem Verhältnis,"

Celan-Jahrbuch 2 (1988): 165.
51. See Peter Szondi, "Eden," in *Celan Studies*, 83–92.
52. See Joel Golb, "Reading Celan: The Allegory of 'Hohles Lebensgehöft' and 'Engführung,'" in *Word Traces: Readings of Paul Celan*, ed. Aris Fioretis (Baltimore: Johns Hopkins University Press, 1994), 185–218.
53. See Matthias Loewen, "Der Heimat ins Garn: Zu einem Gedicht von Paul Celan," *Germanisch-Romanische Monatsschrift* 32, no. 3 (1982): 315–32.
54. See Otto Pöggeler, *Spur des Worts: Zur Lyrik Paul Celans* (Freiburg: Alber, 1986), 41.
55. Johann Peter Hebel, "Kannitverstan," in *Schatzkästlein des rheinischen Hausfreundes* (Stuttgart: Reclam, 1981), 152–55.
56. Paul Celan, *Sprachgitter*, Tübinger Ausgabe, ed. Jürgen Wertheimer (Frankfurt am Main: Suhrkamp, 1996), 89.
57. Lawrence L. Langer, *Holocaust Testimonies: The Ruins of Memory* (New Haven, Conn.: Yale University Press, 1991), 4
58. Jacques Derrida, "Shibboleth: For Paul Celan," in *Word Traces*, 19.
59. Ibid., 59.
60. Szász, "Es ist nicht so einfach," 23.
61. On this disjunction, see also Sidra DeKoven Ezrahi, "Writing Poetry after Auschwitz: Paul Celan as the Last Barbarian," in *Booking Passage: Exile and Homecoming in the Modern Jewish Imagination* (Berkeley: University of California Press, 2000), 141–56.
62. See Otto Lorenz, *Schweigen in der Dichtung: Hölderlin, Rilke, Celan. Studien zur Poetik deiktisch-elliptischer Schreibweisen* (Göttingen: Vandenhoeck and Ruprecht, 1989), 50.
63. See Jean Laplanche, *New Foundations for Psychoanalysis*, trans. David Macey (Oxford: Basil Blackwell 1989).

Conclusion

1. Cathy Caruth, *Unclaimed Experience: Trauma, Narrative, and History* (Baltimore: Johns Hopkins University Press, 1996), 70.
2. Ruth Leys, *Trauma: A Genealogy* (Chicago: University of Chicago Press, 2000), 284.
3. For recent attempts by social scientists to define the traits of diasporic groups, see Gérard Chaliand and Jean-Pierre Rageau, *The Penguin Atlas of Diasporas*, trans. A. M. Berrett (New York: Penguin Books, 1997); and Robin Cohen, *Global Diasporas: An Introduction* (Seattle: University of Washington Press, 1997). See also William Safran's useful critique of Cohen in "Comparing Diasporas: A Review Essay," *Diaspora* 8, no. 3 (1999): 255–91. Among the critics who emphasize aspects of collectivity in diasporic film and literature are Maeera Y. Schreiber, "The End of

NOTES TO CONCLUSION

Exile: Jewish Identity and Its Diasporic Poetics," *PMLA* 113, no. 2 (March 1998): 273–87; John Durham Peters, "Exile, Nomadism, and Diaspora: The Stakes of Mobility in the Western Canon," in *Home, Exile, Homeland: Film, Media, and the Politics of Place*, ed. Hamid Naficy (New York: Routledge, 1999), 17–41; and Hamid Naficy, *An Accented Cinema: Exilic and Diasporic Filmmaking* (Princeton, N.J.: Princeton University Press, 2001), esp. 13–15, 63–100.

4. Gilroy, *The Black Atlantic*, 213.
5. See especially Bhabha's "Dissemi-Nation: Time, Narrative and the Margins of the Modern Nation," in his *The Location of Culture*, 139–70.
6. Gilroy, *The Black Atlantic*, 198.
7. Ibid.
8. Ibid., 203.
9. Letter from August 2, 1948. Quoted in Felstiner, *Paul Celan*, 57.
10. Jean Bollack, "Paul Celan und Nelly Sachs," 119–34.
11. Winfried Menninghaus, "Meridian des Schmerzes: Zum Briefwechsel Paul Celan / Nelly Sachs," *Poetica* 26, no. 1–2 (1994): 169–79.
12. Rolf Michaelis, "Es ist eine Wunschautobiographie: Peter Weiss mit Rolf Michaelis im Gespräch über seinen politischen Gleichnisroman," *Die Zeit*, Oct. 10, 1975. Quoted in Alexander Stephan, "Spätfolgen des Exils: Zwischenbericht zu Peter Weiss: *Die Ästhetik des Widerstands*," in *Exil: Wirkung und Wertung*, ed. Donald G. Daviau and Ludwig M. Fischer (Columbia, S.C.: Camden House, 1985), 248, 255.
13. Eric L. Santner, *On the Psychotheology of Everyday Life: Reflections on Freud and Rosenzweig* (Chicago: University of Chicago Press, 2001), 70.
14. Ibid., 5–6. Emphasis by Santner.
15. See Arjun Appadurai, *Modernity at Large: Cultural Dimensions of Globalization* (Minneapolis: University of Minnesota Press, 1996), 5.
16. Julia Hell, "From Laokoon to Ge: Resistance to Jewish Authorship in Peter Weiss's *Ästhetik des Widerstands*," in *Rethinking Peter Weiss*, ed. Jost Hermand and Marc Silberman (New York: Peter Lang, 2000), 35.
17. Ibid., 30.
18. See Raymond Klibansky, Erwin Panowsky, and Fritz Saxl, *Saturn and Melancholy: Studies in the History of Natural Philosophy, Religion, Art* (Nendeln/Liechtenstein: Kraus Reprint, 1979), 317.
19. James A. W. Heffernan, *Museum of Words: The Poetics of Ekphrasis from Homer to Ashbery* (Chicago: University of Chicago Press, 1993), 7.
20. See also Genia Schulz's insightful remarks on the function of names in Weiss in her *"Die Ästhetik des Widerstands": Versionen des Indirekten in Peter Weiss' Roman* (Stuttgart: Metzler, 1986), 110–11.
21. See Rainer Rother, *Die Gegenwart der Geschichte: Ein Versuch über Film und zeitgenössische Literatur* (Stuttgart: Metzler, 1990), 149. On Weiss's

construction of history and its affinities to Walter Benjamin's allegorical reading of history, see Alexander Honold, "Trümmer und Allegorie: Konstruktion historischer Bedeutung bei Walter Benjamin und Peter Weiss," in *Peter Weiss Jahrbuch* 1 (1992): 59–85.

Works Cited

Adelson, Leslie. "Nichts wie zuhause: Jeannette Lander und Ronnith Neumann auf der utopischen Suche nach jüdischer Identität im westdeutschen Kontext." In *Jüdische Kultur und Weiblichkeit in der Moderne*, edited by Sabine Schilling, Inge Stephan, and Sigrid Weigel, 307–30. Cologne: Böhlau, 1994.

Adorno, Theodor W. *Aesthetic Theory*. Translated and edited by Robert Hullot-Kentor. Minneapolis: University of Minnesota Press, 1997.

———. *Critical Models: Interventions and Catchwords*. Translated by Henry W. Pickford. New York: Columbia University Press, 1998.

———. *Minima Moralia: Reflections from Damaged Life*. Translated by E. F. N. Jephcott. London: NLB, 1974.

———. *Notes to Literature*. Vol. 1. Edited by Rolf Tiedemann. Translated by Shierry Weber Nicholsen. New York: Columbia University Press, 1991.

———. *The Jargon of Authenticity*. Translated by Knut Tarnowski and Frederic Will. Evanston, Ill.: Northwestern University Press, 1973.

Adunka, Evelyn. "Günther Anders und das jüdische Erbe." In *Günther Anders kontrovers*, edited by Konrad Paul Liessmann, 72–80. Munich: Beck, 1992.

Agamben, Giorgio. *Remnants of Auschwitz: The Witness and the Archive*. Translated by Daniel Heller-Roazen. New York: Zone Books, 1999.

Améry, Jean. *At the Mind's Limits: Contemplations by a Survivor on Auschwitz and Its Realities*. Translated by Sidney Rosenfeld and Stella P. Rosenfeld. Bloomington: Indiana University Press, 1980.

———. "Die deutsche Sprachwelt." In *Der Grenzgänger: Gespräch mit Ingo Hermann in der Reihe "Zeugen des Jahrhunderts,"* 83–86. Göttingen: Lamuv, 1992.

WORKS CITED

———. "Jargon der Dialektik." In *Widersprüche*, 53–78. Stuttgart: Ullstein, 1970.
Anders, Günther. *Die Schrift an der Wand: Tagebücher 1941 bis 1966*. Munich: Beck, 1967.
———. *Wir Eichmannsöhne: Offener Brief an Klaus Eichmann*. Munich: Beck, 1964.
Appadurai, Arjun. *Modernity at Large: Cultural Dimensions of Globalization*. Minneapolis: University of Minnesota Press, 1996.
Arendt, Hannah. *Eichmann in Jerusalem: A Report on the Banality of Evil*. Rev. and enlarged edition. New York: Viking Press, 1964.
———. "The Jew as Pariah: A Hidden Tradition" (April 1944). In *The Jew as Pariah: Jewish Identity and Politics in the Modern Age*, edited by Ron H. Feldman, 67–90. New York: Grove Press, 1978.
———. *Rahel Varnhagen: The Life of a Jewess*. Edited by Liliane Weissberg. Translated by Richard and Clara Winston. Baltimore: Johns Hopkins University Press, 1997.
Baer, Ulrich. *Remnants of Song: Trauma and the Experience of Modernity in Charles Baudelaire and Paul Celan*. Palo Alto, Calif.: Stanford University Press, 2000.
Baer, Ytzak. *Galut*. Translated by Robert Warshow. New York: Schocken Books, 1947.
Bahr, Ehrhard. *Nelly Sachs*. Munich: Beck, 1980.
Bakhtin, Mikhail. *The Dialogic Imagination: Four Essays*. Edited by Michael Holquist. Translated by Caryl Emerson and Michael Holquist. Austin: University of Texas Press, 1981.
Benjamin, Walter. *Selected Writings 4: 1938–1940*. Edited by Howard Eiland and Michael W. Jennings. Translated by Edmund Jephcott et al. Cambridge, Mass.: Belknap Press of Harvard University Press, 2003.
Bennholdt-Thomsen, Anke, and Alfredo Guzzoni. "Melusine: Herkunft und Bedeutung bei Nelly Sachs." *Euphorion* 81, no. 2 (1987): 156–70.
Benz, Wolfgang, ed. *Die Juden in Deutschland 1933–45: Leben unter nationalsozialistischer Herrschaft*. Munich: Beck, 1988.
Berendsohn, Walter A. *Aufbauarbeit in Israel*. Berlin: Bernhard and Graefe, 1953.
———. *Nelly Sachs: Einführung in das Werk der Dichterin jüdischen Schicksals*. Darmstadt: Agora, 1974.
Bering, Dietz. *Der Name als Stigma: Antisemitismus im deutschen Alltag, 1812–1933*. Stuttgart: Klett-Cotta, 1987.
Berman, Russell A. "'Der begrabenen Blitze Wohnstatt': Trennung, Heimkehr und Sehnsucht in der Lyrik von Nelly Sachs." In *Im Zeichen Hiobs: Jüdische Schriftsteller und deutsche Literatur im 20. Jahrhundert*, edited by Gunter E. Grimm and Hans-Peter Bayerdörfer, 280–92. Königstein/Ts.:

WORKS CITED

Athenäum, 1985.
Bernstein, Michael André. *Foregone Conclusions: Against Apocalyptic History.* Berkeley: University of California Press, 1994.
Bernstein, Susan. "Journalism and German Identity: Communiqués from Heine, Wagner, and Adorno." *New German Critique* 66 (Fall 1995): 65–93.
Bettelheim, Bruno. *The Informed Heart: Autonomy in a Mass Age.* New York: Avon, 1971.
Bhabha, Homi K. *The Location of Culture.* New York: Routledge, 1994.
Bier, Jean-Paul. "The Holocaust, West Germany, and Strategies of Oblivion, 1947–1979." In *Germans and Jews since the Holocaust: The Changing Situation in West Germany,* edited by Anson Rabinbach and Jack Zipes, 185–207. New York: Holmes and Meier, 1986.
Birus, Hendrik. "Hommage á quelqu'un: Paul Celans *Hüttenfenster*—ein 'Wink' für Johannes Bobrowski?" In *Hermenautik—Hermeneutik: Literarische und geisteswissenschaftliche Beiträge zu Ehren von Peter Horst Neumann,* edited by Holger Helbig, Bettina Knauer, and Gunnar Och, 269–77. Würzburg: Königshausen and Neumann, 1996.
Bobrowski, Johannes. *Gesammelte Werke.* Vol. 1. Edited by Eberhard Haufe. Stuttgart: Deutsche Verlags-Anstalt, 1987.
Bodemann, Y. Michal. "Staat und Ethnizität: Der Aufbau der jüdischen Gemeinden im Kalten Krieg." In *Jüdisches Leben in Deutschland seit 1945,* edited by Micha Brumlik et al., 49–69. Frankfurt am Main: Jüdischer Verlag bei Athenäum, 1986.
Bollack, Jean. "Paul Celan und Nelly Sachs: Geschichte eines Kampfes." *Neue Rundschau* 105, no. 4 (1994): 119–34.
Borowski, Tadeusz. *This Way for the Gas, Ladies and Gentlemen.* Translated by Barbara Vedder. New York: Penguin Books, 1976.
Börsenverein des Deutschen Buchhandels. *Nelly Sachs: Ansprachen anläßlich der Verleihung des Friedenspreises des Deutschen Buchhandels.* Frankfurt am Main: Börsenverein des Deutschen Buchhandels, 1965.
Böschenstein, Bernhard. "Celan und Mandelstamm: Beobachtungen zu ihrem Verhältnis." *Celan-Jahrbuch* 2 (1988): 155–68.
Bower, Kathrin M. *Ethics and Remembrance in the Poetry of Nelly Sachs and Rose Ausländer.* Rochester, N.Y.: Camden House, 2000.
Boyarin, Daniel, and Jonathan Boyarin. "Diaspora: Generation and the Ground of Jewish Identity." *Critical Inquiry* 19, no. 4 (Spring 1993): 693–725.
———. *Powers of Diaspora: Two Essays on the Relevance of Jewish Culture.* Minneapolis: University of Minnesota Press, 2002.
Braun, Michael. "Phasen, Probleme und Perspektiven der Nelly-Sachs-Rezeption: Forschungsbericht und Bibliographie." In *Nelly Sachs: Neue Inter-*

WORKS CITED

pretationen, edited by Michael Kessler and Jürgen Wertheimer, 375–93. Tübingen: Stauffenburg, 1994.

Breuer, Ingo. "Der Jude Marat: Identifikationsprobleme bei Peter Weiss." In *Peter Weiss: Neue Fragen an alte Texte,* edited by Irene Heidelberger-Leonard, 64–76. Opladen: Westdeutscher Verlag, 1994.

Briegleb, Klaus. "Ingeborg Bachmann, Paul Celan: Ihr (Nicht-)Ort in der Gruppe 47 (1952–1964/65)." In *Ingeborg Bachmann und Paul Celan: Poetische Korrespondenzen,* edited by Bernhard Böschenstein and Sigrid Weigel, 29–81. Frankfurt am Main: Suhrkamp, 1997.

———. "'Neuanfang' in der westdeutschen Nachkriegsliteratur—Die Gruppe 47 in den Jahren 1947–1951." In *Bestandsaufnahme: Studien zur Gruppe 47,* edited by Stephan Braese, 35–64. Berlin: Schmidt, 1999.

Brumlik, Michael. "Günther Anders: Zur Existenzialontologie der Emigration." In *Zivilisationsbruch: Denken nach Auschwitz,* edited by Dan Diner, 110–49. Frankfurt am Main: Fischer, 1988.

Burgard, Peter J. "Adorno, Goethe, and the Politics of the Essay." *Deutsche Vierteljahrsschrift für Literaturwissenschaft und Geistesgeschichte* 1 (1992): 160–91.

Cahn, Michael. "Subversive Mimesis: T. W. Adorno and the Modern Impasse of Critique." In *Mimesis in Contemporary Theory: An Interdisciplinary Approach.* Vol. 1, *The Literary and Philosophical Debate,* edited by Mihai Spariosu, 27–64. Philadelphia: Jahn Benjamins, 1984.

Caruth, Cathy. *Unclaimed Experience: Trauma, Narrative, and History.* Baltimore: Johns Hopkins University Press, 1996.

Celan, Paul. "Briefe an Alfred Margul-Sperber." *Neue Literatur* 26, no. 7 (July 1975): 50–63.

———. "Briefe" [to Reinhard Federmann]. *Die Pestsäule* 1, no. 1 (1972): 17–21.

———. *Collected Prose.* Translated by Rosmarie Waldrop. Manchester: Carcanet, 1986.

———. *Gesammelte Werke.* Edited by Beda Allemann and Stefan Reichert. Frankfurt am Main: Suhrkamp, 1983.

———. *Glottal Stop: 101 Poems by Paul Celan.* Translated by Nikolai Popov and Heather McHugh. Hanover, N.H.: Wesleyan University Press / University Press of New England, 2000.

———. *Poems of Paul Celan.* Translated by Michael Hamburger. Rev. and exp. ed. New York: Persea Books, 2002.

———. *Selected Poems and Prose of Paul Celan.* Translated by John Felstiner. New York: Norton, 2001.

———. *Speech-Grille and Selected Poems.* Translated by Joachim Neugroschel. New York: Dutton, 1971.

———. *Werke.* Tübinger Ausgabe. Edited by Jürgen Wertheimer. Frankfurt

WORKS CITED

am Main: Suhrkamp, 1996–.
Chalfen, Israel. *Paul Celan: A Biography of His Youth.* Translated by Maximilian Bleyleben. New York: Persea Books, 1991.
Chaliand, Gérard, and Jean-Pierre Rageau. *The Penguin Atlas of Diasporas.* Translated by A. M. Berrett. New York: Penguin Books, 1997.
Chaumont, Jean-Michael. "Geschichtliche Verantwortung und menschliche Würde bei Jean Améry." In *Über Jean Améry,* edited by Irene Heidelberger-Leonard, 29–47. Heidelberg: Winter, 1990.
Claussen, Detlev. "Eine kritische Differenz: Zum Konflikt Jean Amérys mit Theodor W. Adorno und Max Horkheimer." In *Jean Améry (Hans Maier),* edited by Stephan Steiner, 197–207. Basel: Stroemfeld, 1996.
Clifford, James. "Diasporas." *Cultural Anthropology* 9, no. 3 (1994): 302–38.
Cohen, Robert. "The Political Aesthetics of Holocaust Literature: Peter Weiss's *The Investigation* and Its Critics." *History and Memory* 10, no. 2 (Fall 1998): 43–67.
Cohen, Robin. *Global Diasporas: An Introduction.* Seattle: University of Washington Press, 1997.
Corbea-Hoisie, Andrei. *Czernowitzer Geschichten: Über eine städtische Kultur in Mittelosteuropa.* Vienna: Böhlau, 2003.
Davies, W. D. *The Territorial Dimension of Judaism.* Berkeley: University of California Press, 1982.
de Certeau, Michel. *The Practice of Everyday Life.* Translated by Steven Rendall. Berkeley: University of California Press, 1984.
Derrida, Jacques. "Shibboleth: For Paul Celan." In *Word Traces: Readings of Paul Celan,* edited by Aris Fioretis, 3–72. Baltimore: Johns Hopkins University Press, 1994.
Diner, Dan. "Negative Symbiose: Deutsche und Juden nach Auschwitz." *Babylon* 1 (October 1986): 9–20.
———, ed. *Zivilisationsbruch: Denken nach Auschwitz.* Frankfurt am Main: Fischer, 1988.
Dinesen, Ruth. *Nelly Sachs: Eine Biographie.* Translated by Gabriele Gerecke. Frankfurt am Main: Suhrkamp, 1992.
———. "Verehrung und Verwerfung: Nelly Sachs—Kontroverse um eine Dichterin." In *Kontroversen, alte und neue: Akten des VII. Internationalen Germanisten-Kongresses Göttingen 1985,* edited by Karl Pestalozzi, Alexander von Bormann, and Thomas Koebner, 130–37. Tübingen: Niemeyer, 1986.
Döhl, Reinhard. "Geschichte und Kritik eines Angriffs: Zu den Behauptungen gegen Paul Celan." *Deutsche Akademie für Sprache und Dichtung: Jahrbuch 1960*: 101–32.
Eisen, Arnold M. *Galut: Modern Jewish Reflection on Homelessness and Homecoming.* Bloomington: Indiana University Press, 1986.

―――. "Off Center: The Concept of the Land of Israel in Modern Jewish Thought." In *The Land of Israel: Jewish Perspectives*, edited by Lawrence A. Hoffman, 263–96. Notre Dame, Ind.: University of Notre Dame Press, 1986.

Encyclopaedia Judaica. Jerusalem: Keter, 1972.

Enzensberger, Hans Magnus. "Die Steine der Freiheit." *Merkur* 13, no. 8 (August 1959): 770–75.

Erk, Ludwig, comp. *Deutscher Liederhort: Auswahl der vorzüglichen Volkslieder*. Revised by Franz M. Böhme. Vol. 3. Leipzig: Breitkopf and Härtel, 1894.

Eshel, Amir, and Thomas Sparr. "Zur Topographie der Herkunft in der Lyrik von Dan Pagis und Paul Celan." In *Von Franzos zu Canetti: Jüdische Autoren aus Österreich*, edited by Mark Gelber, Hans Otto Horch, and Sigurd Paul Scheichl, 115–28. Tübingen: Niemeyer, 1996.

Eskin, Michael. *Ethics and Dialogue in the Works of Levinas, Bakhtin, Mandel'shtam, and Celan*. Oxford: Oxford University Press, 2000.

Ezrahi, Sidra DeKoven. *Booking Passage: Exile and Homecoming in the Modern Jewish Imagination*. Berkeley: University of California Press, 2000.

Felman, Shoshana. "Theaters of Justice: Arendt in Jerusalem, the Eichmann Trial, and the Redefinition of Legal Meaning in the Wake of the Holocaust." *Critical Inquiry* 27, no. 2 (Winter 2001): 201–38.

Felman, Shoshana, and Dori Laub. *Testimony: Crises of Witnessing in Literature, Psychoanalysis, and History*. New York: Routledge, 1992.

Felstiner, John. *Paul Celan: Poet, Survivor, Jew*. New Haven, Conn.: Yale University Press, 1995.

Fiero, Petra S. *Schreiben gegen Schweigen: Grenzerfahrungen in Jean Amérys autobiographischem Werk*. Hildesheim: Olms, 1997.

Finkielkraut, Alain. *The Imaginary Jew*. Translated by Kevin O'Neill and David Suchoff. Lincoln: University of Nebraska Press, 1994.

Firges, Jean. *Vom Osten gestreut, einzubringen im Westen: Jüdische Mystik in der Dichtung Paul Celans*. Annweiler am Trifels: Sonnenberg, 1999.

Foschepoth, Josef. *Im Schatten der Vergangenheit: Die Anfänge der Gesellschaften für Christlich-Jüdische Zusammenarbeit*. Göttingen: Vandenhoeck and Ruprecht, 1993.

Freud, Sigmund. *The Standard Edition of the Complete Psychological Works of Sigmund Freud*. Edited and translated by James Strachey. London: Hogarth Press, 1953–75.

Fritsch-Vivié, Gabriele. *Nelly Sachs*. Reinbek bei Hamburg: Rowohlt, 1993.

Gay, Peter. *My German Question: Growing Up in Nazi Berlin*. New Haven, Conn.: Yale University Press, 1998.

Garloff, Katja. "The Emigrant as Witness: W. G. Sebald's *Die Ausgewanderten*." *German Quarterly* 77, no. 1 (Winter 2004): 76–93.

WORKS CITED

Gebauer, Gunter, and Christoph Wulf. *Mimesis: Culture, Art, Society.* Translated by Don Reneau. Berkeley: University of California Press, 1995.

Geier, Manfred. "Poetisierung der Bedeutung: Zu Struktur und Funktion des sprachlichen Zeichens in einem Gedicht von Celan." In *Paul Celan,* edited by Werner Hamacher and Winfried Menninghaus, 239–71. Frankfurt am Main: Suhrkamp, 1988.

Gelber, Mark H. "Nelly Sachs und das Land Israel: Die mystisch-poetischen Funktionen der geographisch-räumlich Assoziationen." In *Nelly Sachs: Neue Interpetationen,* edited by Michael Kessler and Jürgen Wertheimer, 169–78. Tübingen: Stauffenburg, 1994.

Gerlach, Rainer. "Isolation und Befreiung: Zum literarischen Frühwerk von Peter Weiss." In *Peter Weiss,* edited by Rainer Gerlach, 147–81. Frankfurt am Main: Suhrkamp, 1984.

Gilman, Sander L. *Jewish Self-Hatred: Anti-Semitism and the Hidden Language of the Jews.* Baltimore: Johns Hopkins University Press, 1986.

———. "Jewish Writers in Contemporary Germany: The Dead Author Speaks." In *Inscribing the Other,* 249–78. Lincoln: University of Nebraska Press, 1991.

———. *Jews in Today's German Culture.* Bloomington: Indiana University Press, 1995.

———. "Salome, Syphilis, Sarah Bernhardt and the 'Modern Jewess.'" *German Quarterly* 66, no. 2 (Spring 1993): 195–211.

Gilman, Sander L., and Karen Remmler, eds. *Reemerging Jewish Culture in Germany: Life and Literature since 1989.* New York: New York University Press, 1994.

Gilroy, Paul. *The Black Atlantic: Modernity and Double Consciousness.* Cambridge, Mass.: Harvard University Press, 1993.

Goethe, Johann Wolfgang von. *Collected Works.* Vol. 3, *Essays on Art and Literature.* Edited by John Gearey. Translated by Ellen von Nardroff and Ernest H. von Nardroff. New York: Suhrkamp, 1986.

Golb, Joel. "Reading Celan: The Allegory of 'Hohles Lebensgehöft' and 'Engführung.'" In *Word Traces: Readings of Paul Celan,* edited by Aris Fioretis, 185–218. Baltimore: Johns Hopkins University Press, 1994.

Goldsmith, Oliver. *The Citizen of the World.* London: Folio Society, n.d.

Goodrich, Frances, and Albert Hackett. *The Diary of Anne Frank.* New York: Random House, 1956.

Grimm, Jakob, and Wilhelm Grimm, eds. *Deutsches Wörterbuch.* Revised by Karl Euling. Leipzig: Hirzel, 1936.

Habermas, Jürgen. *The Structural Transformation of the Public Sphere: An Inquiry into a Category of Bourgeois Society.* Translated by Thomas Burger with the assistance of Frederic Lawrence. Cambridge, Mass.: MIT Press, 1989.

WORKS CITED

Hall, Stuart. "Cultural Identity and Diaspora." In *Identity: Community, Culture, Difference*, edited by Jonathan Rutherford, 222–37. London: Lawrence and Wishart, 1990.

Halpern, Ben. *The Idea of the Jewish State*. 2nd ed. Cambridge, Mass.: Harvard University Press, 1969.

Hamacher, Werner. "Working Through Working." Translated by Matthew T. Hartman. *Modernism / modernity* 3, no. 1 (January 1996): 23–55.

Hamacher, Werner, and Winfried Menninghaus, eds. *Paul Celan*. Frankfurt am Main: Suhrkamp, 1988.

Hansen, Miriam. "Mass Culture as Hieroglyphic Writing: Adorno, Derrida, Kracauer." *New German Critique* 56 (Spring–Summer 1992): 43–73.

Hebel, Johann Peter. "Kannitverstan." In *Schatzkästlein des rheinischen Hausfreundes*, 152–55. Stuttgart: Reclam, 1981.

Heffernan, James A. W. *Museum of Words: The Poetics of Ekphrasis from Homer to Ashbery*. Chicago: University of Chicago Press, 1993.

Heidelberger-Leonard, Irene. "Jean Améry's Selbstverständnis als Jude." In *Über Jean Améry*, edited by Irene Heidelberger-Leonard, 17–27. Heidelberg: Winter, 1990.

Heine, Heinrich. *Sämtliche Schriften*. Vol. 1, *Schriften 1817–1840*. Edited by Klaus Briegleb. Frankfurt am Main: Ullstein, 1981.

———. *The Rabbi of Bacharach*. Translated by Charles Godfrey Leland. In *Jewish Stories and Hebrew Melodies*, 21–80. New York: Markus Wiener, 1987.

Hell, Julia. "From Laokoon to Ge: Resistance to Jewish Authorship in Peter Weiss's *Ästhetik des Widerstands*." In *Rethinking Peter Weiss*, edited by Jost Hermand and Marc Silberman, 21–44. New York: Peter Lang, 2000.

Herf, Jeffrey. *Divided Memory: The Nazi Past in the Two Germanys*. Cambridge, Mass.: Harvard University Press, 1997.

Hessing, Jakob. *Die Heimkehr einer jüdischen Emigrantin: Else Lasker-Schülers mythisierende Rezeption 1945 bis 1971*. Tübingen: Niemeyer, 1993.

Heym, Stefan. *Ahasver*. Munich: Bertelsmann, 1981.

Hohendahl, Peter Uwe. *Prismatic Thought: Theodor W. Adorno*. Lincoln: University of Nebraska Press, 1995.

———. "The Scholar, the Intellectual, and the Essay: Weber, Lukács, Adorno, and Postwar Germany." *German Quarterly* 70, no. 3 (1997): 217–32.

Honold, Alexander. "Trümmer und Allegorie: Konstruktion historischer Bedeutung bei Walter Benjamin und Peter Weiss." *Peter Weiss Jahrbuch* 1 (1992): 59–85.

Horkheimer, Max. *Gesammelte Schriften*. Vol. 16. Edited by Alfred Schmidt and Gunzelin Schmid Noerr. Frankfurt am Main: Fischer, 1995.

Horkheimer, Max, and Theodor W. Adorno. *Dialectic of Enlightenment*.

WORKS CITED

Translated by John Cumming. New York: Continuum, 1997.

Huyssen, Andreas. *After the Great Divide: Modernism, Mass Culture, Postmodernism*. Bloomington: Indiana University Press, 1986.

Hyman, Paula E. *Gender and Assimilation in Modern Jewish History: The Roles and Representation of Women*. Seattle: University of Washington Press, 1995.

Israel, Nico. *Outlandish: Writing between Exile and Diaspora*. Palo Alto, Calif.: Stanford University Press, 2000.

Jakobson, Roman. "Linguistics and Poetics." In *Language in Literature*, edited by Krystyna Pomorska and Stephen Rudy, 62–94. Cambridge, Mass.: Belknap Press of Harvard University Press, 1987.

Jay, Martin. *Adorno*. Cambridge, Mass.: Harvard University Press, 1984.

———. "Mimesis and Mimetology: Adorno and Lacoue-Labarthe." In *The Semblance of Subjectivity: Essays in Adorno's Aesthetic Theory*, edited by Tom Huhn and Lambert Zuidervaart, 29–53. Cambridge, Mass.: MIT Press, 1997.

———. *Permanent Exiles: Essays on the Intellectual Migration from Germany to America*. New York: Columbia University Press, 1986.

Jenny, Urs. "Abschied von den Eltern." In *Über Peter Weiss*, edited by Volker Canaris, 47–50. Frankfurt am Main: Suhrkamp, 1970.

Kafka, Franz. *Drucke zu Lebzeiten*. Kritische Ausgabe. Edited by Wolf Kittler, Hans-Gerd Koch, and Gerhard Neumann. Frankfurt am Main: Fischer, 1994.

Kant, Immanuel. *The Cambridge Edition of the Works of Immanuel Kant: Practical Philosophy*. Translated and edited by Mary J. Gregor. Cambridge: Cambridge University Press, 1996.

Keilson, Hans. "Die Reparationsverträge und die Folgen der Wiedergutmachung." In *Jüdisches Leben in Deutschland seit 1945*, edited by Micha Brumlik et al., 121–39. Frankfurt am Main: Jüdischer Verlag bei Athenäum, 1986.

Kersten, Paul. *Die Metaphorik in der Lyrik von Nelly Sachs: Mit einer Wortkonkordanz und einer Nelly Sachs-Bibliographie*. Hamburg: Lüdke, 1970.

Kessler, Michael. "Dichte der Abwesenheit: Transzendenz und Transzendieren im Werk der Nelly Sachs." In *Nelly Sachs: Neue Interpretationen*, edited by Michael Kessler and Jürgen Wertheimer, 225–68. Tübingen: Stauffenburg, 1994.

Kirshenblatt-Gimblett, Barbara. "Spaces of Dispersal." *Cultural Anthropology* 9, no. 3 (1994): 339–44.

Klibansky, Raymond, Erwin Panowsky, and Fritz Saxl. *Saturn and Melancholy: Studies in the History of Natural Philosophy, Religion, Art*. Nendeln/Liechtenstein: Kraus Reprint, 1979.

WORKS CITED

Klüger, Ruth. *weiter leben: Eine Jugend*. Munich: Deutscher Taschenbuchverlag, 1997.

Kramer, Sven. "Zusammenstoß in Princeton—Peter Weiss und die Gruppe 47." In *Bestandsaufnahme: Studien zur Gruppe 47*, edited by Stephan Braese, 155–74. Berlin: Schmidt, 1999.

Kuhn, Juliane. *"Wir setzten unser Exil fort": Facetten des Exils im literarischen Werk von Peter Weiss*. St. Ingbert: Röhrig, 1995.

LaCapra, Dominick. *History and Memory after Auschwitz*. Ithaca, N.Y.: Cornell University Press, 1998.

———. *Representing the Holocaust: History, Theory, Trauma*. Ithaca, N.Y.: Cornell University Press, 1994.

———. *Writing History, Writing Trauma*. Baltimore: Johns Hopkins University Press, 2001.

Lachmann, Renate. *Memory and Literature: Intertextuality in Russian Modernism*. Translated by Roy Sellars and Anthony Wall. Minneapolis: University of Minnesota Press, 1997.

Langer, Lawrence L. *Holocaust Testimonies: The Ruins of Memory*. New Haven, Conn.: Yale University Press, 1991.

Laplanche, Jean. *New Foundations for Psychoanalysis*. Translated by David Macey. Oxford: Basil Blackwell, 1989.

Lehmann, Hans-Thies. *Theater und Mythos: Die Konstitution des Subjekts im Diskurs der antiken Tragödie*. Stuttgart: Metzler, 1991.

Lehmann, Jürgen, ed. *Kommentar zu Paul Celans "Die Niemandsrose."* With the assistance of Christine Ivanović. 2nd ed. Heidelberg: Winter, 1998.

Levin, Thomas Y. "Nationalities of Language: Adorno's *Fremdwörter*. An Introduction to 'On the Question: What is German?'" *New German Critique* 36 (Fall 1985): 111–19.

Leys, Ruth. *Trauma: A Geneology*. Chicago: University of Chicago Press, 2000.

Loewen, Matthias. "Der Heimat ins Garn: Zu einem Gedicht von Paul Celan." *Germanisch-Romanische Monatsschrift* 32, no. 3 (1982): 315–32.

Lorenz, Otto. *Schweigen in der Dichtung: Hölderlin, Rilke, Celan: Studien zur Poetik deiktisch-elliptischer Schreibweisen*. Göttingen: Vandenhoeck and Ruprecht, 1989.

Lüttmann, Helmut. *Die Prosawerke von Peter Weiss*. Hamburg: Lüdke, 1972.

Meltzer, Françoise. *Hot Property: The Stakes and Claims of Literary Originality*. Chicago: University of Chicago Press, 1994.

Mendes-Flohr, Paul. "Franz Rosenzweig and the Crisis of Historicism." In *The Philosophy of Franz Rosenzweig*, edited by Paul Mendes-Flohr, 138–61. Hanover, N.H.: University Press of New England, 1988.

Menke, Christoph. *The Sovereignty of Art: Aesthetic Negativity in Adorno and*

Derrida. Translated by Neil Solomon. Cambridge, Mass.: MIT Press, 1998.

Menninghaus, Winfried. "'Czernowitz / Bukowina' als Topos deutsch-jüdischer Geschichte und Literatur." *Merkur* 53, no. 3–4 (March–April 1999): 354–57.

———. "Meridian des Schmerzes: Zum Briefwechsel Paul Celan/Nelly Sachs." *Poetica* 26, no. 1–2 (1994): 169–79.

Mitscherlich, Alexander, and Margarete Mitscherlich. *The Inability to Mourn: Principles of Collective Behavior*. Translated by Beverly R. Placzek. New York: Grove Press, 1975.

Montesquieu, Charles-Louis de Secondat, baron de. *Persian Letters*. Translated by John Ozell. New York: Garland, 1972.

Morris, Leslie, and Jack Zipes, eds. *Unlikely History: The Changing German-Jewish Symbiosis, 1945–2000*. New York: Palgrave, 2002.

Müssener, Helmut. "'Du bist draußen gewesen': Die unmögliche Heimkehr des exilierten Schriftstellers Peter Weiss." In *Die Gruppe 47 in der Geschichte der Bundesrepublik*, edited by Justus Fetscher, Eberhard Lämmert, and Jürgen Schutte, 135–51. Würzburg: Könighausen and Neumann, 1991.

Naficy, Hamid. *An Accented Cinema: Exilic and Diasporic Filmmaking*. Princeton, N.J.: Princeton University Press, 2001.

Naumann, Bernd. *Auschwitz: A Report on the Proceedings against Robert Karl Ludwig Mulka and Others before the Court at Frankfurt*. Translated by Jean Steinberg. New York: Praeger, 1966.

Naumann, Uwe. "Ein Stück der Versöhnung: Zur Uraufführung des Mysterienspiels *Eli* von Nelly Sachs (1962)." *Exilforschung: Ein Internationales Jahrbuch* 4 (1986): 98–114.

Neusner, Jacob. *Self-Fulfilling Prophecy: Exile and Return in the History of Judaism*. Boston: Beacon, 1987.

Nicholsen, Shierry Weber. *Exact Imagination, Late Work: On Adorno's Aesthetics*. Cambridge, Mass.: MIT Press, 1997.

Nolden, Thomas. *Junge jüdische Literatur: Konzentrisches Schreiben in der Gegenwart*. Würzberg: Königshausen und Neumann, 1995.

Nora, Pierre. "Between Memory and History: Les Lieux de Mémoire." *Representations* 26 (Spring 1989): 7–25.

Olschner, Leonard. *Der feste Buchstab: Erläuterungen zu Paul Celans Gedichtübertragungen*. Göttingen: Vandenhoeck and Ruprecht, 1985.

———. "Der mühsame Weg von Nelly Sachs' Poesie ins literarische Bewußtsein." In *Die Resonanz des Exils: Gelungene und mißlungene Rezeption deutschsprachiger Exilautoren*, edited by Dieter Sevin, 267–81. Amsterdam: Rodopi, 1992.

WORKS CITED

Ostmeier, Dorothee. *Sprache des Dramas, Drama der Sprache: Zur Poetik der Nelly Sachs.* Tübingen: Niemeyer, 1997.

Peitsch, Helmut. "Die Gruppe 47 und die Exilliteratur—ein Mißverständnis?" In *Die Gruppe 47 in der Geschichte der Bundesrepublik,* edited by Justus Fetscher, Eberhard Lämmert, and Jürgen Schutte, 108–34. Würzburg: Königshausen and Neumann, 1991.

Perels, Christoph. "Zeitlose und Kolchis: Zur Entwicklung eines Motivkomplexes bei Paul Celan." *Germanisch-Romanische Monatsschrift* 29 (1979): 47–74.

Peters, John Durham. "Exile, Nomadism, and Diaspora: The Stakes of Mobility in the Western Canon." In *Home, Exile, Homeland: Film, Media, and the Politics of Place,* edited by Hamid Naficy, 17–41. New York: Routledge, 1999.

Pickford, Henry W. "Critical Models: Adorno's Theory and Practice of Cultural Criticism." *Yale Journal of Criticism* 10, no. 2 (1997): 247–70.

Pöggeler, Otto. *Spur des Worts: Zur Lyrik Paul Celans.* Freiburg: Alber, 1986.

Postone, Moishe. "Anti-Semitism and National Socialism." *New German Critique* 19 (Winter 1980): 97–115.

Rabinbach, Anson. "The Jewish Question in the German Question." *New German Critique* 44 (Spring–Summer 1988): 159–92.

———. *In the Shadow of Catastrophe: German Intellectuals between Apocalypse and Enlightenment.* Berkeley: University of California Press, 1997.

Rabinbach, Anson, and Jack Zipes, eds. *Germans and Jews since the Holocaust: The Changing Situation in West Germany.* New York: Holmes and Meier, 1986.

Richter, Hans Werner. *Plädoyer für eine neue Regierung.* Reinbek bei Hamburg: Rowohlt, 1965.

Rilke, Rainer Maria. *Duineser Elegien, Die Sonette an Orpheus.* Stuttgart: Reclam, 1997.

Ritter, Joachim, and Karlfried Gründer, eds. *Historisches Wörterbuch der Philosophie.* Basel: Schwabe, 1971–.

Robinson, Benjamin. "*The Specialist* on the Eichmann Precedent: Morality, Law, and Military Sovereignty." *Critical Inquiry* 30, no. 1 (Autumn 2003): 63–97.

Roebling, Irmgard, ed. *Sehnsucht und Sirene: Vierzehn Abhandlungen zu Wasserphantasien.* Pfaffenweiler: Centaurus, 1992.

Rosenzweig, Franz. *The Star of Redemption.* Translated by William H. Hallo. New York: Holt, Rinehart, and Winston, 1971.

Rother, Rainer. *Die Gegenwart der Geschichte: Ein Versuch über Film und zeitgenössische Literatur.* Stuttgart: Metzler, 1990.

Sachs, Nelly. *Briefe der Nelly Sachs.* Edited by Ruth Dinesen and Helmut Müssener. Frankfurt am Main: Suhrkamp, 1984.

WORKS CITED

———. *Fahrt ins Staublose*. Frankfurt am Main: Suhrkamp, 1961.
———. "Leben unter Bedrohung." In Walter A. Berendsohn, *Nelly Sachs: Einführung in das Werk der Dichterin jüdischen Schicksals*, 9–12. Darmstadt: Agora, 1974.
———. *O the Chimneys: Selected Poems*. Translated by Michael Hamburger et al. New York: Farrar, Straus and Giroux, 1967.
———. *Suche nach Lebenden*. Frankfurt am Main: Suhrkamp, 1971.
———. *The Seeker and Other Poems*. Translated by Ruth and Matthew Mead and Michael Hamburger. New York: Farrar, Straus and Giroux, 1970.
———. *Zeichen im Sand: Die szenischen Dichtungen der Nelly Sachs*. Frankfurt am Main: Suhrkamp, 1962.
Sacks, Peter M. *The English Elegy: Studies in the Genre from Spenser to Yeats*. Baltimore: Johns Hopkins University Press, 1985.
Safran, William. "Comparing Diasporas: A Review Essay." *Diaspora* 8, no. 3 (1999): 255–91.
Said, Edward. *Representations of the Intellectual: The 1993 Reith Lectures*. New York: Pantheon Books, 1994.
———. *Reflections on Exile and Other Essays*. Cambridge, Mass.: Harvard University Press, 2000.
Salloch, Erika. *Peter Weiss's* Die Ermittlung: *Zur Struktur des Dokumentartheaters*. Frankfurt am Main: Athenäum, 1972.
Santner, Eric L. *My Own Private Germany: Daniel Paul Schreber's Secret History of Modernity*. Princeton, N.J.: Princeton University Press, 1996.
———. *On the Psychotheology of Everyday Life: Reflections on Freud and Rosenzweig*. Chicago: University of Chicago Press, 2001.
———. *Stranded Objects: Mourning, Memory, and Film in Postwar Germany*. Ithaca N.Y.: Cornell University Press, 1990.
Schlant, Ernestine. *The Language of Silence: West German Literature and the Holocaust*. New York: Routledge, 1999.
Scholem, Gershom G. "Die 36 verborgenen Gerechten in der jüdischen Tradition." In *Judaica* 1, 216–25. Frankfurt am Main: Suhrkamp, 1963.
———. *Die Geheimnisse der Schöpfung: Ein Kapitel aus dem kabbalistischen Buche Sohar*. Berlin: Bücherei des Schocken Verlags, 1935.
———. *Major Trends in Jewish Mysticism*. New York: Schocken Books, 1988.
———. *On Jews and Judaism in Crisis: Selected Essays*. Edited by Werner J. Dannhauser. New York: Schocken Books, 1978.
———. *Von der mystischen Gestalt der Gottheit*. Frankfurt am Main: Suhrkamp, 1973.
Schreiber, Maeera Y. "The End of Exile: Jewish Identity and Its Diasporic Poetics." *PMLA* 113, no. 2 (March 1998): 273–87.
Schubert, Elke. *Günther Anders*. Reinbek bei Hamburg: Rowohlt, 1992.
Schulz, Genia. *"Die Ästhetik des Widerstands": Versionen des Indirekten in Peter*

WORKS CITED

Weiss' Roman. Stuttgart: Metzler, 1986.
Schulze, Joachim. "Rauchspur und Sefira: Über die Grundlagen von Paul Celans Kabbala-Rezeption." *Celan-Jahrbuch* 4 (1991): 193–246.
Schweid, Eliezer. "Land of Israel." In *Contemporary Jewish Religious Thought: Original Essays on Critical Concepts, Movements, and Beliefs*, edited by Arthur A. Cohen and Paul Mendes-Flohr, 535–41. New York: Free Press, 1987.
Sebald. W. G. "Verlorenes Land: Jean Améry und Österreich." In *Text und Kritik* 99 (1988): 20–29.
Seyhan, Azade. *Writing outside the Nation*. Princeton, N.J.: Princeton University Press, 2001.
Silbermann, A. M., ed. and trans. *Chumash with Rashi's Commentary*. Jerusalem: Silbermann Family, 1934.
Söllner, Alfons. *Peter Weiss und die Deutschen: Die Entstehung einer politischen Ästhetik wider die Verdrängung*. Opladen: Westdeutscher Verlag, 1988.
Solomon, Petre. "Briefwechsel mit Paul Celan, 1957–1962." *Neue Literatur* 32, no. 11 (November 1981): 60–80.
Sperber, Manès. "Churban oder Die unfaßbare Gewißheit." In *Die Kontroverse: Hannah Arendt, Eichmann und die Juden*, edited by F. A. Krummacher, 9–32. Munich: Nymphenburger Verlagshandlung, 1964.
Spies, Bernhard. "Exilliteratur—ein abgeschlossenes Kapitel? Überlegungen zu Stand und Perspektiven der literaturwissenschaftlichen Exilforschung." In *Exilforschung: Ein internationales Jahrbuch* 14 (1996): 11–30.
Stephan, Alexander. "Spätfolgen des Exils: Zwischenbericht zu Peter Weiss: *Die Ästhetik des Widerstands*." In *Exil: Wirkung und Wertung*, edited by Donald G. Daviau and Ludwig M. Fischer, 245–57. Columbia, S.C.: Camden House, 1985.
Stern, Frank. "Philosemitismus: Stereotype über den Feind, den man zu lieben hat." *Babylon* 8 (1991): 15–26.
———. *The Whitewashing of the Yellow Badge: Antisemitism and Philosemitism in Postwar Germany*. Translated by William Templer. Oxford: Pergamon, 1992.
Stewart, Susan. *On Longing: Narratives of the Miniature, the Gigantic, the Souvenir, the Collection*. Baltimore: Johns Hopkins University Press, 1984.
Stöhr, Martin. "Gespräche nach Abels Ermordung: Die Anfänge des jüdisch-christlichen Dialogs." In *Jüdisches Leben in Deutschland seit 1945*, edited by Micha Brumlik et al., 197–229. Frankfurt am Main: Jüdischer Verlag bei Athenäum, 1986.
Szász, János. "'Es ist nicht so einfach . . .': Erinnerungen an Paul Celan; Seiten aus einem amerikanischen Tagebuch." *Neue Literatur* 26, no. 11 (November 1975): 22–34.

WORKS CITED

Szondi, Peter. *Celan Studies*. Edited by Jean Bollack et al. Translated by Susan Bernofsky with Harvey Mendelsohn. Palo Alto, Calif.: Stanford University Press, 2003.

Teraoka, Arlene A. *East, West, and Others: The Third World in Postwar German Literature*. Lincoln: University of Nebraska Press, 1996.

Tieck, Ludwig. "Leben und Tod der heiligen Genoveva: Ein Trauerspiel." In *Schriften*. Vol. 2, 1–272. Berlin: Reimer, 1828.

Villon, François. *Complete Poems*. Edited and translated by Barbara N. Sargent-Baur. Toronto: University of Toronto Press, 1994.

Vogt, Jochen. *Peter Weiss*. Reinbek bei Hamburg: Rowohlt, 1987.

Walser, Martin. "Unser Auschwitz." *Kursbuch* 1 (1965): 189–200.

Wasserstrom, Steven M. *Between Muslim and Jew: The Problem of Symbiosis under Early Islam*. Princeton, N.J.: Princeton University Press, 1995.

Weigel, Sigrid. "Die Erinnerungs- und Erregungsspuren von Zitat und Lektüre: Die Intertextualität Bachmann-Celan, gelesen mit Benjamin." In *Ingeborg Bachmann und Paul Celan: Poetische Korrespondenzen*, edited by Bernhard Böschenstein and Sigrid Weigel, 231–49. Frankfurt am Main: Suhrkamp, 1997.

Weiß, Christoph. *Auschwitz in der geteilten Welt: Peter Weiss und die 'Ermittlung' im Kalten Krieg*. St. Ingbert: Röhrig, 2000.

Weiss, Peter. "Bericht über Einrichtungen und Gebräuche in den Siedlungen der Grauhäute." In *In Gegensätzen denken: Ein Lesebuch*, 119–35. Frankfurt am Main: Suhrkamp, 1986.

———. *Exile*. Translated by E. B. Garside, Alastair Hamilton, and Christopher Levenson. New York: Delacorte Press, 1968.

———. *Marat/Sade, The Investigation, The Shadow of the Body of the Coachman*. Edited by Robert Cohen. New York: Continuum, 1998.

———. *Notizbücher, 1960–1971*. 2 Vols. Frankfurt am Main: Suhrkamp, 1982.

———. *Notizbücher, 1971–1980*. 2 Vols. Frankfurt am Main: Suhrkamp, 1981.

———. *Rapporte*. Frankfurt am Main: Suhrkamp, 1968.

———. *Rapporte 2*. Frankfurt am Main: Suhrkamp, 1971.

———. *The Conversation of the Three Walkers and The Shadow of the Coachman's Body*. Translated by S. M. Cupitt. London: Calder and Boyars, 1972.

———. *Werke in sechs Bänden*. Frankfurt am Main: Suhrkamp, 1991.

Werner, Uta. *Textgräber: Paul Celans geologische Lyrik*. Munich: Fink, 1998.

Wiedemann, Barbara, ed. and comp. *Paul Celan—Die Goll-Affäre: Dokumente zu einer 'Infamie.'* Frankfurt am Main: Suhrkamp, 2000.

Wiggershaus, Rolf. *The Frankfurt School: Its History, Theories, and Political Significance*. Translated by Michael Robertson. Cambridge, Mass.: MIT Press, 1994.

WORKS CITED

Young, James E. *Writing and Rewriting the Holocaust: Narrative and the Consequences of Interpretation*. Bloomington: Indiana University Press, 1988.

Index

Abel (biblical), 74, 81
Abraham (biblical), 114–15, 116, 118, 119
acculturation, 6, 46. See also "assimilation"
Adelson, Leslie A., 188n. 18
Adenauer, Konrad, 8, 10, 58–59, 98
Adorno, Theodor, 2, 7, 10, 19, 66, 191–92nn. 3–30; Aesthetic Theory, 30; on Auschwitz and poetry, 98; Dialectic of Enlightenment, 22–23, 28, 29, 32; enlightenment viewed by, 49; "Essay as Form, The," 24–25, 31; exile and, 21–28; family name(s) of, 48; German language and, 26–27; "Heine the Wound," 22, 28–33, 39–41; "Meaning of Working Through the Past, The," 10, 29, 32, 33, 35–39, 193n. 46; Minima Moralia, 24, 34, 66; Notes to Literature, 24, 26; "On the Question: 'What Is German?,'" 22, 26; postwar move to Frankfurt, 18, 21–22; on psychoanalysis and history, 33–39; "Words from Abroad," 24, 26–28, 33
Adunka, Evelyn, 194n. 56

Agamben, Giorgio, 12, 13–15, 190n. 32
agency, 35, 90, 104, 113
Agnon, Shmuel Yosef, 95, 207n. 24
Alba/Aubade (poetic genre), 160
alienation, 28, 33, 48, 62, 199n. 17
Allemann, Beda, 216n. 34
almond tree, symbolic meaning of, 141, 214n. 26
Amenhotep IV (pharaoh of Egypt), 173
Améry, Jean, 2, 42, 47, 196n. 79; on breaking away from origins, 68; "How Much Home Does a Person Need?," 49; At the Mind's Limits, 49, 195nn. 70–72, 196n. 79; postwar move to Belgium, 18; "Resentments," 50–53; Weiss compared with, 57, 58
Anders, Günther, 2, 7, 19, 67, 141; annihilation of memory and, 156–57; "Besuch im Hades" [Visit to Hades], 44–47; postwar move to Vienna, 18; return to landscape of youth, 135; Schrift an der Wand, Die [The Writing on the Wall], 41; significance of name, 48; "Überfall, Der" [The Assault],

237

INDEX

Anders Günther (*continued*) 43; "Wir Eichmannssöhne [We, Eichmann's Sons], 47
Andersch, Alfred, 97, 105, 196n. 76, 207n. 21
Annette von Droste-Hülshoff-Preis für Dichterinnen, 96, 133
antifascism, 10, 179–80, 181
antisemitism, 2, 16, 39, 59, 119; as "false mimesis," 32; image of Jewish hyperintelligence, 24; Marxist view of Holocaust and, 88; postwar revival of, 132; projection mechanisms and, 32; projection theory of, 28–29; stereotypes of Jews, 10, 28, 118
apocalypse, 146, 149, 177
Apollinaire, Guillaume, 155
Appadurai, Arjun, 181, 219n. 15
Arendt, Hannah, 14, 39, 41, 60, 194n. 52, 211n. 63
Argonauts, myth of the, 154
Armenian dispersion, 3
assimilation, 19, 46, 111; as annihilation of difference, 133; capitalism and, 29; chimera of German-Jewish symbiosis and, 103; failure of, 29, 39, 72; gender dynamics of, 46–47; hope for end of anti-Jewish violence and, 139; Jews of Bukovina and, 13, 46; as mimetic behavior, 29, 82
Association of Hebrew Writers, 177
atomic bomb, 41
Auschwitz, 45, 56, 93, 151, 164; Améry as inmate of, 48; Anders's visit to, 43–44; as "break in civilization," 2; Dresden bombing equated with, 35; emancipation invalidated by, 48; place name as metonym for Holocaust, 166; Polish name for, 182; recovery of messianic idea after, 161; survivors of, 16, 18; trial at Frankfurt, 8, 85, 86, 87–92, 99; as turning point of human history, 41; Weiss's visit to, 60, 92
Ausländer, Rose, 136
Austria, 16, 48, 174
authoritarianism, German, 60
autobiographical writing, 51–52, 57; of Sartre, 68; of Weiss, 61–73
avant-gardism, 78, 129

Babylon (journal), 112
backshadowing, narrative, 40, 45, 135
Baer, Ulrich, 33, 134, 193n. 37, 213n. 14
Baer, Ytzak, 207n. 29
Bahr, Erhard, 205n. 3
Bakhtin, Mikhail, 75, 200n. 27, 210n. 56
Bayerdörfer, Hans-Peter, 208n. 34
Belgium, 48
Ben-Gurion, David, 127, 211n. 64
Benjamin, Walter, 35, 39–40, 193n. 44, 194n. 54, 220n. 21
Benn, Gottfried, 102
Bennholdt-Thomsen, Anke, 210n. 53
Benz, Wolfgang, 210n. 59
Berendsohn, Walter, 104, 105, 124, 207n. 28, 207nn. 20;23;28, 208n. 32, 209n. 44
Bergmann, Shmuel Hugo, 111, 208n. 37
Bering, Dietz, 209n. 52
Berlin, 15, 17, 71, 162, 167
Berman, Russell A., 208n. 34
Bernstein, Michael André, 40, 46, 140, 194n. 55
Bernstein, Susan, 192n. 26
Berrett, A. M., 218n. 3
Bettelheim, Bruno, 101, 206n. 13
Bhabha, Homi, 3, 4, 12, 53, 188n. 9, 193n. 31, 219n. 5; on colonial mimicry, 30; on diasporic discourse, 176; on temporality of postcolonial migration, 112
Bible, 97, 106, 114–15; Ecclesiastes, 141; Exodus, 119, 173–74; Genesis, 117; Hosea, 100; Isaiah,

INDEX

127; Jeremiah, 141, 214n. 26
Bier, Jean-Paul, 189n. 21
Bilderverbot (taboo on mimesis), 22–24
Bildung, 34
Birus, Hendrik, 215n. 30
black cultures, transatlantic, 175–77
Bleyleben, Maximilian, 212n. 4
blood libel, 140
Bobrowski, Johannes, 146–47, 149, 215n. 31, 216n. 35; "Heimat des Malers Chagall, Die" [The Homeland of the Painter Chagall], 149; "Pruzzische Elegie" [Prussian Elegy], 147, 149
Bodemann, Y. Michal, 98, 103, 205n. 6
Bohemia, 159, 160, 161, 170
Böhme, Franz M., 215n. 27
Böll, Heinrich, 8
Bollack, Jean, 133, 134, 177, 213n. 12, 219n. 10
Bormann, Alexander von, 205n. 3
Borowski, Tadeusz, 198n. 7
Börsenverein des Deutschen Buchhandels, 100
Böschenstein, Bernhard, 212n. 1, 216n. 41, 217n. 50
Bower, Kathrin M., 210n. 54
Boyarin, Daniel and Jonathan, 4, 5, 12, 175, 188n. 8
Braese, Stephan, 198n. 8
Braun, Michael, 205n. 3
Brecht, Bertolt, 179
Breslau, 43, 44–45
Breuer, Ingo, 60, 61
Briegleb, Klaus, 198n. 8, 212n. 1
Brumlik, Micha, 194n. 56, 196n. 78, 205n. 6
Brundert, Willy, 206n. 11
Buber, Martin, 95, 144, 210n. 54
Bucharest, 132
Buenos Aires, 125
Bukovina, 132, 134; cultural heterogeneity of, 135; remapping of, 136–44

Burgard, Peter J., 192n. 19
Burger, Thomas, 196n. 83

Cahn, Michael, 191n. 8
Cain (biblical), 72
Camus, Albert, 143
Canaan, biblical land of, 128
Canaris, Volker, 199n. 16
capitalism, 29, 34, 88, 180, 204n. 54
Carthage, 38
Caruth, Cathy, 173, 174, 190n. 36, 218n. 1
Catholic church, in Germany, 99
Celan, Paul, 1, 6, 174, 178; Bukovina in imagination of, 136–44; "Contrescarpe, La," 167–69; "Eden," 162; endings absent from poetry of, 151–62; "Es ist alles anders" ["It's All Different"], 155–61, 170–71; "Gauner- und Ganovenweise, Eine" ["A Rogues' and Gonifs' Ditty"], 136–44, 151–52; on German poetry, 129; "Hinausgekrönt" ["Crowned Out"]: 145–146; "Hüttenfenster" ["Tabernacle Window"], 146–51; "In der Luft" ["In the Air"], 144; on "Jewish loneliness," 177; Jewish mysticism and, 144–51, 176; on Jews of Eastern Europe, 7, 11; "Kermorvan," 162–66; "Meridian" speech, 134, 142, 164; "Nachmittag mit Zirkus und Zitadelle" ["Afternoon with Circus and Citadel"], 161–62; place names in poems of, 162–71; plagiarism charge against, 11, 18, 131–35, 212n. 1; reception in Germany, 10, 18; Sachs and, 105; "Todesfuge" ["Deathfugue"], 131; "Und mit dem Buch aus Tarussa" ["And with the Book from Tarussa"], 152–55. See also Niemandsrose, Die [The No-One's Rose]

239

INDEX

cemeteries, Jewish, 8, 71, 132, 150
Central Office for the Investigation of National Socialist Crimes, 8
Certeau, Michel de, 76, 200n. 28
Chagall, Marc, 147
Chalfen, Israel, 212n. 4, 214n. 22
Chaliand, Gérard, 218n. 3
Château de Kermorvan (Brittany), 164
Chaumont, Jean-Michel, 197n. 87
Chelmno death camp, 13
Christian Democrats, 98, 198n. 12
Christians/Christianity, 10, 98–99, 127, 139; German Romanticism and, 119, 122; yearning for transcendence, 156
chronotopes, 75–76
circumcision, 72–73, 167, 202n. 35
Claussen, Detlev, 195n. 73
Clifford, James, 5, 12
Cohen, Robert, 202n. 41, 203n. 49, 208n. 30
Cohen, Robin, 218n. 3
Colchis, 152–55
Cold War, 185, 211n. 63
colonialism, 56
commodification, 28, 39
commodity fetishism, 82
Communism, 179
community, 3, 176, 179, 186
concentration camps, 15, 58, 99
consciousness, 7, 13; diasporic, 56, 175; global versus universal, 180–81; historical, 36; trauma and, 35–36
Corbea-Hosie, Andrei, 214n. 19
cosmopolitanism, 65, 67–68, 73, 198n. 12, 200n. 20; Czernowitz as symbol of, 136; exile and, 56; as inauthentic, 118; Kant's idea of, 69–70; optimism of, 93; remnants of, 61–73; symbolic origin and, 71
cultural studies, Jewish, 3, 12
culture industry, 34
Cumming, John, 191n. 9
Cupitt, S. M., 200n. 26

Czechoslovakia, 55, 182
Czernowitz, 136–38, 167, 168

Dante Alighieri, 59, 86–87, 87, 202–3nn. 45–47; *Divine Comedy*, 59, 86, 91
Daviau, Donald G., 219n. 12
Davies, W. E., 187n. 2
Davy, M. M., 215n. 28
death, poetic figure of, 147, 194n. 61
death camps, 12, 41, 169; instrumental reason and, 49; material remnants of, 92; in metaphorical association, 79. *See also* Auschwitz; Chelmno death camp
Delbo, Charlotte, 166
democracy/democratization, 8, 9–10, 25
Derrida, Jacques, 135, 166, 170, 218n. 58
dialectics, 49
Diary of Anne Frank, The (play and film), 101–2
diaspora, 2–3, 14, 18; Adorno's valorization of, 24, 28, 29; bearing witness to the Holocaust, 174; black and Jewish concepts of, 175–77; community and, 73–81; cultural identity and, 4; diasporic consciousness, 56, 175; exile contrasted with, 2, 7, 175, 188n. 8; genre conventions and, 73; German-speaking Jews in Eastern Europe, 135; Judaism and enlightenment linked to, 22–23; land of Israel and, 108–10; mediation and, 97; messianic redemption and, 111; nostalgia and, 4–5; reconceptualization of, 129; redoubled, 5, 6; retroactive diasporization, 40–41, 47; shift in concept of, 3, 12; as site of remembrance, 107; tradition and, 176
Diner, Dan, 5, 97, 112–13, 114, 115, 187n. 2, 188n. 16; "Negative Symbiose: Deutsche und Juden

240

nach Auschwitz" [Negative Symbiosis: Germans and Jews after Auschwitz], 112–13
Dinesen, Ruth, 124, 204n. 1, 205n. 3, 206n. 15
displacement, 2, 12, 21, 26, 39, 173; DPs (displaced persons), 112–13; essay genre and, 25
Döhl, Reinhard, 132–33, 212n. 8
domestic (private) sphere, 46, 124
Domin, Hilde, 103
Dortmund, 96, 98
Dresden, bombing of, 35
Dreyfus, Capt. Alfred, family of, 39
dualism, creational (kabbalistic doctrine), 151
Dürer, Albrecht, 182, 183

Edfelt, Johannes, 205n. 4, 207nn. 25–27
Edom (biblical), 138, 139
Eichendorff, Joseph von, 23–24
Eichmann, Adolf, trial of, 96, 97, 125; execution of Eichmann, 47, 127, 204n. 1; political dimension of, 211n. 63; remembrance of Holocaust and, 8
Eichmann, Klaus, 47
Eiland, Howard, 193n. 44
Einhorn, Erich, 152
Eisen, Arnold M., 187n. 3, 207n. 30
Ekelöf, Gunnar, 210n. 62
ekphrasis, 182–83
Elbe River, 159–60
emancipation (nineteenth century), 6, 48, 175, 188n. 17; failure of, 28, 39; hope for end of anti-Jewish violence and, 139; medieval Muslim-Jewish "symbiosis" as model for, 140
Emerson, Caryl, 200n. 27, 210n. 56
emigrant, return of, 12, 13, 17–18; psychology of emigrant, 41–42; relation to language, 22
emigration, 12, 15, 27
Encyclopedia Judaica, 2

England, 55, 174
Enlightenment, 22, 23, 34, 69; death camps and, 49; ideal of rational religion, 106; public sphere and, 91; stranger/foreigner's perspective and, 82, 83
Enzensberger, Hans Magnus, 97, 98, 132, 204n. 3
Ephraimites (biblical), 166–67
equivocation, 24–25, 29, 31
Esau (biblical), 139
eschatology, 126, 135, 141, 217n. 44
Esenin, Sergei, 156; "Ioniia," 156
Eshel, Amir, 213n. 18
Eskin, Michael, 217n. 41
ethnic community, 3
ethnocentrism, 3, 69, 200n. 20
eugenics, 175
Europe, Eastern/Central, 6, 7, 43, 47, 184; displaced persons (DPs) from, 112–13; German hegemony in, 67, 135, 136, 146; German refugees from Soviet advance in, 61; heterogeneity in pre-Holocaust times, 143, 146; Jewish mysticism in, 144; Jews of, 118, 136–37; socialism in, 134
Europe, Western, 7, 135
exile, 30, 49, 189n. 19; alienation and, 62; diaspora contrasted with, 175, 188n. 8; family relations and, 62; imposed versus self-chosen, 2–3, 12, 71–72; isolation of, 179; as liberating experience, 174; mythological/theological paradigms of, 122; poetry of, 97; postwar German attitudes toward exiles, 59–60; reification of the past and, 43; as site of critique, 11, 56–57; as site of mediation, 96; testimony and, 13
existentialism, 6, 62, 68, 71
expulsion, mass, 1
Ezrahi, Sidra DeKoven, 218n. 61

INDEX

fascism, 7, 10, 22, 204n. 54; Allied defeat of, 160; false mimesis and, 32; lingering postwar dispositions toward, 25; literary condemnation of, 59; Marxist economistic critique of, 88; plague as symbol of, 143; popular front against, 179; projection mechanisms and, 29; suffering of Germans during World War II and, 37–38; systemic continuity of, 38–39. *See also* Nazism

Federmann, Reinhard, 217n. 49

Feldman, Ron H., 194n. 52

Felman, Shoshana, 12, 13, 14, 15, 91, 175, 189n. 28; on Eichmann trial, 211n. 63; on testimony of survivors, 85, 86

Felstiner, John, 212n. 7, 213n. 17

female body, 46, 47, 63, 64

Fetscher, Justus, 196n. 76

Fiero, Petra S., 195n. 71

Finkielkraut, Alain, 110, 208n. 36

Fioretis, Aris, 218n. 52

Firges, Jean, 216n. 37

Fischer, Gottfried Bermann, 215n. 33

Fischer, Ludwig M., 219n. 12

Fortunoff Archive for Holocaust Testimonies (Yale University), 85

Foschepoth, Josef, 205n. 7

France, 17, 28, 136, 161, 162, 163

Frank, Anne, 8, 101–2, 103

Frank, Otto, 102

Frankfurt, 85, 140

Franzos, Karl Emil, 136

Fremdwörter (foreign words), 26, 29, 33

Freud, Sigmund, 12, 17, 35; "Beyond the Pleasure Principle," 174, 193n. 44; *Moses and Monotheism*, 173–74; on mourning rituals, 160; "Remembering, Repeating, and Working-Through," 36; on taboos, 67; on the uncanny, 42; concept of working-through, 36–37

Fritsch-Vivié, Gabriele, 210n. 58

galut (exile), 2

Garloff, Katja, 190n. 43

Garside, E. B., 199n. 17

Gay, Peter, 15, 16–17, 190n. 39

Gearey, John, 200n. 21

Gebauer, Gunter, 191n. 8

Geier, Manfred, 213n. 18

Geißner, 206n. 15

Gelber, Mark H., 208n. 35, 213n. 18

gender, 46, 95, 101, 181–82

genealogy, 4, 5, 111, 175

genocide, 5, 10, 45, 101, 173; encounter with actuality of, 125; ethical dimension of language and, 13; home as site of, 6; as industrial process, 134, 175; mourning process and, 9; traumatic return of, 1. *See also* Holocaust; Shoah

Gentiles, 27, 102, 106

Gerecke, Gabriele, 206n. 15

Gerlach, Rainer, 197n. 3

German Jewish writers, 1–2, 175, 187n. 1; absence of community and, 179; gender and, 95; in German public sphere, 124–25; "impossible returns" of, 15; multiple affiliations of, 6; postwar return to German-speaking lands, 18; reception in West Germany, 11, 59, 103, 133, 173

German language, 1, 48, 122, 187n. 1; Adorno and, 22; Améry and, 48; Celan and, 131–32, 132, 143; in Eastern Europe, 7, 136; foreign words in, 26; German-speaking lands, 6; Heine and, 29; heterogeneity of, 18; Jewish survivors writing in, 6; Jewish use of High German, 27; as universal language, 6; Sachs and, 119, 205n. 3; "Ur" prefix in, 116, 117, 118; Weiss and, 55, 71, 85, 174

Germans: complacency about Nazi past, 52; guilt of, 49–50; guilt feelings of, 32, 35, 52, 100–101; Holocaust survivors and, 16;

242

INDEX

mourning of, 8–9; national identity of, 7–8; "negative symbiosis" with Jews, 5–6; reconciliation with Jews, 1, 96, 99; suffering during World War II, 37–38
Germany, East (Democratic Republic), 58, 105
Germany, pre–World War II: eastern frontier of, 44–45; Heine as "wound" in culture/history of, 30–31
Germany, West (Federal Republic), 1, 8, 50, 53; Allied occupied zones, 9; democracy in, 25; Entschädigungsamt (Compensation Office), 81–82; fascist persistence in, 22, 132; financial reparations to Jews, 9; Jewish women constructed as conciliatory figures in, 97–105; juridical limitation on Nazi crimes, 169; latent antisemitism in, 32; literary institutions, 55, 58; mass media in, 90; philosemitism in, 87, 133, 198n. 129–10; public sphere in, 10, 56, 57–61
Gesellschaften für Christlich-Jüdische Zusammenarbeit, 98, 104
Gilman, Sander L., 188–89n. 18, 202n. 35, 206nn. 11;19, 209n. 51
Gilroy, Paul, 73, 175–77, 178, 200n. 25, 219nn. 4;6
globalization, 2, 180
God, absence of, 127–28
Goes, Albrecht, 207n. 24
Goethe, Johann Wolfgang von, 69, 99, 200n. 21
Golb, Joel, 162, 218n. 52
Goldsmith, Oliver, 202n. 37
Goll, Claire, 131, 212n. 1
Goll, Yvan, 131
Goodrich, Frances, 101, 206n. 14
Grass, Günter, 8, 59, 198n. 12
Greek dispersion, 3
Gregor, Mary J., 200n. 22
Grimm brothers, 141, 209n. 48

Grimm dictionary, 162
Grimm, Gunter E., 208n. 34
Groddeck, Wolfram, 215n. 34
Grosbard, Ulu, 202n. 41
Group Experiment, 25
Gründer, Karlfried, 200n. 20
Gruppe 47, 1, 10, 55; Celan and, 212n. 1; politicization of, 58–59; Sachs and, 97; Weiss and, 58–60
Guzzoni, Alfredo, 210n. 53
Gypsies, 9

Habermas, Jürgen, 51, 90, 196n. 83
Habsburg empire, 136, 143, 188n. 17
Hackett, Albert, 101, 206n. 14
Hades (Greek mythological), 147, 194n. 61
Hall, Stuart, 3–4, 187n. 7, 188n. 8
Hallo, William H., 209n. 42
Halpern, Ben, 208n. 30
Hamacher, Werner, 36, 37, 193n. 48, 194n. 50, 213n. 18, 215n. 33
Hamburger, Michael, 204n. 2
Hamilton, Alastair, 199n. 17
Hamm, Peter, 104, 105, 207n. 24
Hansen, Miriam, 191n. 8
Hartman, Matthew T., 193n. 48
"Hashkeidia Porachat" [The Almond Tree Is Blooming] (Zionist song), 141
Hasidim, 5, 117, 137, 144, 207n. 24
Haskalah, 144
Haufe, Eberhard, 216n. 35
Hebel, Johann Peter, 164, 218n. 55; Schatzkästlein des rheinischen Hausfreundes, 164
Hebrew language, 95, 116, 146, 150, 151, 174
Hebrews, ancient, 23, 173–74
Heffernan, James, 183, 219n. 19
Hegel, Georg Wilhelm Friedrich, 112, 197n. 87
Heidegger, Martin, 24, 41
Heidelberger-Leonard, Irene, 195n. 72, 197n. 87, 198–199n. 15

INDEX

Heimatlosigkeit (homelessness), 28, 30, 96
Heine, Heinrich, 28–33, 41; Book of Songs, 28; Celan and, 138, 139, 140–41, 159; Deutschland: Ein Wintermärchen [Germany: A Winter's Tale], 159; as pariah, 39; Rabbi von Bacharach, Der [The Rabbi of Bacharach], 139, 140–41, 214nn. 23–24
Helbig, Holger, 215n. 30
Hell, Julia, 182, 219n. 16
Herf, Jeffrey, 8, 189n. 22
Hermand, Jost, 219n. 16
Herz, Henriette, 46
Hessing, Jakob, 206n. 16
Heym, Stefan, 200n. 23
Hildesheimer, Wolfgang, 103
Hiroshima, 41
history: acknowledgment of, 52; alternative courses of, 141, 185; deterministic view of, 40; Holocaust as rupture in, 33; Kant's idea of, 69; reconciliation and, 105; Rosenzweig's understanding of, 111, 116; as text, 40
Hitler, Adolf, 8, 133, 184, 185
Hoffman, Lawrence A., 208n. 30
Hohendahl, Peter Uwe, 28, 29, 191n. 3, 192n. 19
Hölderlin, Friedrich, 78, 217n. 44
Höllerer, Walter, 58
Holmqvist, Margaretha and Bengt, 204n. 1
Holocaust, 1, 5, 27, 43, 176; Auschwitz as metonym for, 166; Dante's inferno metaphor and, 86; dead victims of, 134; diaspora bearing witness to, 174; failure of assimilation and, 39; identities constituted in relation to, 5–6, 112; imagined Jewish revenge for, 32, 100–101, 124; Jewish–German reconciliation after, 96, 99; literal meaning of, 128; Marxist view of, 87–88; material remnants of, 92; poetry and, 95, 98, 104, 106–7, 120; as religious-universal event, 98; remembrance of, 8, 12, 18, 105; as rupture in Western civilization/history, 2, 22, 33, 113; survivors of, 16, 107, 166; "unrepresentability" of, 12–13; witnesses to, 15, 85. *See also* genocide; Shoah
Holquist, Michael, 200n. 27, 210n. 56
homesickness, 67
homosexuals, as victims of Nazism, 9
Honold, Alexander, 220n. 21
Horch, Hans Otto, 213n. 18
Horkheimer, Max, 22–23, 34, 191n. 7
Huhn, Tom, 191n. 8
Hulewitz, Witold, 215n. 34
Hullot-Kentor, Robert, 192n. 29
Husserl, Edmund, 41, 44
Huyssen, Andreas, 92, 203n. 49, 206n. 12
hybridity, 122, 210n. 56
Hyman, Paula E., 195n. 68

identities, cultural and national, 3, 4; absence of homeland and, 12; cosmopolitanism and, 70; hybridity and, 176; performative nature of national identity, 30; split, 175; uncanniness and, 180
identity, German, 9, 32, 48, 112
identity, Jewish, 4, 61, 104, 187n. 1; aporias of, 49; in Celan's poems, 140; constituted in relation to Holocaust, 112; failure of assimilation and, 28–29; German and Eastern European, 118; German culture and Jews, 48; in German public sphere, 103; imposed versus chosen, 95; resurgent antisemitism and, 132
idolatry, Jewish injunction against, 23, 29, 106
intertextuality, 151, 155

INDEX

Isaac (biblical), 115
Isaiah (biblical), 127
Israel, land of, 4, 6, 107; collective gathering in, 108; demystification of, 207n. 30; restoration of, 106; symbolic recovery of, 125, 128
Israel, Nico, 21, 188n. 8
Israel, state of, 2, 10, 100, 108, 207n. 28; Celan in, 177; Eichmann trial in, 127; establishment of, 208n. 32; German relations with, 8, 50, 100; Holocaust survivors in, 13; refutation of stereotypes and, 110–11
Italy, 143

Jacob (biblical), 152, 153–54
Jakobson, Roman, 123, 210n. 210n. 57
Jay, Martin, 191n. 3
Jennings, Michael W., 193n. 44
Jens, Walter, 212n. 7
Jephcott, E.F.N., 192n. 13, 193n. 44
Jerusalem, 125–28
Jewish studies, 3, 12
Jews: black diaspora compared with, 175–77; diasporic consciousness of German Jews, 19; emancipation of, 2, 6; emergence from ancient Hebrews, 174; expulsion from Spain, 106, 140, 146; German liberals and, 147; German patriotism of, 44; as "guardians of memory," 113; historical roles of, 23; intellectuals, 29; "negative symbiosis" with Germans, 5–6; philosemitism as exploitation of, 133; in Poland, 117, 119; postwar minority in West Germany, 103; reconciliation with Germans, 1, 96, 99; relation to history, 111–12; self-hatred and, 72; troubled coexistence with Christians, 139
Johnson, Uwe, 8
Judaism, 4, 49, 107; mystical strains of, 95, 122, 130, 144–51, 178;

nomadism and, 23, 191n. 7; Orthodox, 111, 140, 188n. 17; proscription against idolatry, 29; taboo on mimesis, 22–24; vengeful stereotype of, 100–101

Kabbalah, 106, 145, 146, 150, 151. *See also* Judaism, mystical strains of
Kafka, Franz, 72, 83, 85; "Bericht für eine Akademie, Ein" [A Report to an Academy], 83–84, 85; *Verwandlung, Die [The Metamorphosis]*, 72
Kant, Immanuel, 69–70, 200n. 22; "Idea for a Universal History with a Cosmopolitan Intent," 69–70; *Toward Perpetual Peace*, 70
Kaschnitz, Marie Luise, 132
Keilson, Hans, 196n. 78
Keller, Gottfried, 147
Kersten, Paul, 212n. 70
Kessler, Michael, 205n. 3, 211n. 65
Kirshenblatt-Gimblett, Barbara, 3, 187n. 5
Klibansky, Raymond, 219n. 18
Klüger, Ruth, 15–16, 190n. 37
Knauer, Bettina, 215n. 30
Knowledge: absence of, 170; historical, 36; language and, 22; moral, 18, 47, 51; traumatic, 186
Koebner, Thomas, 205n. 3
Kraus, Karl, 28
Kristallnacht, 167
Krummacher, F. A., 211n. 63
Kuhn, Juliane, 197n. 5

LaCapra, Dominick, 36, 113, 193n. 47, 209n. 40
Lachmann, Renate, 216n. 41
Lagerlöf, Selma, 102, 104, 206n. 15
Lämmert, Eberhard, 196n. 76
Langer, Lawrence, 166, 218n. 57
language, 80, 122–23, 182; assimilation and, 29; concepts in essay and, 25; erotic desire for the exotic and, 33; essentialist notion of, 22;

245

INDEX

language (*continued*)
  Holocaust and failure of, 12–13, 14; historical boundedness of, 131; internal division of, 166; linguistic overdeterminations, 116–17; lost and recovered, 70, 78; symbolic identity and, 185; traumatic experience and, 201n. 31
Lanzmann, Claude, 13
Laplanche, Jean, 170, 218n. 63
Lasker-Schüler, Else, 101, 102, 103
Laub, Dori, 14, 91, 175, 189n. 28; on Holocaust as event without witnesses, 12–13; on return to site of trauma, 15; on testimony of survivors, 85, 86
Lawrence, Frederic, 196n. 83
Lazare, Bernhard, 39
Lebanon, 140
legends, Jewish, 97, 117, 127
Lehmann, Hans-Thies, 204n. 53
Lehmann, Jürgen, 213n. 18
Levenson, Christopher, 199n. 17
Levi, Primo, 13, 14
Levin, Thomas, 26, 192n. 23
Leys, Ruth, 174, 218n. 2
liberalism, 2, 98, 133, 147
Liessmann, Konrad Paul, 194n. 56
lieux de mémoire (places of memory), 92, 166, 170
Loewen, Matthias, 163, 165, 218n. 53
London, 68, 69
Lorenz, Otto, 218n. 62
Los Angeles, 21
Löw, Rabbi, 159
Lübke, Heinrich, 98, 99
Lüttmann, Helmut, 200n. 26
Luftmenschen, 24, 149

Macey, David, 218n. 63
Mahler, Gustav, 39
Mandel'shtam, Osip, 156, 162, 165, 214n. 26
Marat, Jean-Paul, 60, 61, 198n. 6
Margul-Sperber, Alfred, 212n. 9, 213n. 11, 215n. 32
Marxism, 56, 179
mass media, 90
McHugh, Heather, 215n. 29
Meinecke, Dietlind, 215n. 28
melancholia, 8
Melencolia I (Dürer engraving), 182, 183
Meltzer, Françoise, 212n. 2
memory, 74–75, 93; industrial genocide and annihilation of, 157; effacement of, 35; everyday life and, 92; Jews as guardians of, 105–6, 114; kink inhibiting process of, 42; "missing grave syndrome," 165–66; retrieval of, 116; screen memories, 112, 113; silencing of, 8; topological, 75. *See also lieux de mémoire* (places of memory)
Mendelsohn, Harvey, 213n. 14
Mendes-Flohr, Paul, 111, 208n. 208nn. 30, 38
Menke, Christoph, 192n. 29
Menninghaus, Winfried, 136, 177, 213n. 18, 214n. 19, 215n. 33, 219n. 11
messianism, 144–45, 149, 157
Michaelis, Rolf, 219n. 12
migration, 3–4
mimesis, 80–81; assimilation and, 29; Judaic taboo on, 23–24; bodily knowledge and, 182; musical performance as, 30
mimicry, 82
Mitscherlich, Alexander and Margarethe, 8, 36, 42
modernity, 175
monotheism, 173–74
Montesquieu, Baron de, 202n. 37
Morris, Leslie, 188n. 16
Moses (biblical), 173–74
mourning, 19, 40, 135, 144, 156; Freudian *fort-da* ritual, 160, 174; inability to mourn, 35, 42; poetic landscapes of, 96

INDEX

Muselmann (doomed camp inmate), 13, 15, 17
music, 29–30, 176
Müssener, Helmut, 204n. 1
mythology, 122, 123

Nachträglichkeit (deferred action), 12
Naficy, Hamid, 219n. 3
narcissism, 8, 9, 36, 42
Nardoff, Ellen and Ernest H. von, 200n. 21
narrative, 75–77, 201n. 31; screen memories and, 112; Shoah as limit of, 113
nationalism, 3, 27, 176
nation-state, 3, 4
Naumann, Bernd, 203n. 50
Naumann, Uwe, 205n. 5
Nazism, 6, 16, 41, 104; abstraction of, 52; annexation of Austria, 48; anti-Jewish laws, 124; Christian Democratic explanation of, 98; Christian relation to, 98–99; collective identification with, 36; disavowal of crimes of, 35; failure of language and, 12–13; German bystanders to, 59; German folk tradition appropriated by, 143; German industrial elite's support for, 88, 184–85; legacy of, 7, 8, 10; non-Jewish victims of, 9; psychoanalytic theory and, 8–9; public discussion about, 10; refugees from, 50, 55, 57, 58, 59, 61. *See also* fascism; Third Reich
Neues Deutschland (East German party newspaper), 105
Neugroschel, Joachim, 217n. 42
Neusner, Jacob, 208n. 30
New Left (West German), 10
New York City, 45, 68, 69
Nicholson, Shierry Weber, 191n. 12, 192n. 21
Niemandsrose, Die [The No-One's Rose] (Celan), 11, 134, 135, 143, 144, 152; dedication to Mandel'shtam, 156; place names in, 161; plagiarism crisis and, 133
Nimrod (biblical), 114, 116
Nobel Prize, 95
Noerr, Gunzeln Schmid, 191n. 7
Nolden, Thomas, 189n. 18
nomadism, 23, 191n. 7
Nora, Pierre, 92, 166, 169–70, 204n. 57
normalization, discourse of, 53
Normandy-Niemen (Normandy Squadron), 159, 161, 170
nostalgia, 3, 4, 43, 160
nouveau roman, 75

Och, Gunnar, 215n. 30
October Revolution, 181
Oinopion (mythological), 154
Olschner, Leonard, 156, 205n. 3, 217n. 217n. 48
Orion (mythological), 152, 154
Orpheus (mythological), 156
Orthodoxy, religious, 111, 140, 188n. 17
Ostflüchtlinge (German refugees from Eastern Europe), 61
Ostmeier, Dorothee, 209n. 43
Ovid, 154
Ozell, John, 202n. 37

Palestine, 105
Panofsky, Erwin, 183, 219n. 18
Paranoia, 124
pariah, figure of, 60, 72
Paris, 69, 179; Celan in, 132, 137, 152, 167, 168; cosmopolitanism of, 70; existentialism in, 6, 68, 71
pedagogy, 10, 34, 37, 51
Peitsch, Helmut, 58, 59, 196n. 76
Perels, Christopher, 217n. 44
persecution fears, 1, 57, 59, 96
Pestalozzi, Karl, 205n. 3
Peters, John Durham, 219n. 3
philosemitism, 9–10, 11, 87, 133, 198n. 12
Pickford, Henry W., 191n. 4, 192n.

INDEX

Pickford, Henry W. (*continued*) 21, 193n. 49
Pöggeler, Otto, 218n. 54
pogroms, 140, 143
Poland, 44, 117, 119, 182
Poles, 195n. 64
Pomorska, Krystyna, 210n. 57
Popov, Nikolai, 215n. 29
postcolonial criticism, 3, 12, 53, 112, 175
Postone, Moishe, 52, 196n. 86
poststructuralism, 151
progress, idea/ideology of, 40, 139
Promised Land, 4, 114
Protestantism, 55, 99
Prussia, East, 146
psychoanalysis, 8–9, 12, 15, 92, 112; American transformation of, 34; enlightenment and, 34; postwar German resistance to, 33; trauma theory in, 134; universality and, 180, 181
public sphere, 10, 56, 57–61, 90, 103, 124

Rabinbach, Anson, 8, 10, 22, 189n. 20, 191n. 7
racism, 59, 175
Rageau, Jean-Pierre, 218n. 3
Rashi, 209n. 49
redemption, 127, 128, 149, 155, 157
Reich-Ranicki, Marcel, 199n. 19
Reichert, Stefan, 215n. 28, 216n. 34
reification, 24, 32, 43
Remmler, Karen, 189n. 18, 202n. 35
Rendall, Steven, 200n. 28
resistance, 91, 135, 143, 204n. 54; in Belgium, 48; in France, 170; incomplete mourning and, 156; nondeterministic view of history and, 40; poetic, 142
responsibility, 35, 50, 113
return: idea of, 5; of former exiles to Germany, 21–22, 41–47, 58, 60, 66–67, 86–87, 88, 92, 96, 124; to land of Israel, 107, 157; and

"working-through," 12, 13, 15–17
revelation, 116, 180
Richter, Hans Werner, 59, 60, 198n. 12
righteous, hidden thirty-six, 117, 127
Rilke, Rainer Maria, 147
Ritter, Joachim, 200n. 20
Robertson, Michael, 191n. 3
Robinson, Benjamin, 211n. 63
Roebling, Irmgard, 209–210n. 53
Rokeah, David, 104
Roman Empire, 23, 38
Romania, 132, 214n. 22
Romanticism, German, 23, 46, 103; Jewish mysticism and, 122, 178; Sachs's Melusine cycle and, 119–20
Rosenfeld, Sidney and Stella P., 195n. 70
Rosenzweig, Franz, 97, 111–13, 116, 180, 209n. 42
Rosh Ha-Shanah (Jewish New Year), 157
Rother, Rainer, 185, 219n. 21
Rudy, Stephen, 210n. 57
Russia, 136, 152, 156, 161, 162
Russian Revolution, 181
Ruth (biblical), 107–8
Rutherford, Jonathan, 187n. 7

Sachs, Nelly, 6, 95–97, 175; "Aber deine Brunnen" ["But Your Wells"], 108–11; *Abram im Salz [Abram in the Salt]*, 114–15; agricultural imagery in, 105, 107, 110–11; on bearing witness, 174; cultural synthesis and, 178; *In den Wohnungen des Todes [In the Habitations of Death]*, 95; "In der Flucht" ["Fleeing"], 97; divine intentionality of dispersal and, 7; Eichmann trial and, 124–30, 210–11n. 62, 211n. 63; *Eli*, 97, 98, 117–19, 124; as figure of reconciliation, 1, 11, 18, 95–105;

248

INDEX

flight to Sweden, 95, 206n. 15; *Glühende Rätsel [Glowing Enigmas]*, 129–30; "Immer hinter" [Always Beyond], 120–23; "Jäger, Der" [The Hunter], 129; "Land Israel," 107–8; Melusine cycle, 119–20; on memory, myth, and mediation, 105–23; paranoid breakdown of, 124–25, 129; on political conflict in Israel, 208n. 32; on public and private, 206–7n. 20; reception in Germany, 10, 18; *Sternverdunklung [Eclipse of the Stars]*, 107; "Überall Jerusalem" ["Everywhere Jerusalem"], 97, 125–28, 130; *Und niemand weiß weiter [And No One Knows How to Go On]*, 97, 119–23
Sacks, Peter M., 217n. 46
Sadagora (village in Bukovina), 137
Safran, William, 218n. 3
Said, Edward, 21, 189–90n. 31
Salloch, Erika, 203n. 52
Santner, Eric, 9, 36, 124, 180–81, 189n. 23, 210n. 61, 219n. 13
Sartre, Jean-Paul, 68
Saxl, Fritz, 219n. 18
Scheichl, Sigurd Paul, 213–214n. 18
Schilling, Sabine, 188n. 18
Schlant, Ernestine, 189n. 21
Schlösser, Manfred, 103
Schmidt, Alfred, 191n. 7
Scholem, Gershom, 95, 102–3, 112, 144, 146, 206n. 17, 210n. 54, 211n. 64, 216n. 39; *Major Trends of Jewish Mysticism*, 144, 146, 215n. 28
Schreber, Daniel, 124
Schreiber, Maeera Y., 218–219n. 3
Schubert, Elke, 194n. 56
Schulz, Genia, 219n. 20
Schulze, Joachim, 215n. 29, 216n. 37
Schutte, Jürgen, 196n. 76
Schweid, Eliezer, 208n. 30
screen memories, 112, 113
Sebald, W. G., 17, 1196n. 75

secularization, 2
sefiroth (divine emanations), 146
self-determination, national, 3, 112
Sellars, Roy, 216n. 41
Sevin, Dieter, 205n. 3
Seyhan, Azade, 188n. 8
sexuality, 34–35, 63–64, 146, 156
Shakespeare, William, 159
shibboleth, 135, 146, 166–67, 170
Shoah, 1, 6, 44, 50, 85; ghosts of, 134; giving testimony to, 7; as limit of narrative, 113; testimony of, 106. *See also* genocide; Holocaust
Shoah (Lanzmann film), 13
sideshadowing, narrative, 40, 45, 140, 142
Silbermann, Rabbi A. M., 209n. 49
Silberman, Marc, 219n. 16
silence, 178, 183, 203n. 51
Silesia, 41
skekhinah (feminine Divine Presence), 122, 146, 210n. 54
Social Democrats, 60, 198n. 12
Söllner, Alfons, 56, 92, 197n. 5
Solomon, Neil, 192n. 29
Solomon, Petre, 212nn. 3;6, 213n. 15
Song of Songs (biblical), 46
Soviet Union, 181; army air force, 159
Spain, Jews of, 45, 106, 140, 146
Spanish Civil War, 179–80
Spariosu, Mihai, 191n. 8
Sparr, Thomas, 213n. 18
Sperber, Manès, 211n. 63
Spies, Bernhard, 189n. 19
Srebnik, Simon, 13
Stalingrad, battle of, 38
Stein, Edith, 44
Steinberg, Jean, 203n. 50
Steiner, Stephan, 195n. 73
Stephan, Alexander, 219n. 12
Stephan, Inge, 188n. 18
stereotypes, 10, 26, 28, 72; gender, 96; Jewish names, 118, 209n. 52;

249

INDEX

stereotypes (*continued*)
of Jewish versus Christian God, 100; of Jewish women, 101; Jews as thieves and parasites, 132; philosemitic inversion of, 198n. 12; psychoanalytic concepts as, 34; redirection of, 118; refutation of, 110
Sterling, Eleanore, 9, 189n. 26
Stern, Frank, 189n. 25
Stevens, George, 101
Stewart, Susan, 43, 194n. 59
Stockholm, 56, 68, 69, 71, 96, 111
Stöhr, Martin, 205n. 7
subjectivity, 14, 22, 34, 93; of Auschwitz trial defendants, 90, 92; of returning exile, 92
Suhrkamp, Peter, 71
Suhrkamp publishing house, 97
surrealism, 56
survivors, 13, 14, 96; guilt of, 165; *Muselmänner* and, 17; subjective experience as moral category, 50–51; testimony of, 85–86
Swan, Jon, 202n. 41
Sweden, 55, 60, 95, 179
Switzerland, 55
symbiosis, German-Jewish cultural, 102–3, 112–13, 136, 188n. 16
symbiosis, medieval Muslim-Jewish, 114, 140
synagogues, desecration of, 8
Szász, János, 212n. 5
Szondi, Peter, 134, 162, 213n. 14, 218n. 51

Tarnowski, Knut, 191n. 5
Tarusskie stranitsy [Pages from Tarussa], 152
teleology, 123, 127
Templer, William, 189n. 25
Teraoka, Arlene, 56, 197n. 4
territory, 105, 114; polity based on, 5
testimony, 13, 85, 91, 175; as incomplete speech, 12, 13–15; location of, 88

Third Reich, 1, 6, 56, 99. *See also* Nazism
Third World, 56
Tieck, Ludwig, 210n. 54
Tiedemann, Rolf, 191n. 12
time, disrupted sense of, 18–19, 42, 50, 76, 77, 185
Tobias, Rochelle, 216n. 37
Tölölian, Kachig, 187n. 6
Torah, 2, 106
trauma, 15, 37–39, 77, 128; collectivity/community and, 78, 175; historical dimension of, 63; historical predetermination and, 43; Jewish mysticism and, 151; as liberating, 173–74; of perpetrators, 35, 113; return to site of, 16; revelation and, 114–15; screen memories and, 112; temporal disruption and, 185; testimony and, 13–14, 85–86; uncanniness and, 44, 58; witness to, 13; *Wunde* and, 33
trauma theory, 12, 134, 175
Treblinka death camp, 164
Tsvetaeva, Marina, 152
Tu B'shvat (Jewish holiday of trees), 141

uncanny (Freudian concept), 42, 180
United States, 34
universalism/universality, 23, 27, 47, 61; Anne Frank and, 101, 102; global consciousness contrasted with, 180; Jerusalem as symbol of, 127
Ur (ancient city/German prefix), 115–19, 129
utopianism, 31, 34, 52, 135; Cold War and, 185; earthly realization of, 156; ingathering and, 155

Varnhagen, Rahel, 46, 194n. 52
Vedder, Barbara, 198n. 7
Vergangenheitsbewältigung (mastering of the past), 8, 10, 47, 59, 73,

INDEX

169
Vienna, 15, 41, 132
Vietnam War, 59
Villon, François, 136, 137, 142, 214n. 21
Vogt, Jochen, 197n. 5

Waldrop, Rosmarie, 212n. 71
Wall, Anthony, 216n. 41
Walser, Martin, 86, 90, 202n. 44
wandering Jew, 23, 72
Warshow, Robert, 207n. 29
Wasserstrom, Steven, 114, 209n. 41
Weigel, Sigrid, 188n. 18, 212n. 1, 216n. 41
Weiss, Christoph, 202n. 43
Weiss, Peter, 1, 6, 97, 129, 174; *Abschied von den Eltern [Leavetaking]*, 61, 62–65, 67, 70–71, 199nn. 17–18; *Ästhetik des Widerstands, Die [The Aesthetics of Resistance]*, 179–86, 197n. 1; Auschwitz trial and, 125; autobiographical novels, 61–73; "Bericht über Einrichtungen und Gebräuche in den Siedlungen der Grauhäute" [Report on Institutions and Customs in the Settlements of the Grayskins], 57, 81–85; *Besiegten, Die* [The Defeated], 71; cosmopolitan ideal of, 6, 7, 11; critique of West German society, 81–93; diasporic consciousness and, 6; *Ermittlung, Die [The Investigation]*, 57, 81, 85, 87–93, 198n. 6; family background, 55; *Fluchtpunkt [Vanishing Point]*, 6, 62, 65–73, 74, 78; *Fremde, Der* [The Stranger], 71; *Gespräch der drei Gehenden, Das [The Conversation of the Three Walkers]*, 57, 73–81, 178–79; Gruppe 47 and, 58–60; Jewish identity and, 60–61, 201–2n. 35; *Marat/Sade*, 90,

198n. 6; "Meine Ortschaft" [My Place], 92–93; *Notizbücher, 1960–1971*, 57, 76, 197n. 1; reception in Germany, 10, 18; *Rekonvaleszenz* [Convalescence], 79; *Schatten des Körpers des Kutschers, Der [The Shadow of the Coachman's Body]*, 55, 58, 71, 74; search for diasporic community, 73–81; transitory community and, 178; "Vorübung zum dreiteiligen Drama divina commedia" [Preparatory Exercise for the Three-Part Drama Divina Commedia], 86–87, 91; West German literary scene and, 55–56, 197n. 1; in West German public sphere, 56, 57–61
Weissberg, Liliane, 194n. 52
Weltbürgertum (world citizenship), 69, 71, 199n. 19
Werner, Uta, 133, 213n. 13
Wertheimer, Jüegen, 205n. 3, 213n. 18, 218n. 56
Wiedemann, Barbara, 212n. 1
Wiedergutmachung (reparations treaty), 9, 50
Wiggershaus, Rolf, 190–191n. 3
Will, Frederic, 191n. 5
Winston, Richard and Clara, 194n. 52
Wittig, Friedrich, 100, 101
Woche der Brüderlichkeit (week of brotherhood), 10, 98, 103
women, Jewish, 45–47, 97–105, 182, 206n. 11
working-through (Freudian concept), 36–37
World War I, 38, 111, 170
World War II, 30, 43, 127, 163, 167, 182; destruction of Vitebsk, 149; German soldiers in, 146; German suffering in, 37–38; humiliation of Orthodox Jews in, 140; Normandy Squadron in, 159;

251

INDEX

World War II (*continued*)
  revisionist view of, 195n. 64
Wulf, Christoph, 191n. 8

Yiddish language, 142, 170, 214n. 22
Young, James, 87, 88, 203n. 49

Zionism, 107, 111, 144, 177, 188n. 17, 207n. 28; diaspora in view of, 3, 4–5; exile and, 2. *See also* Israel, state of
Zipes, Jack, 188n. 16, 189n. 20
Zuidervaart, Lambert, 191n. 8